CLERGY WOMEN
An Uphill Calling

BARBARA BROWN ZIKMUND
ADAIR T. LUMMIS
PATRICIA M. Y. CHANG

Westminster John Knox Press
Louisville, Kentucky

Scripture quotations from the New Revised Standard Version
of the Bible are copyright © 1989 by the Division of Christian Education
of the National Council of the Churches of Christ in the U.S.A.
and are used by permission.

Book design by Jennifer K. Cox
Cover design by Pam Poll
Cover photograph by Greg Schneider

First edition
Published by Westminster John Knox Press
Louisville, Kentucky

This book is printed on acid-free paper that meets the
American National Standards Institute Z39.48 standard. ∞

PRINTED IN THE UNITED STATES OF AMERICA
98 99 00 01 02 03 04 05 06 07 — 10 9 8 7 6 5 4 3 2 1

Library of Congress Cataloging-in-Publication Data

Zikmund, Barbara Brown.
    Clergy women : an uphill calling / by Barbara Brown Zikmund, Adair
T. Lummis, Patricia M.Y. Chang.— 1st ed.
        p.   cm.
    Includes bibliographical references and index.
    ISBN 0-664-25673-2 (alk. paper)
    1. Women clergy.   2. Ordination of women.   3. Women in church work.
I. Lummis, Adair T.   II. Chang, Patricia M. Y.   III. Title.
BV676.Z55   1998
262'. 14'0820973—dc21
                                                                    97-39966

THIS BOOK IS DEDICATED TO CLERGY WOMEN
WHO ENVISION NEW FORMS OF MINISTRY
FOR TOMORROW'S CHURCH

Contents

Figures, Indexes, and Tables

Introduction and
Acknowledgments

Since the early 1980s, when the earlier Hartford Seminary-sponsored study of clergy women entitled *Women of the Cloth* was published, more and more women have gained clergy status and are serving as ordained leaders in American Protestantism. By 1990 it was time for a follow-up study.

This research began with a planning grant from the Lilly Endowment, Inc., to determine the scope and best methodology for a new clergy women study. In connection with the planning grant, several consultations were held with key denominational leaders to discuss research options. The following people assisted in various ways during the project planning phase: Edith Blumhoeffer, Marilyn Breitling, Lataunya Bynum, Jackson Carroll, Joy Charlton, Helen Crotwell, Celia Hahn, Barbara Headley, Nancy Jo Kemper, Penny Marler, William McKinney, Paula Nesbitt, Connie Parvey, Mary Pellauer, Kathy Ragsdale, Nancy Richardson, Lynn Scott, Mary Serovy, Jeanette Sherrill, Allison Stokes, Ruth Wallace, Mary Paula Walsh, and Miriam Therese Winter.

Soon thereafter a major project proposal was developed suggesting a lengthy survey of clergy women and clergy men from a wide spectrum of Protestant denominations—complemented with additional information from appropriate female and male laity. The project was generously funded by Lilly Endowment, Inc., and supported by program director Jeanne Knoerle. Within several months a research associate, Patricia M. Y. Chang, was hired to work on the project, along with Barbara Brown Zikmund and Adair T. Lummis, who were already at Hartford Seminary.

During the first six months of the project a questionnaire was prepared and pretested. The following people assisted with the development of the questionnaire and/or participated in pretesting: Linda Barnes, Laurie Etter, Nancy Faus, Laine Hawxhurst, Shirley Hoover, Ellen Fay-Johnson, Elizabeth Fisher, Olivia Hayes, Lois Kennedy, Ginny King, Mary Klaaren, Janet Mackey, Beth Thompson, Jann Cather Weaver, along with students in classes and small groups related to Hartford Seminary.

At the same time negotiations began with various denominations to obtain names for a representative sample. The following denominational staff assisted in providing names and addresses: Craig Collemer (American Baptist Churches), Sheri Doty (Assemblies of God), Toni Bynum (Christian Church/Disciples of Christ), Robert Faus (Church of the Brethren), Keith Huttenlocker (Church of God, Anderson, Indiana), Pat Warren and Rebecca Laird-Christensen (Church of the Nazarene), John Docker (Episcopal Church), Mary D. Pellauer and Kenneth Inskeep (Evangelical Lutheran Church in America), Carolyn Ellis (Free Methodist Church), Ida J. Smith (Presbyterian Church (U.S.A.)), Ellen Mers (Reformed Church in America), Jim Shull (Southern Baptist Convention), Sarah Frances Anders (Southern Baptist ordained women), M. Lynn Scott (United Methodist Church), Mary Sue Gast and Edith Guffey (United Church of Christ), Ellen Brandenburg (Unitarian-Universalist Association), Kenneth Heer (Wesleyan Church).

Once the questionaire/survey was returned the following persons coded the nearly five thousand returned questionnaires and/or assisted with follow-up telephone interviews: Marie Alston, Judy Anderson, Sandra Douglas, Shirley Dudley, Angie Dunnham, Muriel Dupree, Frederick Green, Margaret Lezak, Jason Roozen, and Sheryl Wiggins.

As the research findings became clear and the manuscript of the book took shape, we distributed drafts of the manuscript to people for feedback. We visited several ecumenical meetings to report on our work; we gave representatives of the media "press releases" with preliminary findings; we presented professional papers at the Society for the Scientific Study of Religion, the Religious Research Association, and other professional societies; and we held an educational outreach event at Hartford Seminary to get feedback from local women clergy. The following people gave us written feedback on early drafts of the manuscript or shared informally their reactions to our work in small-group settings: Joanne Chadwick, Nancy Faus, Sister Helena Marie, Kathy Manis Findley, Jean Hendricks and Rebecca Laird, Valentine Royal, Nancy Sanders, Peggy Shriver, and Rebecca J. Tollefson.

On February 9–10, 1996, we held a national consultation on the project in Chicago. At that session an editor of Westminster John Knox Press, Jon Berquist, was present, as well as denominational leaders, sociologists, and local women pastors. The following people attended the consultation: Catherine Brekus, Deborah Bruce, Joy Charlton, Mark Chaves, Mary S. Donovan, Deborah Kapp, Rebecca Laird, Edward Lehman, Linda Moody, Paula D. Nesbitt, Mary Ann Neevel, Laura Rey, Lynn Rhodes, Faith Rohrbough, Susie Stanley, Peter A. R. Stebinger, Denise D. Tracy, Barbara B. Troxell, Catherine Wessinger, and Margaret Wiborg.

In addition we would like to thank Richard Schoenherr, Rachel Rosenfeld, Jackson Carroll, Ed Lehman, and Aage Sorensen for sharing their research experience and advice along the way. We are especially grateful to our colleagues in the Center for Social and Religious Research at Hartford Seminary: Nancy Ammerman, Carl Dudley, David Roozen, Mary Jane Ross, and Sheryl Wiggins. We also wish to thank the staff in the Hartford Seminary library, president's office, and business office who have assisted us in finding books and reports, in providing needed computer support, in handling budgets and financial matters with speed and good spirits: Jackie Ammerman, Lilyne Hollingworth, Loreli Jenkins, Marie Rovero, Carolyn Sperl, and Nancy Wood.

Finally, we offer special words of thanks to our supportive and growing families: Patty Chang's husband, Jesper Sorensen, has provided crucial support during the project—especially given the fact that their sons, Nikolaj and Benjamin, were both conceived and born during its duration. Adair Lummis is grateful to her family who understand and appreciate her commitment to research. Barbara Brown Zikmund's husband, Joseph Zikmund II, must be lauded for his patience—as "BBZ" balances the demands of being the president of Hartford Seminary and her work on this book.

Above all, however, we thank the hundreds of women and men who took the time to fill out the questionnaire or talk to one of us on the phone. The full survey and the percentage results for each question may be found on the Hartford Seminary web page, http://www.hartsem.edu. As we come to the end of this project we affirm that the service and commitments of clergy women are forging new understandings of ministry, even as ordained ministry for clergy women remains "an uphill calling."

Barbara Brown Zikmund
Adair T. Lummis
Patricia M. Y. Chang

1

A NEW SITUATION

One of the most significant changes in church life in the twentieth century has been the movement of ordained women into recognized settings of ministry in American Protestantism. For centuries, clergy were male. No one thought too much about it. In recent decades, however, the situation has changed. Today, more and more women are serving as pastors and clergy leaders in Protestant churches.

Church members asked what they think about this situation offered a mixed reaction.

> I am very happy with a woman minister. She is very easy to talk with. Right there when needed and very concerned about people's feelings. I have worked or chaired many committees of the church working with many ministers. Working with a woman minister has been a new and rewarding experience.
>
> (United Church of Christ lay woman)

Not everyone is pleased, however:

> In my opinion, women who desire ordination as ministers of the gospel are usurping the man and the place of helpmeet is too lowly for their ego. Too many women reject the idea of being in subjection, they want to be the head instead of the support of a man as head. Any woman who truly wants to serve will have more opportunities than she can handle. The problem is that they want to direct or have top authorities which are rightfully man's role, since God placed them [men] as head of church and family.
>
> (Southern Baptist lay man)

Laity in the churches obviously differ in their assessment of women in ministry settings. With firsthand experience, attitudes are changing; but it is a difficult process. Some lay leaders who support and affirm the pastoral leadership of women are worried. Others believe that women make better pastors than men do. Still others insist that gender is becoming irrelevant.

> Our experience with a woman pastor in a small rapidly growing congregation has led me to the conclusion that women are in many ways superior to men when it comes to doing ministry. Perhaps because they are more intuitive and relational. At any rate,

our experience has been that our woman pastor has been better at discerning the voice of the congregation than male pastors who often have trouble getting their own agenda in this area.

(Church of the Brethren lay woman)

Another lay leader noted:

Women can certainly be good pastors as I have seen personally. However, there is a danger that churches with female pastors will not address the needs of men. Men are not self-sufficient (though many of us think that we are) spiritually. If a church has a female pastor, that pastor must encourage the men of the church to meet together to uplift one another, make one another accountable, and pray and study God's word together. This is why, I feel, churches with female pastors may lose men. Men and women are different. We both have different needs, and the needs of both sexes must be met for the church to thrive.

(American Baptist lay man)

Increasingly, however, lay leaders do not think gender will matter:

There is no doubt in my mind that many characteristics of the church and its constituents are determined by the minister. Our current female minister speaks to a special crowd because of her age and sex. However, her talents go far beyond. . . . I doubt that sex or age will be a criterion in our next ministerial search, since the most important features of a minister are how they complement the existing talents of the lay members.

(Unitarian-Universalist lay woman)

For the immediate future, however, the gender of clergy does make a difference. Men and women experience differently the demands of being clergy. Laity, denominational leaders, and the general public are variously antagonistic, confused, ambiguous, and affirming in their attitudes toward women clergy. The career paths of men and women follow different routes. Even understandings of authentic religious leadership and ordination itself are being transformed by the growing numbers of women clergy.

We have based this study on data collected from almost five thousand surveys that ordained women and men from sixteen Protestant denominations provided in 1993 and 1994. In addition, we were able to supplement the survey results by doing short telephone interviews with 124 women and the same number of men in parish ministry (distributed over all of the denominations). To explore some issues in depth, we also conducted thirty longer interviews (of approximately one hour or longer) with clergy in a variety of ministry settings (twenty-six women and four men). Finally, we asked a small sample of key lay leaders in congregations served by clergy in our sample (six hundred) to respond to a modified form of the questionnaire that we had given to clergy.

The denominations surveyed vary in size, polity, and theology—they are mainline Protestant denominations, Unitarian-Universalists, Southern Baptists, and members of several small Holiness denominations that trace their origins to early Methodism. This study builds on a smaller multidenominational study, conducted by Hartford Seminary between 1979 and 1982, involving nine mainline Protestant denominations. (Four of these denominations have since merged, reducing the number to seven.) The results of the Hartford Seminary research were published in a book titled *Women of the Cloth,* by Jackson W. Carroll, Barbara Hargrove, and Adair T. Lummis (San Francisco: Harper & Row, 1983).

In our 1993–94 study, we have been able to examine both the general and the particular in the experiences of ordained clergy in the 1990s. Whereas previous studies often have been limited to the experiences of clergy within one or a few denominations, our sample, by its breadth, allows us to see how different denominational features influence the experiences of clergy. By virtue of that same breadth, we are able to interpret what is common to the experiences of clergy in different institutional contexts. This research will help denominational leaders see the impact of specific institutional procedures and practices and also allow pastors to recognize common issues and problems that they share with their colleagues in other traditions.

Further, this study, when compared with the earlier *Women of the Cloth* research, provides a unique viewpoint on how things have changed over time. We are able to show what difference twelve years makes in the situation of clergy women and men. We are able to compare career decisions and experiences, views toward work, family issues, and theologies of ordination. We are also able to assess how successfully denominations and congregations are handling the rising numbers of clergy women.

WHO ARE THE CLERGY IN THIS STUDY?

The 1993–94 research contains information from female and male clergy across fifteen predominantly white Protestant denominations.[1] We have not included clergy in Roman Catholicism or clergy in the historically black Protestant denominations. However, information about ethnic minority women and men within our sixteen predominantly white Protestant denominations is included.

Finding a workable definition for *ordained clergy* in this research is a challenge. Ordination is practiced and delineated in a variety of ways in different denominational traditions. Some denominations have several "kinds" of ordination: ordination to deacons' orders; ordination to lay eldership; ordination to sacramental authority, without full standing or access to denominational decision making; ordination with full membership in conference or diocesan structures.

In this study, we have used a definition for *ordained clergy* that Constant H. Jacquet Jr. at the National Council of Churches of Christ (NCCC) developed in his study "Women Ministers in 1986 and 1977: A Ten Year View."[2] Jacquet classifies "ordained clergy" as those having "full ministry," or holding that office "having the most complete and unrestricted set of functions relating to the ministry of the Gospel, administering the Word and Sacrament or carrying out the office of pastor or priest in the church." In 1986, at the time of Jacquet's report, twenty-one NCCC denominations gave "full ministry status" to women.

First, we began our research with the twenty-one denominations that Jacquet had studied. We decided not to include (of those he surveyed) the two Mennonite churches, the Moravians, the Christian Congregationalists, and the Church of the Foursquare Gospel because these have very few women clergy, they are very small, or we anticipated that obtaining a sample would be difficult. Second, we discovered with our pretest groups that it is almost impossible to develop a common questionnaire that both is useful for the various denominations and works with the Salvation Army (which has a militaristic structure). According to Jacquet's data, the Salvation Army had more women clergy than any other denomination in 1977 (3,037) and ranked second among those with women clergy in 1986 (3,220). We think that a study of women clergy in the Salvation Army is needed, but we decided that it was impossible to include them in this study. Third, we added the Unitarian-Universalists. They are not members of the National Council of Churches of Christ, but they have large numbers of women clergy and have been ordaining women for many years. And fourth, we included the Southern Baptists. The Southern Baptist Convention (SBC) is the largest Protestant denomination in the United States. Although the SBC does not officially endorse the ordination of women, individual Southern Baptist congregations have been ordaining women since 1964. When we discovered that we could get a good sample of ordained Southern Baptist women, we were delighted to include them. Finally, the American Lutheran Church (ALC) and the Lutheran Church of America (LCA), on the one hand, and The United Presbyterian Church in the U.S.A. (UPCUSA) and the Presbyterian Church U.S. (PCUS), on the other—four of Jacquet's twenty-one denominations in 1986—have created two new denominations: the Evangelical Lutheran Church in America (ELCA) and the Presbyterian Church (U.S.A.). After these adjustments, then, the questionnaire was mailed to approximately ten thousand male and female clergy in sixteen denominations, resulting in a good sample from fourteen denominations. (See Appendix 1.1, "Number of Respondents in the Hartford Seminary Study by Gender and Denomination" [1994].)

For two denominations we ended up with an inadequate sample: the Reformed Church in America (RCA) and the Assemblies of God (AOG).[3] From time to time we have been able to include data from these denominations in the denominational clusters we use to report our work, but the low numbers make it impossible to make any independent statements about these two denominations.

HOW MANY CLERGY WOMEN ARE THERE?

Before we turn to the particularities of our research, it is helpful to get a historical sense of the ways in which women have moved into the clergy vocation during recent decades. Women have long been a pillar of the institutional church—supporting its clergy, educating its children, maintaining its altars, volunteering for various projects and causes, and speaking from its pulpits. Yet only recently have women entered the ranks of the professional "clergy" in significant numbers. Data from the U.S. Census demonstrate revealing historical trends of male and female clergy between 1910 and 1990.

As early as 1910, 685 women identified their occupation as "clergy" in the U.S. Census. In 1920, this number climbed to 1,787; in 1930, it was reported as 3,276; and in 1950, the number reached 6,824.[4] Relatively little is known about these women except that they clearly identified themselves as "clergy," not as lay volunteers or religious workers. After 1970, the numbers rose significantly. Although this study focuses especially on women ordained after 1970, it is clear that the experiences of earlier, "pioneer" women clergy paved the way for later generations.

Figure 1.1
Male and Female Clergy, 1910–1990

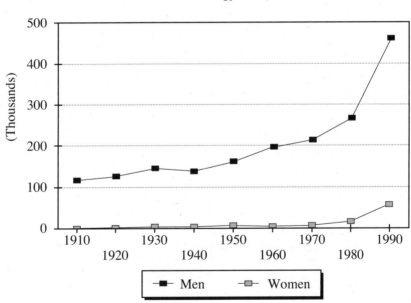

The surge in numbers of both male and female clergy after 1970 appears to belie any generalization that American religion overall is experiencing a clergy shortage. While the fortunes of particular denominations vary, the interest and participation of men and women in professional leadership within the church as a whole have increased dramatically from 1970 to 1990. Comparisons of our 1994 data with Constant Jacquet's data from 1977 and 1986 yield interesting insights.[5] (See Appendix 1.2, "Changing Numbers of Clergy in Major Protestant Denominations," and Appendix 1.3, "Change in Number of Clergy Women as Percent of Total Clergy," examining those denominations where we have comparable information for 1977, 1986, and 1994.)

For virtually all of the denominations we have studied, the absolute number of female clergy has increased since 1977. However, the percentage of growth seems to have slowed somewhat in the 1990s. Because increases in the numbers of women clergy are reported as percentages of total clergy in the denomination, it is important to note that in some cases the magnitude of growth has been amplified by the decline in the number of men, rather than representing a strong increase in the number of women.

From our collection of denominational figures in 1994,[6] we find that the United Methodists report the largest number of ordained women overall (3,003), followed by the United Church of Christ (1,843) and the Assemblies of God (1,574). However, if we look at women as a percentage of all ordained clergy in a particular denomination, the Unitarian-Universalist Association has the highest percentage of women, 30 percent, in their clergy workforce. The United Church of Christ has the second highest percentage at 25, followed by the Christian Church (Disciples of Christ) at 18. The Free Methodist Church had the smallest percentage of female clergy, less than 1 percent. Taken together, the denominations in our sample have an average of 10 percent female clergy.[7]

In spite of overall growth in numbers, female clergy remain a minority in almost every area of church life. Although some observers may lament that "women are getting all the best jobs for political reasons," the numbers indicate that clergy women remain significantly underpaid and underemployed relative to men. Women are more likely to serve part-time, to leave parish ministry, and to serve in specialized ministries.

Despite the fact that more women are enrolled in seminaries today than at any other time in history, the number of female students reported by the Association of Theological Schools (ATS) in the United States and Canada in its *Factbook* (1993–94) has grown only from 19 percent of total seminary students in 1978 to slightly over 30 percent in 1994. These statistics include Roman Catholic seminaries, which do not prepare women for the priesthood, so the percentage of women enrolled at Protestant seminaries is a bit higher. Nevertheless, 70 percent of seminarians are still men, and men continue to enter the ministry in majority numbers.[8] Also, when we examine the changes in the percentage of women clergy across time, the proportional increase between 1986 and 1994 is, in most cases, lower than the proportional increase between 1977 and 1986. This suggests that while the percentage of women clergy continues to increase, it is doing so at a slower rate.

It is also important not to equate increasing seminary enrollments automatically with increasing numbers of female clergy. The number of females preparing for ministry represents only one side of the equation. Many women who attend seminary do not seek church employment. Those who do often end up leaving church positions, at higher rates than men. Furthermore, seminary-trained women are often unemployed and underemployed. And if perceptions of sexism and discrimination within the institutional church persist, qualified women are less likely to choose denominational ordination to legitimatize their particular sense of a call to ministry.

Setting these difficulties aside, our interviews with women clergy show that they have a deep and abiding commitment to ministry. It is important to understand that even when women leave the employment of the institutional church, they likely have not forsaken their call or their sense of vocation. Rather, they have become disenchanted with the institutional church. Although the situation for women clergy has improved, the women in our research testify that many of the institutional contexts within which women serve remain hostile.

We are convinced that patterns of institutional discrimination continue to limit the ministries of women. Although increasing numbers of women are in seminaries, and many of them are seeking ordained status in Protestant denominations, congregations and denominational systems consistently, whether overtly or unconsciously, thwart the ministries of women. It is our hope that this research will raise the awareness of church leaders in such a way as to enable congregations and denominations to accept and benefit from women who feel called to ministries in their midst. It is our further hope that this research will give women who feel that God is calling them to new forms of service new hope and sufficient courage to find meaningful expressions for their ministry within and beyond the churches.

DENOMINATIONAL VARIATIONS

Survey responses and interviews from all these different denominations clearly reveal important denominational patterns that inform ministry and shape the experiences of male and female clergy. Although gender remains an important variable in ministry, denominational differences are extremely important.

For this reason, we have grouped many of the responses to our questions into three denominational clusters that reflect the differences in how authority is perceived and located within these denominations. The resulting typology divides our sample as follows:

> Congregation-centered denominations
> Institution-centered denominations
> Spirit-centered denominations

In using this typology, we are aware that all typologies are artificial constructions and must be interpreted carefully. By nature, typologies are arbitrary and often break down against the complexity of reality. We have grouped our data, therefore, sensitive to the limitations of these denominational clusters but convinced that the clusters enable us to make information from our research accessible and usable.

It is possible to argue that all the denominations in our study are more or less congregation-centered, institution-centered, and Spirit-centered. Nevertheless, patterns of church practice suggest that denominations do vary in their views about the sources of authority in church practice.

> Some traditions insist that the essence of the church is found in the gathered people, the congregation. In these denominations, authority centers on local congregations.
>
> Some traditions ground ecclesiastical life in an institutional, churchly legacy established by the biblical and historical experience of the institutional church. In these denominations, authority comes from the apostolic witness as preserved through the centuries in specific institutional forms.
>
> Still other traditions insist that the work of the Holy Spirit constitutes the church anew in every age. In these denominations, authority comes from direct, often personal spiritual experience.

These three clusters move beyond the classic categories of church governance, or polity: episcopal, presbyterial, and congregational. They take into account the ways in which leadership authority is recognized, as well as who makes the decisions. Furthermore, because these three clusters also follow patterns that echo the historical struggle of women for ordination in the history of Protestantism in the United States, they are useful for our work.

The efforts of women to become ordained in American Protestantism unfolded over several hundred years. The journey began when lay women in local congregations began to ask questions. Were women allowed to speak in church meetings? This was an important question, because in the early nineteenth century there was a prohibition against women speaking in mixed groups, or "promiscuous assemblies" as they were called. Next, women wanted to know if they were allowed to vote or to serve on the governing boards or councils in local congregations. Eventually, it was debated whether women could represent local parishes or congregations at regional, diocesan, or national meetings. In most Protestant denominations, no progress was made toward affirming women clergy until lay women gained basic power and influence.

CONGREGATION-CENTERED DENOMINATIONS

The congregation-centered denominations were the first Protestants to expand opportunities for women's leadership in the churches. Congregation-centered denominations vest decision-making responsibilities in local congregations and do not require regional or national approval for many actions. Women in congregation-centered denominations generally exercised lay citizenship privileges in these denominations by the late eighteenth and the early nineteenth century. The Congregationalists (now United Church of Christ), Unitarian-Universalists, Christian Church (Disciples of Christ), and Northern Baptists (now American Baptists) were the first denominations in our sample to recognize and authorize the ministries of strong female lay leaders, itinerant female preachers, female educational and medical missionaries, and ordained female clergy. For these four congregation-centered denominations it was a small step, usually a local and functional one, to ordain a woman.

The first woman formally ordained to the Christian ministry in a major Protestant denomination in America was Antoinette L. Brown. She was ordained by the Congregationalists in a small church in upstate New York in 1853.[9]

The Church of the Brethren and the Southern Baptists are also included in our congregation-centered denominational cluster, but their story is more complicated. Sometimes we find that these two denominations are very different from the other congregation-centered denominations; at other times they fit into a common pattern. Sometimes a split is evident between women's and men's opinions in these two denominations that is not apparent with the other four congregation-centered denominations.

The Church of the Brethren, rooted in the rural Anabaptist immigrant heritage of central Europe, for centuries resisted creating a class of ordained leaders in favor of what it called "free ministry." Until very recently (1930s and 1940s), most congregations in the Church of the Brethren simply "set apart" someone in each congregation to serve as pastor without pay—expecting him (invariably a male) to earn a living outside his pastoral responsibilities. To help these clergy leaders in their ministry, Church of the Brethren clergy took short training courses, but seminary education as a requirement for ordination was rare.

Today, Church of the Brethren members remain ambivalent about ordination, arguing either that everyone should be ordained or that no one should be ordained. As one Church of the Brethren pastor put it, "We are just now beginning what other denominations are moving away from . . . seminary-trained clergy. . . . This means that the prestige of the occupation of pastor has not had the same history of status and decline [as in other Protestant denominations]." In this situation, the increased numbers of women clergy are a good thing; they "strengthen the tradition of the 'priesthood of all believers,' removing some of the barriers between clergy and laity."[10] Nationally, the Church of the Brethren affirms the ordination of women, but informal resistance to female pastors persists at the grass roots. In our study, Church of the Brethren clergy women, many of whom have been to seminary, are some of the most progressive respondents in our sample, whereas male clergy in this denomination remain quite conservative.[11]

Southern Baptists are another congregation-centered denomination with uneven support for women's leadership. In terms of church polity, or governance, Southern Baptists are rabid congregationalists. All decisions and authority in a Baptist church rest with the local congregation, yet very few Southern Baptist women have been ordained.

The reasons are contextual. Southern Baptists, grounded in the "Old South," have come to limit their radical congregationalism and concern for religious liberty with deep (some would say "rigid") biblical fundamentalism. In the years since the Civil War, Protestants in the North and in the South have handled questions of biblical authority very differently. In northern colleges, universities, seminaries, and churches during the latter part of the nineteenth century, the scholarly development of modern biblical criticism was welcomed. As a result, attitudes of northern Protestants about women's ministries underwent significant change, supported by biblical scholarship that became increasingly open to flexible interpretations of scripture texts that had earlier limited women. In the South, however, Southern Baptists, southern Methodists, and southern Presbyterians became increasingly preoccupied with conservative and fundamentalist views of the Bible and the role of women. The South became known as the Bible Belt, and southern churches of all denominations resisted new forms of women's leadership and ministry.

In recent decades, the southern Methodists and southern Presbyterians have reunited with their northern counterparts. It has not been easy, but the reunited denominations have upheld the importance and legitimacy of women's leadership. Southern Baptists, however, have remained steeped in the biblical conservatism of the region. The Southern Baptist Convention, a voluntary alliance of individual congregations, has taken a strong biblical-theological stand against the ordination of women, insisting that women clergy are not biblical.

At the same time, Southern Baptists continue to uphold a congregation-centered understanding of religious authority. As a consequence, local congregations can (and sometimes do) make independent decisions against the Southern Baptist Convention. Exercising their Baptist freedoms, since the early 1960s a small number of progressive Southern Baptist congregations have ordained and called women pastors. One ordained Southern Baptist clergy woman stated her conviction that the "ministry of women is essential to symbolizing the purpose of God," concluding that "as long as women are excluded from ministry, we are speaking an untruth in regard to God's nature and God's promises." Our study contains a sample of 116 ordained Southern Baptist women.[12]

The six congregation-centered denominations in our study are the American Baptist Churches, the Christian Church (Disciples of Christ), the Church of the Brethren, the Southern Baptist Convention, the Unitarian-Universalist Association, and the United Church of Christ. In many responses, clergy from these denominations hold shared values and attitudes about ministry. In some instances, however, we report survey results from Church of the Brethren and Southern Baptist clergy separately, given their unique histories.

INSTITUTION-CENTERED DENOMINATIONS

The second major cluster of respondents in our sample comes from what we call institution-centered denominations. These denominations approach the issue of church leadership with high liturgical and ontological assumptions. Historically, they have often been reluctant to ordain women, drawing on arguments from tradition. Most of these denominations began ordaining women only in the mid–twentieth century, and then only after long institutional and theological debates. This is because these institution-centered denominations place a high value on church order. They believe that when the church sets someone "apart by prayer and laying on of hands" for ordained ministry, it does something that is more than functional. Institution-centered denominations feel connected, in some denominations through the concept of apostolic succession, with the institutional expressions of the Christian church in all times and places.

Institution-centered denominations often follow a polity (governance system) that is presbyterial or episcopal. As one Presbyterian male pastor put it, "In the church I grew up in, good ministry was 'good administration.' "[13] On the American scene, institution-centered denominations combine patterns of local congregationalism with representative and oversight structures. Regardless of the "church order," however, whether episcopal or presbyterial, these denominations have a "high" view of ordination. When someone is ordained, it is a "churchly" event, linking to ecclesiastical practice in all times and places. One pastor noted that the Lutheran persuasion places a heavy emphasis on Word and sacrament in ministry and in the ministry of the church. He said he valued that, but after many years in ministry, he is moving beyond his training as a theologian to develop personal and pastoral skills. In our study, the institution-centered denominations are the Episcopal Church, the Evangelical Lutheran Church in America, the Presbyterian Church (U.S.A.), and the United Methodist Church.

These four denominations wrestled long and hard with the question of women's ordination, and decisions leading to ordination came in incremental steps. In many cases, women were first given temporary leadership and status through license. In other instances, these denominations developed separate credentials for women, authorizing women as educators and missionaries—commissioning, rather than ordaining, women to lesser ministries, still setting them apart from the laity. Following institutional needs, institution-centered denominations ordained women to lay eldership, consecrated them as deaconesses, and credentialed them as religious educators.

In some of these denominations, where a split existed between northern and southern Methodists, northern and southern Presbyterians, or Scandinavian and German Lutherans, ecclesiastical practice has had to overcome regional and ethnic differences. Northerners were generally more open than southerners to clergy women, and Scandinavians were more willing than northern Germans to accept women's leadership. With their various mid-twentieth-century reunions, southern Methodists and southern Presbyterians and some conservative Lutherans who had previously not ordained women were forced to change their practices within reunited denominations. Some exceptions for conscience among denominational leaders have been temporarily tolerated (e.g., bishops who objected to women's ordination have not been required to ordain women), but denominational reunions have been a powerful force leading to the acceptance of full-status ordination for women.

Interestingly, even when institution-centered denominations agreed that no biblical or theological reason existed to deny women ordination, they still moved slowly. All justified the election or ordination of women as lay leaders before voting approval of women as clergy. And sometimes, even after these denominations had come to agreement that no biblical or theological reason justified keeping women from ordained leadership, practical questions about women clergy caused them to hesitate. Institutional debates raged over whether a married woman could do the job and over the relationship of ordained ministry to mission and educational work. People worried that local churches might not want women pastors or that a woman might become a bishop. Leaders in the institution-centered denominations hesitated to take any action without looking at all the institutional consequences.

For example, in connectional systems, such as the United Methodist Church, where full-status clergy belong to a structure or professional entity beyond the local congregation (a conference), the decision to ordain does not grant "full status." Northern Methodist Episcopal women were ordained as "local pastors" in 1924, but they were not granted full conference membership in Methodist annual conferences, with guaranteed appointment privileges, until 1956.

Institution-centered denominations care deeply about church order. They insist that setting apart persons for leadership by prayer and the laying on of hands is serious business, not to be taken lightly. One Methodist pastor stated that he never misses the ordination service at his annual conference because it is "like a birthright to me." As a consequence, once institution-centered denominations make the decision to affirm the ordination of women, they live out the new order with remarkable vigor. In all four of these denominations, women gained full ordained status after 1955: Presbyterians (northern) in 1956, Methodists (already reunited) in 1956, Presbyterians (southern) 1964, Lutherans (Scandinavians and southern Germans) in 1970, and Episcopalians in 1976. Since 1955, hundreds of women clergy have been ordained by these denominations, and the situation of women clergy in these denominations is often considered better than in congregation-centered denominations.[14]

SPIRIT-CENTERED DENOMINATIONS

The third major cluster of respondents we call Spirit-centered denominations. These denominations have links to the Holiness and Pentecostal movements: the Church of God (Anderson, Indiana), the Church of the Nazarene, the Free Methodists, and the Wesleyan Church. They are combined with the Assemblies of God in the Pentecostal tradition.

Unfortunately, these Spirit-centered denominations are not well known or understood on the American religious landscape. Although they are often linked with biblical fundamentalists, such as the Southern Baptists, their heritage is very different.

Spirit-centered or Holiness denominations began with the great Wesleyan revivals in England and America during the mid–nineteenth century. They set out to reclaim the fervor and biblical grounding of early Methodism. Generally speaking, Holiness denominations hold to a high doctrine of the Holy Spirit, believing that through a second blessing or baptism by the Holy Spirit, God blesses men and women to enliven their faith.

From the very beginning, many Holiness leaders were women. Churches were not institutions but communities of the Spirit. They remembered how the apostle Peter quoted from the prophet Joel, "In the last days . . . I will pour out my Spirit upon all flesh, and your sons and your daughters shall prophesy" (Acts 2:17). Indeed, the leadership of popular Holiness preacher Phoebe Palmer was an inspiration to early women in the movement.

By the early twentieth century, however, the Holiness movement had organized into several denominations, and women were relegated to more conventional roles. In this institutionalizing process, questions of church order and biblical authority diluted the radical egalitarian assumptions about women's leadership that had prevailed during the revivals. The Spirit was tamed by institutional practice and denominational assumptions about the nature of the church.

This change is evident in statistics showing the numbers of women clergy in these Spirit-centered denominations over the twentieth century. In the Church of the Nazarene, the percentage of women clergy dropped from 20 percent in 1908 to 6 percent in 1973. In 1992, almost one-third (197) of the women clergy in the Church of the Nazarene were retired. By 1989, only forty-nine Nazarene women were pastors in local churches (less than 1 percent of the congregations in that denomination). In the Church of God (Anderson, Indiana), the story is the same. The highest percentage of women pastors in that denomination reached 32 percent in 1925. By 1992, the percentage of Church of God women clergy had dropped to 15 percent.

Wesleyan and Holiness church historian Susie Stanley believes that "sect analysis" explains the reduction of women clergy in these denominations. In the early stages of development, sects value prophetic leadership and are open to women's leadership. As they institutionalize, men move toward more priestly understandings of authority while women remain charismatic leaders. All of our Spirit-centered denominations ordained women when they were founded. Women's ordination was not even a question. As these denominations matured and became more institutional, however, male leaders (and even some women) were increasingly reluctant to grant priestly authority to women at the institutional level.

Furthermore, the decline of clergy women in these denominations is directly linked to the increased professionalization of leadership in American Protestantism and the linking of ordination to seminary training. Rebecca Laird, a Church of the Nazarene scholar, argues that increases in ordination requirements (especially

educational requirements) in her denomination since 1950 have significantly reduced the number of Nazarene women in ordained ministry. Today, very few
women hold executive positions at the national level in any of the Wesleyan Holiness or Pentecostal churches, with the exception of the Salvation Army.[15]

The decline of women clergy in the Spirit-centered denominations comes from
the tendency of these denominations to embrace the general cultural stereotypes
in American society that support males in leadership roles in and, at least until recently, have limited women's participation in positions of authority. One Church
of God author writes that his church "has traditionally seen women in a supportive rather than a decision-making leadership capacity. In this we have pretty much
reflected prevailing social standards."[16]

Our research contains a good sample from the two largest Holiness denominations, Church of the Nazarene and Church of God (Anderson, Indiana). Unfortunately, we were not able to obtain as strong a sample from Pentecostal
denominations. Nevertheless, it is important to note that Pentecostal denominations, such as the Assemblies of God, also began with the egalitarian blessing of
the Holy Spirit—affirming the power of the Spirit to call anyone, male or female,
to leadership in the church.

In the late twentieth century, Holiness and Pentecostal denominations have
been ideologically linked to southern religion, with its biblical literalism and re-
jection of women's ministries. Church of the Nazarene historian Paul Bassett
calls this the "Fundamentalist leavening" of Holiness and Pentecostal churches.
Like the fundamentalists, some twentieth-century Holiness and Pentecostal leaders have come to oppose the leadership of women in the church by holding to lit-
eral interpretations of key biblical texts from 1 Corinthians 14 and 1 Timothy 2
which insist that women must be subservient to men. Uninformed Holiness and
Pentecostal clergy, unaware of their heritage and the importance of the Holy
Spirit in authorizing leadership, end up unwittingly embracing a narrow biblical
stance promoting male headship in all areas of life. In this environment, Holiness
and Pentecostal women find it extremely difficult to claim their call to ordained
ministry.[17]

In our study, by clustering data from the five Spirit-centered denominations together, we have made it possible to see how attitudes toward women clergy in this
group have a distinct character, shaped by Wesleyan Holiness and Pentecostal history.[18] It is important to keep this group distinct from the Calvinist conservative denominations found in some of the congregation-centered and institution-centered
denominations, for example, the Southern Baptists and conservative Presbyterians.

Our study findings are organized around these two realities: gender and denomination. Sometimes our research shows great differences between the circumstances and the experiences of men and women, regardless of denomination.
Sometimes, however, the differences have to do with denominational culture and
the understandings of clergy or patterns of authority that prevail in congregation-

centered, institution-centered, and Spirit-centered denominations. At other times, additional criteria are needed to explain various patterns of responses. The sample of clergy in our study has a good balance between men and women and a critical mass of respondents in each denomination. In reporting our results, we present information by comparing women and men and by examining denominational clusters—"congregation-centered," "institution-centered," and "Spirit-centered." (See Appendix 1.4, "Ordained Women and Men in the Hartford Seminary Study [1994] [15 Denominations Clustered].")

A FEMINIST PERSPECTIVE

The term *feminist* has a mixed history. In some circles it is viewed as a positive description of a movement to support equality for women in contemporary society. In other settings it has become associated with rabid radicals who try to disrupt and upset family patterns and tear down patriarchal institutions. At the beginning of the 1970s, feminism became widely associated with the "women's liberation movement" and its critique of any system that used female gender as a basis for denying women the societal advantages and rewards permitted men. The 1970s have been characterized by Jessie Bernard as the decade of "Feminist Enlightenment," when young, educated women realized that "sexism was the 'invisible paradigm'" accounting for men's ascendancy in top professional, executive, and governmental positions. The 1970s were "an extraordinary and amazing decade for women and a stunning foil for men."[19]

Whether or not they actually called themselves feminists, beginning in the 1970s, increasing numbers of women entered graduate school, preparing for jobs in the professions of architecture, dentistry, engineering, law, medicine, and ministry and for executive positions in large corporations. Laws were passed equalizing women's access to higher education. It was a heady time of change, and many of these women were inspired to hold and achieve career goals in male-stereotyped occupations. "Feminist" literature, media publicity, and the political and legal successes of the women's movement were impressive.[20]

As the women's movement matured and expanded, its influence in academic, literary, and political circles—and the definition of *feminism*—became more complex. Although all varieties of feminism basically agree with the premise that societal rewards should not be denied to women on the basis of gender, major differences exist among feminists over the cause of the inequity between women and men and what remedies should be used to correct this situation.

Differences among feminist positions in both the secular world and the world of the church are further complicated as women of diverse nationalities, races, and ethnicities take up the "cause." Feminist theologies now include "Asian feminist theology," "Latin American feminist theology," "black feminist theology" (or "womanist theology"), and "ecofeminist theology." For example, theologians holding to diverse feminist perspectives differ as to how far religious language and liturgy need to be changed to include women explicitly, as well as men. When feminists speak of God, they differ about whether Christians should ever refer to God using female imagery. Those feminists who believe that God should be seen and named at least in part as "female" are sometimes called "spiritual feminists."[21]

The movement of women into ordained ministry over the past twenty-five years has taken place in this diverse landscape. It is dangerous to call women clergy feminists, but it is also impossible *not* to call many of them feminists. It is important, therefore, to make very clear at the beginning of this study how we have incorporated the issue of feminism. We believe that many of the women in our sample are feminists, and we define our use of this word, *feminist,* in very precise ways.

To develop a contextually valid understanding of "feminist issues" at the beginning of our research, we decided to avoid using the specific word *feminist* in our survey instrument and in our telephone interviews. Clergy respondents were never asked if they were feminists or what they thought of feminism. The term has too many meanings. Some clergy who do not identify themselves as feminists strongly endorse values that others would term "feminist." Others who use the word give it various definitions.

In our research, we have sought to measure how clergy feel about certain issues related to women's lives. Furthermore, we link clergy opinions with active advocacy for certain things or specific practices in work or private life. Where possible, we try to ascertain if there have been changes in the degree to which clergy advocate certain positions that might be labeled "feminist."

For example, in the mid-1970s and early 1980s, the women's movements in many mainline Protestant denominations actively lobbied for more female lay leadership in local churches, for more ordained women, for more female staff in regional and national denominational offices, and for the use of inclusive language in publications and worship. Comparisons on these issues show that the zeal for many of these things has moderated through the late 1980s and the 1990s.

Advocacy for more female leadership in the church is one way of defining feminism. Our research shows that, by this definition, female pastors are more "feminist" than male pastors. Yet both male and female clergy in 1993–94 were less concerned about including more lay women in church governance, ordaining more women among the clergy, advocating for more female denominational staff, or even promoting the use of inclusive language than they had been in the late 1970s and early 1980s. This decline is probably due to the fact that more and more women are exercising leadership in the churches and hence such leadership has become more acceptable, rather than to a real reduction in the strength of commitment to female leadership by contemporary men or women.

Table 1.1
Pastors in Seven Protestant Denominations,
1980–1981 and 1993–1994[22]

% = % saying "agree"	Clergy Women		Clergy Men	
	1980–81	1993–94	1980–81	1993–94
1. My congregation should appoint or elect an equal number of lay women and lay men on the parish governing board.	75%	62%	58%	46%
2. More women should be ordained to full ministerial status in my denomination.	81%	72%	59%	46%
3. There should be more women in executive staff positions in regional and national offices of my denomination.	85%	80%	49%	44%
4. Inclusive language should be used in church publications and services.	87%	84%	53%	59%

The issue of "inclusive language" is more complex. There was a pervasive—we would say "feminist"—concern for inclusive language among women clergy in our 1980–81 study, and that concern continues in several ways in our more recent study. This is probably because inclusive language, despite some new denominational hymnals and liturgies, is still elusive. Church services in the 1990s are not any more likely to use inclusive language than they were in the late 1970s. Using inclusive language during worship to refer to humans—rather than speaking about *mankind* and using *man* as a generic term for all humanity—was a very radical notion in the late 1970s; many women in the churches who probably did call themselves feminists strongly advocated for more inclusive language, arguing, "Language is . . . one of our most powerful cultural institutions, and it is the shaper of consciousness and behavior. When religious language uses predominantly male images . . . consciousness is shaped in the direction of excluding women."[23]

In our 1993–94 survey, we revisited the inclusive language issue with another question about whether clergy believed that "there should be more hymns and prayers using female imagery and names for God." Both female and male pastors in the seven Protestant denominations studied in the early 1980s are today considerably less likely to feel positive toward using inclusive language when speaking about God than about inclusive language in relation to humanity. Among those pastors, however, clergy women are twice as likely as men to be advocates for using female God imagery. Eighty-four percent of the women and 59 percent of the men favor using "inclusive language" in church services, but no more than 66 percent of the women, compared to 37 percent of the men, want an increase in the use of female imagery for God. We believe that clergy, male and female, who advocate female imagery for God exhibit a form of feminism, whether or not they want to be called feminists.

Even in the 1990s, many clergy women who visualize God in female form are still unlikely to use female images for God in the church services they conduct. Joy Charlton's interviews with clergy women who were ordained in the 1970s and who are still active in ministry in the 1990s indicate that although these "pioneer women" take care as they lead worship to use language that clearly includes women whenever possible, they eschew any reference to God as other than male in their congregations.[24] Another study of feminism in the church, by Miriam Therese Winter, Adair T. Lummis, and Allison Stokes, shows that women pastors may not use inclusive language in large public settings, but they do feed themselves spiritually by using female God-language in their private prayers and in small-group liturgies with like-minded women.[25]

Catherine Wessinger's study *Religious Institutions and Women's Leadership* suggests that although educated women fighting for full leadership opportunities in the church support female God-language, many of these women know that language alone will not cause patriarchal church structures to disintegrate. There must also be a widely held norm of gender equality that allows women in the community, if not in a particular congregation or denomination, to achieve some measure of economic independence and access to greater influence through higher education.[26] Women who have an image of God as female and who are well educated consistently become ardent activists for both the structural and the theological transformation of the church.[27]

DEFINING FEMINISM

When examining clergy opinions gathered through survey research, an analysis of answers to several related questions is much more reliable and revealing than a summary of responses to each question. For this reason, we have grouped together several attitudinal items that are related to one another—in content or in a statistical way—to create an "index" on various topics. We believe that this is a helpful way to summarize survey results.[28]

In certain responses by clergy women and clergy men in our survey, we have isolated two kinds of "feminist" orientation: (1) those persons (male or female) who advocate for more women in church leadership positions and (2) those persons (male or female) who advocate for inclusive language about humans and about God in church services. The first group of responses gives us an index for what we are calling "structural feminism"; the second group of responses gives us an index for what we are calling "spiritual feminism."

Each index is created by grouping a number of related questions together. Interesting relationships emerge between clergy who score high on both indexes, low on one and high on the other, or low on both.

Index 1.1
Structural Feminism Index
Items scored: 1 = "Agree" 2 = "Feelings Mixed" 3= "Disagree"

1. Men should (not) hold the top national and regional executive positions in my denomination.
2. There should be more women in executive and staff positions in regional and national offices of my denomination.
3. More women should be ordained to full ministerial status in my denomination.
4. Women (should) be concerned with attaining top leadership positions in church or society.
5. My congregation should appoint or elect an equal number of lay women and lay men on the parish governing board.
6. Congregations (should) be pressured by denominational officials to hire a woman as pastor (even) if they would prefer to hire a man.
7. For now, in hiring, job promotions, and salary increases, women should be given preference over men with equal abilities.

standardized item alpha: clergy women .67; clergy men .76

Index 1.2
Spiritual Feminism (Inclusive Language) Index
Items scored: 1 = "Agree" 2 = "Feelings Mixed" 3 = "Disagree"

1. Inclusive language should be used in church publications and services.
2. I (would not) find inclusive language during scripture reading disruptive to my worship.
3. There should be more hymns and prayers using female imagery and names for God.

standardized item alpha: clergy women .78; clergy men .79

Clergy women and clergy men who are strong structural feminists are far more likely also to be strong spiritual feminists than are those who are indifferent to or opponents of putting more women in church leadership positions. The two indexes measure different ways of defining *feminism*. In some cases, clergy who are strong structural feminists do not agree with clergy who are strong spiritual feminists. Nevertheless, clergy women are significantly more likely than clergy men to be both strong structural and strong spiritual feminists.

Many clergy women are not feminists by either of these measures. They may be like certain clergy women as Susan Hiatt described. These are clergy women who feel so relieved that they are ordained and have any church job that they either overlook obvious inequities in their situations or feel that if they are "truly called" by God, they should not attempt to change God's church from its present holy state.[29]

Table 1.2
Responses on Feminist Indexes by Gender of Clergy

	Women (2,411)	Men (2,078)
Structural Feminism		
Very/quite strong scores (7–10)	52%	23%
Moderate, mixed (scores 11–12)	25%	24%
Low to opposed (scores 13–21)	23%	53%
	100%	100%
Spiritual Feminism		
Very strong (score 3)	56%	30%
Quite strong (score 4)	17%	16%
Moderate, mixed (scores 5–6)	17%	25%
Low to opposed (scores 7–9)	10%	29%
	100%	100%

Differences in culture among the denomination's regarding what is appropriate also shape clergy responses to these feminist issues. Sometimes the severity of sanctions for nonconforming clergy behavior will determine how feminist clergy become in their personal views, as well as influence their advocacy in ministry. Pentecostal clergy women, as reported in a study by Susan Kwilecki, are found to be indifferent to gender equality issues, especially in the church, because they see the principal struggle as otherworldly rather than an issue of gender justice. For them, the conflict is between the saved and the lost, the obedient and the disobedient. Faithful Christians are called to accept God's will and gifts and to accept without doubt Holy Scriptures which say that wives should be submissive to their husbands.[30] Even in more liberal denominations which do *not* share the ethos that wives should be submissive to their husbands, ordained women who are identified as feminists may be denied placement and promotion and not so subtly forced out of ministry altogether.[31]

In our study, we find substantial differences between clergy women and clergy men from different denominations in relation to their support for structural feminism and spiritual feminism. Clergy, especially women clergy, in the congregation-centered and institution-centered denominational clusters are substantially more likely than those in the Spirit-centered denominations to endorse feminist values about women's leadership in the church and inclusive language in worship.

Clergy men in the Southern Baptist and Spirit-centered denominations are equally unenthusiastic about structural feminism and spiritual feminism. Clergy women in the Spirit-centered denominations resemble clergy men in these denominations in their lack of interest in feminism of any variety. In fact, ordained women in the Spirit-centered denominations are less supportive of structural feminism and spiritual feminism than ordained men in every denomination surveyed but their own and the Southern Baptists. Clergy women in the Assemblies of God, as described by Margaret Poloma,[32] and generally in all Spirit-centered denominations, as Susie Stanley[33] explains, have been relegated to subservience to the authority of ordained men, who now run the denominational structures. Furthermore, because ordained women in the Spirit-centered denominations infrequently obtain graduate-level education (theological or otherwise), they miss the encouragement for career mobility that many women get during their Master of Divinity studies. Women in the Spirit-centered denominations simply accept without question the antifeminist cultural stance of their denominations.

In contrast, ordained women in the Southern Baptist denomination are more like the clergy women in the congregation-centered and institution-centered denominations than like their sisters in the Spirit-centered denominations. Southern Baptist clergy women tend to be strong advocates for more women in church leadership positions and very much in favor of using inclusive language in church services. This creates a sharp contrast between Southern Baptist clergy women and Southern Baptist clergy men around structural feminism and spiritual feminism. This split between male and female clergy among the Southern Baptists is at least five times greater than the gender split on feminist values in any other denomination as measured by our two indexes.

Although Southern Baptist clergy women have encountered negative experiences in their efforts to serve as pastors, unlike clergy women in the Spirit-centered denominations, they expect more. They are not willing to settle for structural or spiritual limitations as biblically justified or divinely ordained. Currently, it seems that the greater educational attainment of present Southern Baptist clergy women combined with the publicized controversies occurring within this denomination, have raised the sensitivities of Southern Baptist women clergy and seminarians about the unfair way women are treated, fueling their feminist consciousness and ire.[34] (See Appendix 1.5, "Responses on Feminist Indexes by Gender and Denomination.")

Women clergy are creating a new situation in many ways. The analysis of our surveys and interviews provides important new insights into the future of Protestant churches and their leadership. Whether clergy use the word or not, many clergy women and clergy men are *feminists*. What they think about the structural nature of the church and how they envision the spiritual language of the faith shape their ministries. These clergy feel genuinely called to serve the church and to serve God.

The call to ordained ministry for women, however, remains an uphill struggle. Feminist views are only one measure of the situation. Further analysis of our research provides important insights into how feminist opinions (or lack thereof) held by clergy and laity affect the abilities of clergy women to carry out their calling. To do so is a complex vocation, requiring great skill and grace. These clergy women do not live easy lives. By looking more closely at their experiences, we gain important insights to inform the work of church leaders and future clergy.

2

A COMPLEX LIFE

Modern life is complex. Not only do people have many roles and relationships with a variety of persons, but when expectations call for conflicting behaviors or management of time, private and public roles become entangled and confused. Persons who enter the ordained ministry take on a particularly complex life.

In the early 1970s, church consultants and sociologists of occupations described the "occupation of divinity" as a profession in which its practitioners (clergy) were particularly apt to suffer severe "role strain," due to ambiguous and conflicting expectations about what their priorities should be and how the pastoral role should be enacted on a daily basis.[1] These researchers warned that the more role strain clergy are under, the greater difficulty they will have fulfilling the clergy role effectively and the more likely they will be to suffer a physical or mental breakdown. The situation has not changed dramatically. Today, role conflict for clergy is no different than it was in the 1970s, and clergy role strain and burnout continue.[2]

MAINTAINING BOUNDARIES

Clergy often have a more difficult time than people in other occupations claiming private space for themselves away from the demands of the church job. This is because, for many people, "being in the ministry" is a way of life, not just a job. Although this holistic concept of the clergy calling is attractive, it is also dangerous. Too often, for both ordained and lay persons, the idea that a clergy career is a special "calling from God" leads to unrealistic expectations that clergy should devote all of their waking time to ministry. Furthermore, parish ministry, compared with all other settings for ministry, is the most "embedded employment," as sociologist Teresa Marciano puts it.[3] By this she means that many parish ministers are expected and expect themselves *not* to have a life that is distinct from their church work. This makes it difficult for clergy to find sufficient personal, family, or social time away from the demands of the church to enable them to be whole, healthy individuals. Even when mental health professionals convince denominational executives and clergy that they must establish "boundaries" between their church work and their private lives,[4] actually doing so is extremely difficult. As one clergy woman put it:

> My leaving ordained ministry was *not* about being female. It was about having a personal life, a job with professional boundaries and time limits. I *need* a job *separate* from my life! . . . I am troubled by the lack of professional boundaries in the church. To me, that connects with clergy sexual abuse and other unhealthy behaviors. I believe very few clergy can handle the diffusion of boundaries in the church.
>
> (clergy woman)

Another, often unrecognized difficulty that clergy face in balancing and bridging different aspects of their lives is that churches, for clergy, are typically places where they work, not places where they volunteer their time as they choose or find nurture or help in bringing together the different aspects of their distracted, complex lives. This situation is clearest to clergy who enter the ministry late in life, having spent many years in churches as active lay persons before taking on their responsibilities as ordained ministers. As one woman explained:

> This small suburban church I pastor was declining when I came a couple of years ago. During the time I have been here, membership and finances have improved greatly, though we still have a long way to go. This is my first position; I did not get ordained until my mid-forties. I like the people in this church and the feeling seems mutual. But I am coming to realize fully the meaning of "self-care"—that it is *not* the same as religious involvement. When I was employed full-time in a scientific career, I was also very, very active in the church music program and as a lay leader. The church was both my support and my "hobby." Involvement in the church before ordination was a good way of "self-care." I am realizing that I must "get my jollies" *outside* of the church. . . . I am trying to discover ways of nourishing myself, but I am not sure quite how to do that yet.
>
> (clergy woman)

To assess the ways in which clergy manage the time and role demands of their chosen career, we have developed an index of items that clusters together a group of responses to our questionnaire that may measure the ability of clergy to manage the various roles and boundaries in their lives.

Are clergy women more or less likely to be able to handle role conflicts and maintain boundaries between their church work and private lives? From one vantage point, it might be anticipated that the relative newness of ordained women in pulpits and other church positions makes them more vulnerable to pressures to overwork. From another vantage point, however, because clergy women have been ordained more recently than many clergy men, they might hold to newer, professional understandings of the clergy role rather than to the older views of ministry as a twenty-four-hour, seven-day-a-week immersion. Women may also be less constrained to model the "male image" of clergy.

Index 2.1
Boundary Maintenance Index
Items scored from 1, "usually true," to 4, "usually false"

---

1. I was able to maintain a separation between my ministerial duties and my private life.
2. I felt I did have enough time to do what was expected of me by my family or spouse/partner.
3. I usually had enough time to be alone for reflection, hobbies, reading, and recreation.
4. I felt I did (not) impose unrealistic expectations on myself.

---

standardized item alpha: clergy women .68; clergy men .70

Our findings indicate that although substantial differences exist among ordained women and men in their ability to establish boundaries in and between their church work and personal life, clergy women do not significantly differ from clergy men in how well they do this.

Table 2.1
Responses on the Boundary Maintenance Index by Gender

	Women	Men
Very high, good (scores 4–7)	21%	21%
Quite high (scores 8–9)	21%	23%
Moderately fair (scores 10–11)	27%	26%
Low, poor ability (scores 12–16)	31%	30%
	100%	100%

Difference between women and men not significant

CLERGY WITH SPOUSES

Family circumstances vary greatly among clergy. Some clergy believe that marriage is essential to effective ministry. Others view children as a drawback, especially for women clergy. Marital status and whether clergy are parents of minor children greatly affect the complexity of their lives and how they handle role demands emanating from their church employment. Balancing church and personal time is often more difficult for women clergy:

When I was first ordained, I firmly believed that my career would take priority in my life. Even in my last parish position when my child was two years old, I held to my conviction that I was a "pastor who also happened to be a mother." It was very difficult carrying on a full-time ministry with a toddler, even though my husband helped a lot with child care and was supportive of my ministry. Then with the church crisis, many hours away from home in evening meetings, days when I only saw my family for an hour or two, if that, I realized my priorities were screwed up. My relationship with my child did suffer due to my absence five evenings a week. I was burning out from all the strain at the church, the long hours of work, and the guilt. . . . The problem is that so many women, and men for that matter, do not really understand what they are getting into in the parish ministry. They are naive about what the system will demand of them.

(clergy woman)

My first church I hope will be my last. This church was a small church of mainly elderly members, in a "transitional" urban neighborhood that has been rapidly changing economically and racially. The older members who remained after the majority moved to the suburbs clung to the memory of a flourishing church in the sixties. I hated much of the job: the boring committee meetings, the conflicts, the apathy, the passive-aggressive stodgy folk with their crisis mentality. Too, I am introverted. The fishbowl existence of pastor and family I found almost an unendurable invasion of privacy. My wife, also ordained, had a baby soon after we got there. *She* wanted to do more than stay home with the baby. *I* wanted to have a life very apart from church work. So I gave my notice to the church, and made a career change to "housedad." We moved to another state so my wife could accept a good pastoral position. I am taking care of our child and the home full-time now. I am thinking about going back for a doctorate so I can teach when we do not have preschool children.

(clergy man)

Not only am I working full-time for this church, but we live right next door. This makes it a little difficult to carve out uninterrupted family time from church demands. We have two teenagers, who are pretty independent but do need some attention. My husband, who is also ordained, had not been able to get a full-time church job in this area, and has been doing consulting and part-time administrative work from an office in our home—so he also has some geographical difficulty in separating work and family life. Fortunately, when both of us were working full-time, we bought a vacation home. In my present church, this is still within driving distance. We go up there at least a weekend or two a month and spend a week or so there in the summer. This vacation home has helped us do things together as a family for extended periods of time. Also, I *always* take my day off!

(clergy woman)

As a wife, mother, and pastor for nearly fifteen years, I have taken care to ensure that my children are not ignored for the "bottomless pit" demands of congregations. True, I was not very good at doing this when my children were very young and I was new to the parish ministry. But I think I have learned over the years how to balance the roles of *mother* and *pastor* quite well. But I am still having less success in balancing the *wife* and *pastor* role. That is, I have trouble finding time for my husband and me to be together without the church or children. I am in a clergy woman support group, and other "married-with-children" clergy women I know also have this problem. Somehow, it is a lot easier making it clear to the congregation that I am going to spend time with my children rather than go to some church activity, than to say I would prefer not to come because I want to spend time with my husband *alone*.

(clergy woman)

Each of the preceding stories illustrates the variety of components that may affect the ease with which married clergy balance their personal life roles and clergy roles. Marriage is demanding for both men and women. By itself, however, all other things being equal, marriage has no effect on the ability of clergy men to maintain boundaries in their lives (as indicated by their scores on the Boundary Maintenance Index), and it seems to make boundary maintenance only slightly more difficult for clergy women.[5]

We found in our sample that clergy women are more likely to be single than clergy men — 38 percent of the clergy women in our sample were single, compared to 8 percent of the men. Interestingly, being single seems to reduce the prevalence of cross-pressures between church and personal life slightly for clergy women but has no effect on clergy men's ability to manage boundaries.

When clergy marry, the majority marry someone who is not ordained. However, clergy women are more likely to have an ordained spouse than clergy men. Among the married clergy, 42% of the clergy women and 8% of the married clergy men are part of "clergy couples" in our study. Whether or not their spouse is ordained, however, has no direct effect on the ability of married clergy to maintain boundaries between church work and private life.

CLERGY COUPLES

It seems to be easier for clergy couples to understand and deal with each other's needs than it is for couples where one spouse is working in secular employment or not working outside the home at all. Sociologist Edward Lehman, who has written numerous books and articles on clergy women, found that ordained men who are part of clergy couples are more equitable in their leadership and styles than other clergy men.[6] Similarly, clergy men in our study who are married to clergy women are more likely than those married to nonordained women to endorse women's taking leadership in the church and methods to achieve their doing so. That is, clergy men married to clergy women tend to score high on the Structural Feminism Index. It is also true that if the wives of clergy men work outside the home *at all,* these clergy husbands are more apt than those whose wives remain at home to adopt a liberal view of women's role and score high on our Structural Feminism Index.

With clergy women, however, commitment to feminism is unrelated to whether their spouse is ordained. For both married clergy men and clergy women, having an ordained spouse is unrelated to the ability to manage boundaries between church and personal life. As with other married women who work outside the home, clergy women do not significantly reduce the time they give to maintaining a home and home life; they simply struggle in new ways to balance all their commitments to work and family.

This does not necessarily mean that the husbands of clergy women fail to share in the housework and care of young children. Our interviews, supported by other studies, suggest that married clergy women often have very egalitarian marriages that are personally fulfilling. To maintain an egalitarian marriage, however, takes commitment and time from both partners, even when both partners are clergy.[7]

> My husband and I sought a co-pastorate because of our situation with two preschool children. We made the following time arrangement with the parish. We would share the position and alternate weeks. For example, one week my husband would take over *all* the ministerial duties, and I would take care of the children and home. The next week we reversed roles; I was the only minister, and he was the homemaker. It was good for a time. . . . But money was tight, and after a while it was also evident that my husband liked this co-pastorate situation better than I did. I was restless, I wanted something more challenging. I needed a lot more independence and personal freedom in my work, as well as more income, than this position provided. My husband and I finally decided we could live together, work together, but not do both at the same time. We are still married, my children are teenagers still in the home, but I work in denominational headquarters and he is the pastor of a small congregation.
>
> (clergy woman)

It is not surprising that married clergy women are somewhat better able to manage role demands and maintain boundaries between work and private life when they have a househusband caring for the home more or less full-time. When we look at the situation from the other side, however, if the wife of a clergy man works outside the home, it has no impact on his capacity to maintain boundaries.[8] Most clergy men are married to wives who, if they work at all, work in secular occupations to augment the family income.

In contemporary society, career decisions are increasingly difficult in any marriage where both the husband and the wife work outside the home. Our study shows, however, that married clergy women are accorded less consideration in their career decisions by their husbands than they give to their husbands' career decisions. Married clergy, especially clergy men, whose spouse is not fully salaried are most apt to report that their own career needs are given priority. However, among married clergy with fully employed spouses, clergy women are less likely than clergy men to say that their career needs are given as much weight when compared with that of their employed spouses.

CLERGY WITH CHILDREN

When a clergy woman's husband is working full-time, she is apt to have a problem keeping her own life on schedule, especially if she also has a child at home. Fortunately, because a higher proportion of clergy women than clergy men are presently single and because ordained women tend to be older than ordained men, in our study, fewer clergy women (37 percent) than clergy men (56 percent) had a child under age eighteen presently living at home.

These same respondents reported, however, that nearly half (48 percent) of the clergy women and a great majority (89 percent) of the clergy men recall a time when they had at least one child at home while they were working full-time in ministry. Among these ordained parents, clergy men are more than twice as likely as clergy women to report that it was "relatively easy" to carry on their full-time ministry with a young child at home (43 percent to 18 percent). Three times as many clergy women as clergy men (30 percent to 9 percent) recall that it was "very difficult" to carry on their full-time ministry when they had to care for a child under ten. The reason for this discrepancy is obvious—child-care responsibilities are not evenly shared.

Our study shows that responsibility for child care falls primarily on the mother, regardless of whether she is ordained. Fully 43 percent of the clergy women who were working in full-time ministry when their child was young had the major responsibility for care of the child, but only 3 percent of the clergy men in the same situation were the primary caretakers.

Older children and teenagers do not need the near-constant oversight that children ten years of age or younger require, but preteens and teens present their own special set of pressures on any family. It is understandable why both clergy women and clergy men who have any children at home under age eighteen are less likely than those without minors at home to have high scores on the Boundary Maintenance Index. They simply are less able than clergy who do not live with children or teens to handle role and time conflicts successfully and to maintain boundaries between their church work and private life.[9]

It may also be the case that clergy men who currently have children at home, and younger clergy fathers generally, are actually more interested than older clergy men in spending substantial amounts of time with their children.[10] Unfortunately, when clergy men do become more involved with their children and teenagers, they become as likely as clergy women to encounter greater difficulties in time and role management. Sometimes clergy couples take co-pastorate positions precisely so both can parent their young children. Sometimes this works, but our interviews show that balancing the ministry career, marriage, and family is very difficult, even in a co-pastorate.

> After seminary my husband and I (with our baby) were very enthusiastic about the idea of sharing a parish and parenting. We got the parish, but then we had to struggle with finding the ideal way to share the position. We tried alternating weeks— with one of us being sole minister and the other the parent-caretaker, and then

reversed it. But we did not like this arrangement. . . . We moved and got different positions—my husband in a social service agency, and me as the sole pastor of a small church. During my pastorate there I had my second child. Taking care of two children and a church just became too much, especially since my husband was also working long hours. My husband and I wanted to spend some time with our children and each other, as well as do ministry. Both my husband and I left these positions. He is not fully employed as yet, and may leave ministry altogether for secular work. I am now an associate in a large church with good pay and good hours (no more ever than 40 hours a week). It's hard to think ahead what I will do when my children are through high school, but right now I am happy.

(clergy woman)

Having one pastor or even a clergy couple with young children is not always easy on members of the congregations these clergy are trying to serve. Lay leaders want to be supportive, but often they feel cheated, as illustrated in the following comments from three different congregations:

Our ministers are co-pastors, equally sharing the position and family responsibilities of three children under six. Yes, this brings problems. Communication is hard sometimes. Neither is number one leader—however, if they disagree, they never make an issue of it at meetings. But their life is very stressful, and the workload here is demanding. I would not recommend this for a young family. The female is the stronger and better leader. This does not settle well with some people. The congregation is tiring of this arrangement. The lay leadership is overworked trying to work with them.

(lay leader)

We have a very small congregation with a woman pastor with a young child. The burdens of motherhood and pastoral responsibilities should not be underestimated with regards to its effects on the pastor's health and the availability of the pastor to the church.

(lay leader)

I have come to know our pastor and love her dearly, admire her talents and abilities, consider her a good friend, and almost a daughter. . . . She was voted for by the majority of the congregation and I admire her for the way she handled the twenty percent who were openly pro–male pastor. When their baby was born, she moved to a three-quarter time pastorate. . . . It has been my job as chair of the commission to see that the pulpit is filled and worship services planned during her three-month maternity leave. I support her right to have a family. But it does complicate things and call for much compromise and planning as we face, what for us, are uncharted waters.

(lay leader)

Sometimes the struggle to balance church work and family life, for the clergy woman especially but also for young married clergy men with children, is just too much, and they leave ministry. The women who leave, however, would probably stay in ministry if more flexibility and acceptance of combining motherhood and ministry in a church career were possible. One clergy woman suggests that the solution may require us to overhaul the expectations of ordained ministry itself:

> One of my great hopes for the church is that we will return to an understanding of ordination as "functional ministry." Presently, we ordain for life and there is great pressure to maintain that ordained status. As a clergy woman approaching full-fledged motherhood, I want the freedom to choose my lifestyle and career path without the stigma of having "left the ministry" to raise a family. If we return to an understanding of ordination for functions in a specific time, place, etc., then ordained men and women can feel more freedom to do secular work, take a part-time church position, or other family options. Sounds good to me!
>
> (clergy woman)

In their efforts to balance personal and church work in an optimal fashion, clergy women still must take into account, to a far greater extent than clergy men with spouses or children, how lay committees or regional denominational executives will assess the adjustments and solutions they devise. Sometimes spouses take turns giving priority to each other's career. Sometimes a clergy woman may insist that the time has come for "her turn," regardless of whether her husband is working for the church or for a corporation. But even when a clergy woman's husband is supportive, or at least not in open opposition, she may have trouble convincing her denominational executive or the congregational search or hiring committee that she can be a successful pastor if she has children at home or must maintain a commuter marriage:

> In order to take this very good appointment . . . wealthy church in a lovely community . . . recently, I had to convince the bishop that neither the church, my marriage, nor teenage children would suffer, if I had a commuter marriage. For the past twenty years, I had always sacrificed my career so our family could be near where my husband, a federal government executive, works. Now it is his turn to make some adjustments. I am working fifty hours a week and Sunday is of course a busy day. He comes up here most weekends so far, during my first year here. We'll see how it goes.
>
> (clergy woman)

ECONOMIC AND GEOGRAPHIC PRESSURES

Married clergy usually have a major advantage over single clergy, because they tend to have considerably higher family incomes. This is especially true for clergy women.[11] Clergy women are typically married to spouses who work in some profession or managerial position, pushing total family income into a fairly comfortable range. Unfortunately, income alone does not guarantee financial security. Many times, other expenses cause additional stress. Even at the higher income brackets, analysis shows that when clergy say that they experience some difficulty living comfortably on their income, they are likely to have more role strain and difficulty setting boundaries than clergy who can make ends meet without too much fuss. Still a spouse with a good salary enables clergy, especially clergy women, to take church positions where they are needed but that do not pay much. Yet, even with sufficient income, married clergy women may experience difficulty in balancing church work, family responses, and time for themselves.

> I have put a lot of vision and effort into this, my first church. It is the most liberal church in a very conservative town. Efforts have paid off, in less than four years this church has doubled in size (though still under 150 members). Yet, I get a lot of spiritual sustenance and satisfaction from the many hours a week I put in—but a very modest church salary. I can afford to work here because my husband has an excellent managerial salary. The congregation knows they have a deal.
>
> How do I balance church and private life? *Very poorly.* The commute to this church from our home is between thirty and sixty minutes. That, on top of a sixty-hour workweek, doesn't leave a lot of time for a private life. My social life with those outside of my immediate family is practically nil during most of the year. *But* every July and August I *take* two months' vacation with my family.
>
> (clergy woman)

> Balancing ministerial work and private life is something I have had to learn to do to survive. In my first positions in a church social service agency, I was in burnout and suffering a severe emotional and physical breakdown because I could not stop my ministerial work from consuming all my waking hours.
>
> Now, as pastor of this little congregation, I am having a relatively easy time setting these boundaries. This particular church situation makes it easy: (1) My husband works in a higher educational institution, and I live near his work—a half hour away from this church. Distance helps keep boundaries, especially since most members live close to the church. (2) This little church has been used to so little from its pastors for so long—they never complain when I take my weekly day off regularly, never demur when I say I am going to be away for a few days.
>
> (clergy woman)

The clergy women above overlook their low salaries because they are getting other intrinsic rewards from these parish positions, not the least of which are lay members showing appreciation for them and allowing them time away from the church to pursue private and family interests. These parish situations are relatively free of cross-pressures and conflicts concerning what the pastor should be doing. These are congregations in which women pastors have been able to establish clear boundaries between their church work and private life. Unfortunately, other clergy women—and especially clergy men—who need more income or clergy with families that demand more time do not find the ministerial rewards of such parish ministry worth the costs of time and lost income. Nor are single clergy likely to find that an appreciative congregation and time off are enough compensation for putting in fifty or more hours a week at low salary, especially if the congregation is located in an area where it is difficult for a younger person to have a social life.

Low income is only one factor leading to job dissatisfaction among clergy. Location is extremely important. Clergy serving in rural and small-town settings are often very unhappy because these settings lack other clergy. For women, the lack of other women clergy to talk with about parish situations, managing time, stress, loneliness, and trying to establish boundaries exacerbates their unhappiness. Clergy women in suburban and urban areas can be lonely too, but the situation for women who serve rural congregations leads to severe geographic isolation.

Geographic realities are especially significant for clergy women. Ordained women are more often found in the smaller, more isolated parishes, in part because they are more willing to pastor such churches. Ordained men are often focused on the higher salaries and enhanced opportunities for career advancement which come from experience in larger, better paying suburban and urban churches. These wealthier churches often prefer to hire a clergy man as senior or sole pastor on the grounds that richer, older lay members are more likely to support a church headed by an ordained man rather than a woman. Small-town and rural churches, which typically have less status-conscious members as well as less material advantages to offer their pastors, sometimes choose the better qualified woman over the less qualified man among those clergy who are willing to come to congregations in less populated areas. This may be good for the church, but it creates difficulties for the female pastor.[12]

Julie Kanaar's study of Lutheran clergy women in rural pastorates found that these women "often have difficulty finding friends and occasions to socialize outside of the context of being pastor," and their preferred sources of support—other Lutheran pastors—are not easily accessible. Seminary students are often not well prepared for the realities, both negative and positive, of rural pastorates. Rural clergy need to develop support networks with other clergy on a regional basis and use electronic mail to communicate with their far-flung clergy colleagues.

In spite of the problems, research on clergy in rural congregations documents some important job satisfactions: "experiencing the sense of community that exists in rural areas," "having time available to visit parishioners and to study," "enjoying the affirmation and support found in the rural setting," "living in a scenic area and feeling a connection to the land," and "enjoying the freedom in scheduling that comes with serving a small parish and being able to work on 'flextime.'" Working on flextime is important.[13] It helps clergy avoid role strain and overload in their pastoral roles and may even help them establish boundaries between church and personal life—if they exert themselves to find sources of support beyond the local area.

As growing numbers of women seminary graduates accept vacancies in small congregations in sparsely populated areas, new support networks with other clergy women are developing. This has already occurred in the Berkshire hills and valleys of western Massachusetts, where, according to Allison Stokes, "there is a geographic concentration of women pastors unprecedented anywhere in the country." Because of this concentration, Stokes, who is one of these rural pastors, explains, there is now a "critical mass of clergy sisters within a mixed association of clergy." In the Berkshires, clergy women have a strong support network, which, Stokes says, "has made us more able to claim our authority and move forward because we have the encouragement, support and affection of one another."[14]

SINGLE CLERGY

The combination of long hours and low pay in an isolated church situation is particularly difficult for single clergy, especially women. This is evident in the following story by a "formerly single," overworked, impoverished, lonely clergy woman—now happily married and financially secure:

> During my first two pastoral positions after seminary, I gave my all to my ministry. One day I came to realize that my work was my *whole* life. This did not make me happy. Also, I was poor—financially and emotionally. I was working fifty to sixty hours a week for low pay and little appreciation. I found myself becoming a bitter person who could not be effective in any kind of ministry. So I tried to do something about it. I tried to make some friends outside the church and also to start dating. But it is hard to date men as a single woman pastor . . . they are scared of you as a professional "religious person." Getting time for any social life was difficult too: the church acted as if it owned you twenty-four hours a day. But I kept at it—went to social clubs and hobby groups—any event that I could attend which looked promising and did not cost much. At one of these events I met my husband! Marriage has dramatically improved my personal life and my professional life.
>
> (clergy woman)

Marriage usually supports good health, for clergy and for laity. Marriage also sometimes enhances a woman's credibility as a colleague. One associate minister reported that the senior pastor was "more comfortable with me after I married than when I was single. He liked my husband, and we did things with the senior pastor and his wife as couples." The members of the congregation also treated her better after her marriage, knowing that she had a husband. The biggest change, however, was in her personal attitude toward her ministry:

> I was better able to put my ministry into perspective. Before marriage—when the ministry was my *whole* life—any little negative thing someone said upset me for hours. Now I just brush it off and do not overreact like I once did. I feel I am more effective in ministry now because I want to go home to my husband and young children—so I organize my work well.
>
> (clergy woman)

Single clergy often have more difficulty than married clergy in establishing boundaries between their church and personal lives because (1) lay members of their congregations are not as likely to understand or legitimate the need or desire of single pastors for time away from congregational concerns as they would be for married pastors, and (2) single clergy, if they do not have much personal or social life outside their work setting, may not be as motivated to establish boundaries as they would be if they were married.

While single clergy are divided on what effect they think their ordained status has on their general social life, most single clergy are more likely to see their occupation as an obstacle than as an advantage in having opportunities for a "sustained intimate relationship." Single clergy women consistently believe that it is more difficult for them than it is for single clergy men to have a healthy social life and, especially, a romantic relationship.

Table 2.2
Effect of Being Clergy on Personal Relationships of Singles

	General Social Life		Intimate Relationships	
	Women (744)	Men (147)	Women (710)	Men (142)
Positive effect	18%	36%	9%	22%
Mixed or no effect	41%	30%	30%	32%
Negative effect	41%	34%	61%	46%
	100%	100%	100%	100%

About one-fourth of all single clergy, male and female, who answered the survey explained why they thought their ordained status was an obstacle to meaningful romantic friendships. The major reason for single ordained men is that they live in a fishbowl. Close scrutiny by one's parishioners makes it hard to be open about dating or wanting to meet someone. Another, less important reason for considering their occupation to have a negative impact on developing romantic relationships is that they have no available time and little opportunity to meet other singles who are desirable or interested in intimate friendships.

Some of the single ordained women also gave these reasons, but their major explanation for the negative effect of their clergy status on finding intimate companionship was that men are threatened by the thought of dating an ordained woman. The second most cited explanation was that the time demands on them as clergy are so overwhelming that they have little time to meet anyone.

Parish ministry is a demanding career for both men and women in terms of the sheer number of hours expected in a normal workweek. There are also wise prohibitions against clergy forming romantic affiliations with lay members of their congregations, regardless of whether both are single adults. For single or formerly married clergy, therefore, finding the time and the opportunity to develop romantic friendships is difficult—even for male pastors who are eligible and attractive.

Single clergy women have an even harder time cultivating satisfactory social lives and meaningful romantic relationships. Unlike eligible clergy men, who may be hounded by hopeful women and can pursue those they like if they can find the time, single clergy women must be far more circumspect in showing interest. The women find that being an ordained woman is more of a turnoff than a come-on to many of the interesting men they find attractive. For men, the situation is the opposite:

> In my first congregation I tried to do everything people wanted. I found that was impossible even in that small church and even if I put in 120 hours a week. . . . After I was divorced and serving another church, I did find it a bit difficult to have a romantic life. Of course I make it an absolute rule not to get involved with a member of my congregation. Still, I had to laugh when my daughter came to visit one weekend, and said: "Dad, I am worried. Do you realize there are lots of women in this church hitting on you?!"
>
> (clergy man)

Another clergy man commented:

> I now counsel clergy that yes, the parish ministry *is more than a full-time job,* but they should never, never put in more than fifty hours a week on the average, and forty-five would be better. In fact I tell clergy that if they feel overwhelmed, it is their *own fault.*
>
> (clergy man)

Living a balanced life is difficult for clergy. They have every good intention, but the expectations of laity and their own sometimes inflated ideas of what God expects can leave them exhausted and lonely. For women, who often have been socialized to be sensitive to the needs of others, recognizing their own needs is sometimes the hardest challenge:

> How do I balance my ministry with time for myself? I *don't!* I have never been able to do this well. One of the questions parish search committees always ask you is: "How do you plan to nurture yourself?" Good question! Getting a social life as a single woman pastor is very difficult. It is hard to meet people and socialize freely if you are the local pastor. No matter where you go, you are always "on call." Not only do female clergy intimidate men on a social level, it is hard to find time to put into a relationship. I expect that single clergy men have some of the same problems. But in this culture it is all right for men—even clergy men—to be aggressive in dating. Whereas for women—particularly clergy women—it would be considered far too aggressive if they took the initiative in dating.
>
> (clergy woman)

> My child was in primary school when my clergy husband and I were divorced. At one point I thought about giving up on church employment altogether, and working for McDonald's so I could be there when my child came home from school. . . . Getting a social life for myself was difficult when I was first divorced, in finding awake

time that was not devoted to church and child, as well as money for baby-sitters, etc. Although I am dating more now, I find that my profession and commitment to it either leaves men "confessing" that they lack religion, or what I do confuses or threatens them, or they cling to me for the wrong reasons. . . . I would not change my career or do anything really different with my life—except find some easier way to put all these pieces together!

(clergy woman)

Life is complicated for all clergy, but it is stories of single clergy women in rural areas and small towns that show how difficult things are for many women clergy. Some may think that it is easier to distinguish between work and private life if people know each other in both settings; in fact, it makes it more difficult to set boundaries—especially if one is a single clergy woman. Single clergy women in rural churches, for example, find that having a private life away from the concerns of the church or the curiosity of church members and community leaders is virtually impossible. Not only are these women pastors like prize fish in the community fishbowl, but often no other fish of their species are in the bowl. The women make jokes about it, but it is not a funny situation:

What social life? People in the church forget their minister is single, and so I do not get invitations to Thanksgiving or Christmas dinners. At the same time, people here drop in to visit unannounced. People stop in to see me anytime they see my car near the house— and since there is no garage, they can always see the car. In this small farm community with fewer than 150 people, I have had to be very careful about boundaries between church work and my time "off." Making such "boundaries" is not easy for people here to understand. This is a farm community, and farmers do not take a weekly "day off." Most have never had a "vacation." I am younger and more educated than most in this community. It is somewhat hard to find congenial social friends. This isolation is a significant source of stress in my life. My major way of getting support is through telephone conversations with former seminary classmates and others who live at a distance. My telephone bill is huge, but an absolute necessity of life.

(clergy woman)

Being single in a rural parish affects social life—at least romantic life—negatively. I have made friends with women in the parish, which is nice, but I want more than a celibate life and all my social life within the congregation. Even in a rural area, I do feel that married clergy have an easier time getting away from the demands of the parish. But I am learning to handle this. First, I *always* take my day off, go on retreats, and vacation *away* from the area.

(clergy woman)

My first and only church position, right after seminary, was at a small church in a small town where most of the members and residents were over age sixty. Being a single young woman in a small-town parish is really "swimming in a fish bowl." There were few unmarried men anywhere near my age in the town, and those I did meet seemed intimidated by a woman minister. I had no personal life. After five years in this town, I realized that I might never "get a life" if I stayed. One problem for women in this denomination is that young women are supposed to stay celibate until marriage—especially if they are seminarians or pastors. Another problem is that most of the churches open to women are rural churches. So I left this church, and I left ministry for an administrative job. I have a relationship now, I have "a life"!

(clergy woman)

LESBIAN AND GAY CLERGY

Life in the ministry is even more complex and difficult for lesbian and gay clergy. While single heterosexual clergy have difficulty having a personal life in parish ministry, this difficulty is compounded for gay and lesbian clergy. In our study, four lesbian and gay clergy who decided to leave the active ministry were clear that their sexual orientation was a major factor. The situation for these clergy is very complicated.

First, lesbian and gay clergy compete fiercely for the few congregations that will call an openly homosexual pastor. This makes it very difficult to get a job where one's known sexual preference will not jeopardize a call. Second, if a clergy woman or clergy man is not "out," or open about her or his sexuality, that pastor experiences an ongoing inner struggle over whether it is fair or right to work in authorized church leadership (ordained ministry) while hiding one's sexual identity. As one lesbian put it:

> I have become rather anti-clerical of late and am seriously considering surrendering my credentials. Ordination seems to me to be too power-oriented; it tends more to divide than to join clergy and laity. . . . Then there's the issue of sexuality, which the church wants to condemn—when it doesn't ignore it. I'm tired of having to hide myself as a lesbian in the church, especially being ordained.

(clergy woman)

A gay man wrote:

> I enjoy a deeply rewarding and affectionate pastoral bond with my parishioners. I am also gay and celibate . . . my orientation would not be acceptable to many of my parishioners. The love and support which mean so much to me are conditional. If they knew, I would experience some devastating rejection.

(clergy man)

Sometimes chaplaincies, which typically have set hours and are located in hospitals, prisons, and other institutions in more urban areas, allow greater freedom for clergy with nontraditional lifestyles. Some lesbian and gay clergy, however, say that it is easier to get employment in a secular position, where being gay or lesbian is fairly irrelevant:

I prefer chaplaincy. Even if I were suited to parish ministry, and liked it, I would have a more difficult time finding a job because I am lesbian, and refuse to hide it in order to work. Most chaplaincy positions have less of a "fishbowl" environment for their clergy—which helps. My partner and I have been together two and a half years. She works in a hospital setting too, but not in chaplaincy. . . . I have become very selective in the type of work I will do, and the conditions with which I will work, and the role I have to play if I accept certain positions. Therefore, there aren't a whole lot of jobs out there which fit my qualifications.

(clergy woman)

For some gay and lesbian clergy, there are simply no professional jobs in church-related ministries that are acceptable. This is very painful. Ironically, in spite of its refusal to accept the gifts of these clergy, the church does benefit. By making pastoral ministry so difficult for gay and lesbian clergy, it forces them to avoid employment in local congregations, but it does not keep them from involvement in church. One gay man wrote:

I left the church voluntarily because they were prejudiced against my sexual orientation. . . . I am an executive now in a large corporation. . . . [My companion for ten years] owns a small company. If I were to resume ordained ministry, they would have to dismantle their structure of anti-gay restrictions. I doubt this will happen in my lifetime, if ever. . . . I think you might profit from looking at gays and lesbians who have had to leave the church either for conscience sake or for scandal/rumor. The churches have wasted huge assets in letting us go. On the other hand, the churches have empowered significant lay ministry, because we were generally well prepared with a wide range of skills.

(former clergy man, now lay leader)

Fortunately, not all church leaders are against gay and lesbian clergy. Many recognize and value their gifts for ministry. Many are impressed with the way in which this issue calls the churches to accountability. And sometimes church leaders are inspired by the capacity of the church to change and grow. One lay leader wrote:

I have just served on the search committee for my UCC [United Church of Christ] congregation in which we selected a lesbian for associate minister. Amazingly, our tradition allowed us to present her to the congregation and provide the historical framework to further discuss this. It was painful. Many will probably leave the church. I am not a lesbian, but the selection of this woman has so renewed my faith in the organized church. . . . We have chosen a powerful, spirited woman and I feel pulled back into "my family."[15]

(female lay leader)

In our study, only a small sample (under 5 percent) of the clergy identified themselves as being in a committed relationship with another person of the same gender: 147 clergy women and 64 clergy men. When we look for possible differences between lesbian and gay clergy in committed relationships and other clergy women and clergy men in our study, we find very few. Although partnered gays and lesbians tend to be slightly younger than other clergy, usually more difference exists between women and men than between homosexuals and heterosexuals. Lesbians with partners are slightly less likely than other clergy women to be employed in parish ministry; but clergy women, whatever their sexual preference, are less likely to be in parish ministry than clergy men. Not surprisingly, gay and lesbian clergy are more likely than other clergy to anticipate difficulty in getting another church job that is better than the one they now have, and gay and lesbian clergy are more likely than other clergy to have given serious thought to leaving the ordained ministry. The differences here are slight. Overall, no significant difference is apparent between partnered lesbian and gay clergy and other ordained women and men in terms of how much difficulty they have in time management or in maintaining clear boundaries between church work and private life. Gay and lesbian clergy have complex lives, but when we look at all of the issues, we find that their lives are not much different from those of other clergy. (See Appendix 2.1, "Lesbian and Gay Clergy in Committed Relationships.")

EVER-DIVORCED CLERGY

Currently divorced clergy are, of course, single, but many clergy have been divorced and are now remarried. In our study, only 8 percent of the clergy were presently divorced, but 22 percent had been divorced at some point in their lives. Therefore, "ever-divorced" information is a better measure than any "currently divorced" rate to explain the impact of divorce on male and female clergy and its significance for church leadership.

Until a few years ago, for a clergy man or clergy woman to get a divorce was unusual. Often divorce forced the end of his or her career in ministry. Because marriage is a sacrament, or rite blessed by the churches, and understood in relationship to scripture, divorce presents a theological as well as a human crisis in the church. Many Protestant denominations have modified earlier harsh judgments against divorced people, but it is still difficult when clergy divorce.

Attitudes toward divorce vary dramatically—among denominations, across different regions of the country, and even in local congregations. It would be nice if Protestant clergy could exemplify in their own lives the absolute sanctity of marriage vows, but like other people, they are human. As a consequence, divorce is yet another complicating factor in the lives of clergy.

Some congregations and denominations still do not knowingly accept a divorced man or woman as pastor. Clergy wonder, therefore, how much they should reveal about their past when seeking a job. When an active pastor divorces, judgments and divisions may arise in the congregation and in the wider church. Several clergy divorces in a year in a diocese, presbytery, region, conference, synod, or judicatory can have repercussions that reach far beyond the particular clergy family in crisis.

In our study, approximately 24 percent of the clergy women (or 586 out of the 2,485 clergy women in our sample) and 18 percent of the clergy men (or 389 of the 2,116 clergy men responding) had ever been divorced. This rate is very similar to that found among lay persons in contemporary society. The best divorce statistics available to the public come from the U.S. Census Bureau's most recent survey on the national divorce rate, conducted in 1985. That survey states that 23 percent of women and 22 percent of men in the United States have been divorced.[16]

It is important to note that divorce is not the norm among active clergy. In our large sample of clergy, most ordained women and men were in their first marriage—50 percent of the women and 75 percent of the men.

The divorce rate among clergy women, however, is still cause for concern. The divorce rate for clergy women not only is slightly higher than that for clergy men but has increased somewhat since the early 1970s. Furthermore, of the clergy in our study who have been married, three out of ten of the clergy women have been divorced, compared to two out of ten of the clergy men. It is important to note, however, that the divorces of women clergy often have no connection to their work as clergy. Divorced clergy women are nearly twice as likely as divorced clergy men to have been divorced years before they entered the ministry. Whatever their reasons, clergy women do not divorce more frequently due to the stresses or problems related to their work as clergy. By contrast, most divorced clergy men get divorced in the midst of their ministry careers, often causing great trauma in their congregations and denominations. Clergy men are more likely than clergy women to go through the kind of divorce that upsets denominational executives and disrupts church life.

We also found that the ever-divorced rate is far higher among clergy serving in liberal denominations than among those in the more conservative ones. Nearly half of the Unitarian-Universalist clergy women and only slightly fewer Unitarian-Universalist clergy men have been divorced. Over one-fourth of Episcopalian clergy women and clergy men have been divorced. In contrast, no more than one-sixth of the Southern Baptist and Church of the Brethren clergy women and clergy men have ever been divorced. Some divorced clergy may have left the ministry after their divorce and hence are not likely to be in our sample of active clergy. For this reason, in the more conservative denominations, where divorce spells the end of a ministerial career for clergy, the divorce rate in our sample probably underrepresents the "true divorce" rate. We believe, however, that for most of our sample, the divorce rate reported here is an accurate reflection of reality. (See Appendix 2.2, "Ever-Divorced Clergy by Gender and Denomination.")

From the answers of divorced clergy to our survey, we can say that the impact of divorce on clergy careers is limited. Even the negative effects of divorce after ordination on the career and salary of clergy men and clergy women in most denominations are of short duration. Divorce may hurt job prospects for clergy of both genders during the year or two immediately after divorce, but most divorced clergy in our sample, whether divorced before, during, or after seminary or remarried, continue their careers in ministry. The types of positions they get and the salaries they earn are comparable with those for clergy who have never been divorced and who have been in ministry for similar periods of time. The Reverend Diane Miller, director of ministry for the national office of the Unitarian-Universalists, has taken the stand that UU is a caring, open denomination that does not stigmatize either clergy or laity for undergoing the pain of marital breakup. She has made the statements to the press that Unitarians do not take marriage "any less seriously than other people do."[17] Southern Baptist executives, however, feel that divorce is evidence of moral failing and renders a pastor unfit to continue in ministry. In the UU denomination, however, clergy do not suffer negative career consequences, as Miller explains, because "our congregants don't view divorce as an issue in their minister's credibility or effectiveness."[18]

Recognizing that ordained ministry brings unique stresses and strains to marriage, we were curious to see if clergy couples divorced more or less frequently than other clergy. Since clergy couples were few in number until the 1970s, when denominations began ordaining more women, a higher proportion of ordained women than of ordained men are in clergy couples. Not surprisingly, then, a higher proportion of clergy women than of clergy men in our sample are divorced from another ordained person. Among divorced clergy women, 21 percent of their ex-spouses were also ordained at the time of their divorce, compared to only 4 percent of wives of divorced clergy men. Nonetheless, no evidence exists that marrying a person who is ordained will result in a greater likelihood of divorce for a clergy woman or clergy man. In addition, neither clergy women nor clergy men with ordained spouses and who divorce are more likely than those with nonordained spouses to say that ministry pressures contributed to the divorce. For ordained women and men married to other clergy, numerous factors in their lives and personalities create or exacerbate the conflicts in their marriages that lead to divorce.

Overall, 34 percent of the clergy women and 29 percent of the clergy men could not say what impact their divorce has had or will be likely to have on their career. Either they have not tried to get a new job since their divorce or they are not sure what impact their divorce will have when compared with other factors. Several divorced clergy women interviewed were unclear as to whether the fact that they had been divorced or simply the fact that they were women or something else about them turned off a particular search committee. Persons on search committees who are usually the most upset about calling a divorced man or woman to be their pastor are often the same persons who have reservations (even if unvoiced) about women pastors.

Another reason that clergy have difficulty assessing the consequences of their divorce relates to attitudes some laity have toward single clergy. If a divorced clergy woman or clergy man has not remarried, the fact that she or he is currently single may be the problem. As one divorced clergy woman pointed out, single clergy may be viewed by search committees as potential homosexuals or, almost as bad, swinging heterosexuals—and either lifestyle is unacceptable to some people. Others applaud singleness, objecting to remarriage after divorce as morally more offensive than divorce followed by celibacy.

The impact of divorce on a particular clergy career varies with the circumstances surrounding the breakup of the marriage and decisions made immediately after the divorce. For example, seminarians or clergy who carry on an affair with the spouse of a well-known or well-liked person in the same community and then divorce their spouse to marry their lover may be far more likely to find their career blocked than if their divorce does not include scandal and does not involve others known in church circles.

In contrast, divorce without obvious problems can backfire if clergy are seen as divorcing for frivolous reasons and not taking marriage seriously. Obviously, the divorced clergy woman or clergy man being viewed as the "injured party" in the divorce, alleviates the stigma of divorce in the eyes of many. Not being an injured party in a divorce can make things very difficult for clergy. The story of one clergy woman illustrates this problem.

This woman had received awards for excellence and a series of promotions in her church system but was forced out of her position soon after her divorce and turned down for other positions within her denomination. She was later told (by insiders) that her divorce would not have hurt her career if her husband had abandoned her and their preteen child or was an adulterer, batterer, or drug addict. There had been no scandal, however; she and her husband, after a great deal of thought, simply decided to divorce because they were not in love with each other. The church found this unacceptable. Further, her divorce still might not have been a problem if she had been dowdy, obese, or a safe-looking sixty-year-old. But she was in her early thirties and very attractive. Finally, she was too successful. She was told that if she had not attained such a significant position in her denomination, she might have been forgiven for the divorce, at least after a time. She was, however, a highly visible denominational leader, and everyone knew her. She told us that she had no idea that her divorce would have such a negative impact on her career.

Sometimes the impact of divorce on a clergy career is not known immediately. Our research, however, shows no indication that clergy who divorce, regardless of when they divorce or whether they remarry, are any more or less likely to be in parish ministry than in some other church-related or even secular employment. Clergy seem to divorce at much the same rate as laity, and probably for about the same reasons.

STAYING WITH
ORDAINED MINISTRY

Ordained ministry is a challenging vocation. When we asked clergy serving in parish ministries how they spend their time and how they wish they *could* spend their time, their answers were predictable. They were able to rank activities in which they spend their time in terms of the number of hours involved each week (from the most to the least time):

> preaching (preparation and delivery)
> church administration and staff supervision
> attending church meetings
> home and hospital visitation of members
> education and teaching
> pastoral counseling
> worship preparation
> private prayer for church and spiritual guidance
> facilitating small groups
> attending denominational meetings/conferences
> serving on the community boards/committees

A few denominational and gender differences appear in this ranking. For example, clergy in the Spirit-centered denominations engage more often or longer in private prayer for the church. However, a majority of clergy of both genders, in all three denominational clusters, say they would like to spend more time in prayer for their church's life and members than they presently do. Clergy women in the Spirit-centered denominations are least likely to spend much time in sermon preparation and delivery or in church administration and staff supervision. This may be because clergy women in the Spirit-centered denominations are somewhat more likely than women in other denominations to be working under a male senior pastor. In such situations, more of the teaching and counseling falls to an associate or assistant pastor.

Among all of their responsibilities, those dealing with administration and organization (including meeting attendance) are the activities clergy women and clergy men in every denominational cluster would most like to reduce. And they generally agree that preaching, teaching, and visitation are areas where they want to spend more time. These findings echo research on pastoral ministry since 1950. Samuel Blizzard's studies of Protestant parish ministers, done mainly in the 1950s, found, for example, that while the "administrator" role took the most time for clergy, it was their least satisfying ministerial activity.[19]

The priestly task of conducting worship and administering the sacraments is among the six tasks that clergy most highly value overall—especially clergy women in the institution-centered denominations. And finally, clergy women and clergy men in the Spirit-centered clusters are more than eight times more likely than clergy women and clergy men in the other clusters to say that "personal salvation of individuals" is one of their three most satisfying ministries.

Generally speaking, job satisfactions for all of the clergy in our study are similar, with a major exception that about one-fourth of the women pastors in each cluster (twice as many women as men) say that acting as a "positive role model and guide for youth" is one of their three most fulfilling roles. Furthermore, although "changing traditional images of church" is one of the lower-ranked sources of fulfillment in general for clergy, nearly one-fourth of the women pastors in the congregation-centered denominations cited this as one of their three most satisfying ministerial activities. It may be that of all the clergy women in our study, these women have made the most impact in changing traditional images of church, and as a consequence, they have some real satisfaction in recognizing that fact. (See Appendix 2.3, "The Most Satisfying Aspects of Ministry.")

AGE AND HEALTH

Learning how to juggle role demands and manage time—for ministry, for family, and for self—is difficult. Clarifying boundaries between service to the church and private life is complicated. Coping with the economic and geographic pressures on ministry is not easy. Dealing with being single, being homosexual, or being divorced generates anxiety. It may be possible to help clergy learn how to balance their lives more effectively through their seminary studies and in continuing education experiences, but in the end, experience is the best teacher.

We have found that older clergy have an easier time than younger clergy in negotiating conflicting role demands, time management, boundaries, contextual difficulties, and lifestyle questions.[20] Is this because older clergy have lived longer? Perhaps specific experiences that make life easier have been shared by older clergy. Increasingly, clergy, especially women, are entering ordained ministry later in life. It is possible to explore whether living a balanced and healthy life as ordained persons relates to how long they have been ordained or to how old they are.

Our research shows that chronological age is consistently more important than length of ordained service in predicting how well clergy handle role conflicts and set boundaries. One explanation for the greater ease that older clergy have in juggling church and family demands may be that they find themselves in less demanding (and less prestigious) church positions. Another possibility is that older clergy are able to maintain boundaries more easily because they are less likely to have responsibilities for children at home.

In a study of Episcopal and Unitarian-Universalist clergy, Paula Nesbitt indicates that older clergy men, especially those who were ordained as mature adults rather than as young men, are less likely to get top church positions. Further, Nesbitt found that for clergy men, being married, with or without children, has a positive impact on the probability that these men will "move up" the church career ladder. By contrast, clergy women, whether ordained as young women or in middle age, whether married or single, with or without children, are extremely unlikely to get top church positions. For clergy women, being older, single, or having children to care for limits their careers as much as being female.[21]

Looking at age specifically, it is important to note that the general chronological maturity of clergy women in most denominations is viewed positively and rewarded. Many small congregations actually prefer hiring mature women—so much so that younger clergy women sometimes feel a lack of acceptance because they are "too young":

> One of the biggest issues for me in my formative years of ministry was my age. I began the ministry at age twenty-five. I did not always get support from other women clergy or laity who were in their forties. There seemed to be some resentment toward me. Also, many seminaries these days seem to assume that good ministerial candidates are "second career." Those of us entering straight from college got short shrift. I think that's changing a bit. We will see.
>
> (clergy woman)

> While I have found being female to be a problem with a few church members, I have had a much greater problem overcoming the stigma of age—in my case—youth. People seem to have more of a problem in my being—"so young!"—than with my being female. The combination probably doesn't help. I am sure age can be a factor on the other end of the spectrum as well.
>
> (clergy woman)

If there is an age bias favoring the chronologically mature, it may be because older clergy, especially women, have learned how to gain the support of other clergy and parishioners. They are older and wiser. Mature clergy women are able to handle the lack of support and negativity that sometimes undermine effective ministry. In the total sample of clergy in our study, younger women were more likely than older women to say they had "seriously considered" leaving church-related work for some other career over the previous year. Age is not related to actually leaving church work, but apparently, young women think about it more frequently than do older women clergy.

With clergy men, the situation is different. The age of clergy men is unrelated to either thoughts of quitting or actually leaving active ministry. For both clergy men and clergy women, chronological age, time in the ordained ministry, and age at ordination work together to support their "success" as clergy. The longer clergy live and survive as clergy (i.e., do not leave active ministry), the greater likelihood that age will have a salutary effect on their ability to handle the pressures of life and to live as whole, healthy human beings.

Having clergy who are healthy in mind, body, and spirit—and who can develop and sustain sound relationships with colleagues, parishioners, and intimates—is important to any congregation or denomination. Clergy who exploit trust and destroy others or who destroy themselves through substance abuse, emotional breakdowns, or physical illness due to emotional conflicts, overwork, and poor self-care weaken the church.[22]

Aging gracefully and keeping healthy involve physical health, spiritual health, and emotional health. For example, feelings of loneliness experienced by clergy women initially might not seem important. Our study shows, however, that such feelings are a particularly sensitive barometer of clergy health. Loneliness and isolation for clergy have a broader existential meaning. James Fenhagen writes, "Loneliness is a particular problem in the ordained ministry because we are forever moving between the experience of profound intimacy and the experience of intimacy lost. . . . When clergy speak honestly about stress in the ordained ministry, the subject of loneliness always seems to emerge. Yet *loneliness* is the secret word that is not much talked about in clergy circles. Unless dealt with honestly, loneliness can be the force that drives us to seek release by substituting the illusion of intimacy for the real thing."[23]

To explore the health of clergy as a mixture of physical, spiritual, social, and emotional factors, we have created a Clergy Health Index. This index groups answers to four questions as a measure of overall clergy health.

Index 2.2
Clergy Health Index
Items scored from 1, "usually true," to 4, "usually false"

---

1. I felt physically healthy and energetic.
2. I felt spiritually whole and growing in spiritual depth.
3. I (did not) feel the need for confidential counseling.
4. I (did not) feel lonely and isolated.

---

standardized item alpha: clergy women .66; clergy men .68

When we compare clergy scores on this index with the Boundary Maintenance Index, we discover, not surprisingly, that clergy who are consistently better able to establish clear boundaries between their church work and personal lives are more likely to be healthy—enjoying spiritual, mental, social, and physical well-being.[24] This is true for both clergy men and clergy women.

No particular reason exists that clergy women should be more or less healthy than clergy men on the average. Clergy men and clergy women show no significant difference in their ability to manage role demands or to set clear boundaries. Yet, although the ways in which clergy describe their health cover a wide range, when measured by our overall Clergy Health Index, clergy women appear to be slightly less healthy than clergy men.

Table 2.3
Responses on the Clergy Health Index by Gender

	Women (2,322)	Men (2,035)
Very good overall health (scores 4–5)	17%	22%
Quite good overall health (scores 6–7)	24%	30%
Moderate, fair health (scores 8–10)	36%	32%
Low, poor health (scores 11–16)	23%	16%
	100%	100%

Difference between women and men −.11, significant at the .0001 level

Although clergy men generally report themselves in better health than do clergy women in each age group, for both men and women, the older they are, the healthier they are in every area of life. They feel better about themselves, they have friends, and they relate well to other family members, if not always to their denominational executives or church lay leaders.

The largest group of clergy in our study is between forty and fifty-five years of age. Clergy over fifty-five years of age comprise about 24 percent of both genders in our sample, and clergy under age forty account for 25 percent of the women and 19 percent of the men in our sample. In certain denominations, especially the Spirit-centered denominations, the age distribution is different.

Clergy women in the Spirit-centered denominations tend to be considerably older than those in the congregation-centered and institution-centered denominations. By contrast, although little difference overall appears among clergy men in the three denominational clusters, the clergy men in the Spirit-centered denominations tend to be younger than clergy men in the other two denominational clusters. This makes the age difference between clergy women and clergy men far greater in the Spirit-centered denominational cluster than in either of the other two denominational clusters.

The healthiest clergy women—spiritually, physically, and socially—are in the Spirit-centered denominations. Perhaps the fact that most of them are older overwhelms the general tendency for clergy women to feel less healthy. It may be that clergy women in these Spirit-centered denominations are healthier because they are less likely either to smoke or to drink alcohol than are clergy women and clergy men in other denominations. It may be that the majority of clergy women in the Spirit-centered denominations have not really confronted the gender inequities of their denominations and are simply naive and healthy.

We say this because we have discovered an interesting relationship between feminist commitments and the health of clergy women—the more feminist they are in certain denominational clusters, the somewhat poorer their overall spiritual, mental, physical, and social health. This is especially true for clergy women in the Spirit-centered denominations. When we compare the scores of Spirit-centered clergy women who are "feminists," as measured by our Structural Feminism Index (clergy who long for equality of opportunity between women and men in getting church positions), with the scores of clergy women on the Clergy Health Index, we discover that feminists in the Spirit-centered denominations feel the most dispirited and isolated in ministry and score the lowest on our Clergy Health Index. In view of the fact that equality of opportunity for women in the Spirit-centered denominations is more distant and limited than it is in most of the other denominations, it is not surprising that these clergy women experience slightly higher levels of stress in their lives.[25]

Some people who are suspicious of feminism may conclude that feminism makes clergy women sick. Such a conclusion, however, is too simplistic. This relationship between strong feminist values and the health of clergy women is found mainly among feminist clergy women in the Spirit-centered denominations. In these denominations, the clergy men are younger and the clergy women older. Even adjusting for their higher age, however, it appears that the overall health of clergy women in the Spirit-centered denominations suffers in direct proportion to their degree of commitment to feminism.

Being an ordained minister in contemporary society is a hard job. Overall, our research shows that clergy women and clergy men are doing rather well in managing their complex lives. For the most part, they are healthy and think well of themselves as clergy.

3

A RELIGIOUS LEADER

Being a religious leader is an "awe-some" role. The biblical book of Exodus tells the story of Moses, who saw a burning bush and turned aside, only to be told by God, "Come, I will send you to Pharaoh to bring my people, the Israelites, out of Egypt." Moses responded as most of us would: "Who am I that I should go to Pharaoh, and bring the Israelites out of Egypt?" He did not set out to be a religious leader; he did not want to do what God was asking. God, however, had a different idea, reassured Moses, and gave him signs that God would be with him in his new "ministry" (Ex. 3:10–12).

Every clergy man or clergy woman wrestles with this feeling: "Who am I, that I should offer sacraments, preach, teach, pray?" Why me? Religious leadership draws on divine power, and power is both a blessing and a curse.

In a study on pastoral power, Martha Ellen Stortz suggests that individual clergy exercise "power with" the members of their congregation, "power within" themselves as charismatic leaders who provide ideas and inspiration in congregational life, and "power over" members by virtue of their ordained status in ecclesiastical systems.[1] Although each of these sources of power offers potential benefits and contains pitfalls that influence the effectiveness of pastoral leaders, Stortz argues that clergy who primarily share "power with" members of their congregations are best able to develop strong, committed lay leadership.

CLERGY LEADERSHIP STYLES

Today, "sharing ministry" and decision-making power *with* lay members is promoted as the preferred pastoral style—it is theologically justified, and it is expected by educated lay members.[2] This leadership style is also supported because it is an effective way for pastors to develop and maintain congregational vitality. Research shows that when a pastor has a "genuinely collegial style of ministry," the mission and outreach of local congregations flourish. This is because, goes the argument, "members of the congregation take real responsibility, and not just responsibility for the less important aspects of the congregation's life."[3]

Churches are like many institutions in contemporary life—they need effective management and visionary leadership. In corporate America in recent years, a great deal of research into various leadership styles has been done. What makes a good leader? What style of decision making will accomplish the goals of an organization or bring profit to a company?

Discussion has revolved around two styles of leadership. First is the traditional leadership style, which emphasizes power *over* things and people. It is often described as *transactional,* command-and-control, and directive. Although in the past this traditional and more directive leadership style has been commonly used, especially by men, the situation is changing. Increasingly, in business and in the church, a more democratic style of leadership is sought and rewarded. This second leadership style is often described as *transformational,* interactive, collaborative, and democratic, emphasizing power *with.* Flexible and collegial leadership, often associated with women, is seen as more conducive to staff motivation, creativity, and productivity.[4]

This more democratic, "power with" leadership style, however, has real limitations, in the corporate context and in the church. It is often considerably more time-consuming than the traditional, directive style. It usually takes longer to make decisions collaboratively and to work collegially than it does to make decisions authoritatively or to direct the work of others. An interactive, enabling leadership style also assumes that others want and are able to participate in the decision making. This is not always the case. Consequently, when collaborative leadership does not succeed, it may be seen as weak and ineffective in motivating others to attain needed goals. Finally, with a more democratic leadership style, organizations sometimes degenerate—and no leader or group takes responsibility for anything. Moving in a common direction becomes very difficult when opinions are deeply divided. Enabling others to lead is good, but such a leadership style becomes totally inadequate if others do not share a vision about where they want to go. As Stortz puts it, "Mere facilitation neither challenges nor empowers the group to transcend itself and seek possibilities that lie beyond it."[5]

Modern clergy are caught in these debates about leadership styles. Traditional religious leadership was male and directive. People expected clergy to be religious "authorities" and to interpret the truth of scripture and the traditions of the church. In recent decades, clergy in all denominations have adopted more democratic and inclusive leadership styles and find they are very satisfying. Furthermore, many clergy believe that a democratic and inclusive leadership style is more in keeping with the message of the Christian gospel.

A high proportion of all clergy in our research, male and female, say that they *want* to use a "power with" style of leadership, fully incorporating members of their congregations in developing mission, setting goals, and carrying out the work of the church. Unfortunately, many clergy discover that although they would like to use a democratic style of pastoral leadership, they cannot. In fact, sometimes congregations most in need of shared leadership are congregations where a "power with" style of leadership is the least effective. What clergy want to do, what congregations will respond to, and what actually works are not all the same. As one clergy woman reflected on her experience:

> This is my third position, but first as a full-time pastor. This is a two-hundred-member congregation in an upper-middle-class New England town, which is very isolated from urban problems and resolved to remain so! There are many strong people in this congregation, but all determined to go in different directions! For example, take the hymns used on Sunday morning—no matter what I choose there is always someone who will complain about one of them. When I came here not quite a year ago, the members were interested in being "entertained" on Sunday morning, but were not very involved otherwise. The lay leaders wanted me to "do something" about this church, get it more active *within* and visible *without* in the community—but they didn't mean actually involving *them,* or going in ways they would find threatening! . . . Trying to get them involved in planning for the congregation's future is not easy; at church meetings some complain that I am taking "too much of their time."
>
> (United Church of Christ clergy woman)

Clergy who experience this tension between how they want to lead and what the laity expect are worried. In the future, when small congregations have fewer resources to hire full-time pastors to provide directive leadership, the very future of the church will be at stake:

> If I just acted as a laid-back pastor, this church would not do *anything*. For almost any decision in this church, I can almost guarantee that there will be two hundred somewhat different ideas about what direction this church should take. In that kind of situation, unless the pastor makes a decision, the church is going to go *no* where. They *expect* the minister to "take charge." "Taking charge" in this church means the pastor not only makes the decisions, but has to carry them out all by him or herself! It is my conviction that unless lay members of these small New England churches are trained and motivated to take more responsibility for the ministry of their congregations, these congregations will fail—because increasing numbers are not able to afford a full-time pastor.
>
> (United Church of Christ clergy woman)

> In seminary, I saw myself being the kind of enabling pastor who would develop a collegial leadership team with enthusiastic lay members ministering along with me. The reality is that my first appointment is two small congregations, whose regular attenders are farm folk and store clerks close to retirement. Most of the young people leave for the city, and the others do not come to church. Since this two-point charge had been without any minister for six months, they were glad to get me—even though I am their first woman pastor. . . . If I did not come to meetings with some ideas for them to discuss, the meeting would be very short. Very rarely do they initiate ideas or plans for anything other than a church supper. They wait for the pastor to take care of all the details and run the show.
>
> (Lutheran clergy woman)

Clergy women and clergy men expect to exercise professional leadership in the church. That is what they sought ordination for. They are realizing, however, that many church members see a seminary-educated pastor as a "professional" leader and the rest of the congregation as passive "clients" or "amateurs." Habits of church leadership and membership are deeply embedded in local congregational life, and they do not change easily. In some ecclesiastical and ethnic traditions, clinging to the "old ways" is seen as part of keeping the faith. This creates problems for clergy men as well as clergy women. As one clergy man wrote:

> I envisioned my pastoral role in church as a "theological interpreter" of ministries needed and wanted in the church and in the community. My first real parish position was in a small, elderly Lutheran church in an urban neighborhood, which preferred me [a man] over the woman they were also considering. They said they wanted a pastor who would bring new life to the church. But when I tried to enable them to do the kinds of ministry they said they wanted, to think about things theologically, some resisted apathetically and some undercut me behind my back. Some saw me as too laid back, others as too controlling. Their perceptions of me were less based on anything I did, but more out of their own perceptual set—whether they see the pastor as a hireling of the congregation to carry out their wishes, or *Herr Pastore,* an absolute patriarchal authority figure. The kind of leadership pastors use has a lot to do with what the congregation expects, and the kind of situation pastors find themselves in.
>
> (Lutheran clergy man)

In spite of these practical difficulties cited by both male and female pastors, the collaborative "power with" leadership style has emerged as the preferred pattern of leadership for all ministry. It is promoted by various feminist theologies because it is the least controlling leadership style and the style that tries, more than any other, to include other people in decision making,[6] a key feminist value. Unfortunately, it is also a traditionally *feminine* style.

For clergy women, therefore, the "leadership dilemma" exerts double pressures. When the increasingly preferred democratic leadership style is also a more stereotypical "female" leadership style, clergy women are faulted when they use it, and faulted when they do not use it. In fact, sometimes clergy women are forced to use democratic, "with others" styles of leadership to be accepted at all.[7] Many women, however, are delighted to move beyond historical leadership patterns. Their theological horizons have been broadened, and they have a passion to share new understandings of the gospel and to nurture new understandings of the church. Nevertheless, these clergy women with strong feminist inclinations consistently find themselves in a double bind as they try to lead congregations to develop greater sensitivities to social justice issues and inclusive language:

> I was a feminist during seminary, sort of left of Rosemary Ruether, but not as far out as Mary Daly. I tried to adopt a "facilitative" rather than a "directive" style in church positions, checking out everything with people involved before doing something. The third church position was my first as full-time solo pastor, and in

many ways seemed ideal. It was a church in a college town with many well-educated parishioners. When I interviewed with the calling committee, I was up front with them that I liked inclusive language in church services and that I would occasionally use the "Sophia" image for God. They agreed. So not too long after I happily started as pastor there, I did use inclusive language in worship and had a few services where I talked about Sophia. . . . Well!!! There were some in the church who were incensed. They wanted me to stop expressing my overt feminism and views of biblical authority. But I was committed to my personal integrity and convictions. It got worse. We had to call in a church conflict consultant. . . . It didn't help much . . . but it did allow dissident members to voice their anger and objections, get closure and leave. This traumatic experience resulted in a church split. They could no longer pay me a full-time salary. I eventually left and entered a doctoral program.

(clergy woman)

Some clergy who value a democratic leadership style but find themselves in congregations where this style cannot be used effectively develop a mixed leadership pattern. By alternating between democratic and directive leadership styles, they are able to support a more inclusive, collaborative ministry of clergy and lay leaders:

When I came to this small church, it had been without any priest for a while. Like other congregations in this situation, members are both eager to have some professional leadership and at the same time do not want to "take orders" from an expert who comes in from the outside. So consequently, I bounce back and forth between a directive and democratic leadership style in the following way: I take the initiative in leading the discussion in a certain area, lay out some alternatives—then step back. I let them discuss it, make suggestions, and hopefully come to some agreement. From there I go on suggesting further goals, stepping back, and let them talk about what they agree to do in this area.

(Episcopal clergy woman)

I have been disappointed with how stodgy this church is on issues of racial and social justice. They will have nothing to do with the black church in the area. I have learned to adopt the following strategy in coming to a new church: First, see what things have been done and the way they have been done. Then, do what has been done in the usual ways during the first year, but do it better than it has ever been done before or at least a very good job. This ideally will have the effect of persons in the congregation saying, "I think I can get used to having *you* around!" Then slowly try to suggest changes, but always in a collaborative, inclusive way. For example, in my second year for the first time I began stating my own opinions of what I would like to see happen in the church, saying something like: "This is my perspective on this. But this church is for all of us. I want to hear what you have to say. What do you think about it?" Although there is a limit on how far this will work—I haven't gotten them to the point of linking themselves in any ongoing way with the black church—I have gotten them to make changes in the worship service and be more concerned with the community.

(Disciples of Christ clergy woman)

These stories illustrate that clergy, both women and men, have learned how to use a power *with* leadership style alongside a modified power *over* style to advance the mission and ministries of their congregations. And of course, many clergy, both women and men, continue to rely most heavily on directive leadership. They do so because they feel more comfortable with it and because their church members like and benefit from an authoritative minister. Two clergy women with self-defined directive styles of pastoral leadership explain why they choose to lead in more traditional ways:

I believe that it is the Christian duty of pastors to help discern the *right* vision for the church and hold this up to the people, moving them with a gentle but firm hand. The pastor should be less of a facilitator and more of a leader for the good of the people and the congregation.

(United Methodist clergy woman)

I frankly am more comfortable with an authoritative style and am more successful in using this style. I have far more expertise in leadership and a better vision of what the congregation might be than any of its members. That's why they hired me! I set my agenda and then exude a "bossy" confidence that gets people enthusiastically working toward achieving the outcome I have assigned them. This church has doubled in size within the few years I have been here.

(Unitarian-Universalist clergy woman)

GENDER AND CLERGY LEADERSHIP STYLES

Contemporary clergy are finding creative ways to exercise leadership, both in traditional and in more democratic patterns. As more and more women become pastors, the question arises as to whether male and female clergy differ in approaches to leadership. Are female pastors leading their congregations differently? If so, how?

To examine this issue, we selected a random sample of 250 pastors of both genders from all of our fifteen denominations and called them on the telephone. We asked, "From your experience, do you feel women clergy approach or do ministry differently on the average than clergy men?"

The answers we collected are fascinating. Both women and men think that significant differences exist between male and female clergy in this area. Many clergy believe that women clergy are more caring than men about the individual lives of members of the congregation, more pastorally sensitive, more nurturing, and more likely to draw on personal experiences in preaching, teaching, and counseling. Everyone also agrees that clergy women are less interested than clergy men in congregational politics, power over others, and job prestige. The women pastors we talked with were considerably more likely than their male counterparts to volunteer their perception that clergy women's leadership style is different from that typically used by clergy men. Furthermore, all of our denominational clusters show fairly high agreement about the nature of this difference in leadership style:

> Although everyone approaches ministry differently, clergy women are more relational than clergy men, making decisions more cooperatively instead of using a hierarchical or authoritarian approach.
>
> (Wesleyan clergy woman)

> My clergy women colleagues approach ministry in a less hierarchical, more cooperative manner, and they see themselves more as *empowerers* of laity than as *leaders* of laity.
>
> (Unitarian-Universalist clergy woman)

> Clergy women tend to be more collegial in my experience. They tend to use more of a partnership-based than hierarchical leadership style.
>
> (United Church of Christ clergy woman)

> Clergy women have a different focus and style. Women clergy are more interested in sharing power; they work with laity.
>
> (United Methodist clergy woman)

Do clergy women leaders share power more than clergy men in leadership positions? A three-fifths majority of women clergy *think* women clergy do—which is an opinion not shared by most clergy men, only one-fifth of whom agree. Ordained men may have some justification in rejecting the notion that clergy men are less willing to share power than are clergy women. A three-fifths majority of both clergy women and clergy men see themselves as more democratic than directive in leadership style. Clergy women, however, are slightly more likely than clergy men to assess clergy women's leadership style as very democratic. These findings hold whether the clergy are in parish ministry or in some other kind of work.

Table 3.1
Perceptions of Women's Leadership Styles by Gender
("Women leaders tend to share power more than men leaders.")

	Clergy women		Clergy men	
	Parish (1,410)	Other (1,029)	Parish (1,562)	Other (500)
agree	65%	60%	18%	24%
mixed	26%	27%	37%	39%
disagree	9%	13%	45%	37%
	100%	100%	100%	100%

It may be that whatever discrepancy exists between ordained women's and men's perceptions of whether clergy women are more willing than clergy men to share power is present because neither clergy women nor clergy men are basing their opinions on current observations and interactions with clergy of the opposite gender now active in ministry. More than likely, clergy women are remembering the actions of a male senior pastor when they themselves were associates some years ago or are resenting lay men in their congregations who are giving them grief. Clergy men may also be thinking about how open and enabling they themselves are, especially when they compare themselves to some of the autocratic women in their local congregations. Opinions vary:

> Clergy men tend to work for a hierarchical system from the top down. Clergy women try to work from concentric circles. We try to bring lay people also into equality in decision making.
>
> (Episcopal clergy woman)

> Clergy women have a vision for more inclusiveness . . . and use a participatory leadership style. Clergy men that I have known for the most part are not drawn to that kind of leadership.
>
> (Southern Baptist clergy woman)

> Clergy women are more apt to work circularly, not hierarchically. They are more apt to work toward a team effort.
>
> (American Baptist clergy woman)

> From my experience . . . clergy women are far more likely to empower people and work with people. But when it comes right down to taking authority, it is harder for them. Whereas clergy men tend to overseize authority sometimes and act more powerful than they really are.
>
> (American Baptist clergy man)

These attitudes are not new. Clergy leadership style preferences in the 1990s have remained virtually unchanged from those expressed in the 1980–81 research results published in *Women of the Cloth*. Furthermore, these preferences are consistent with additional studies of clergy done by Edward Lehman and others. Lehman found that although clergy women were slightly more likely than clergy men to value empowering laity, clergy women did not differ from clergy men in their use of formal authority within the church.[8] (See Appendix 3.1, "Clergy Self-Perceived Leadership Styles, 1980–1981 and 1993–1994.")

Another study, by Mary Clair Klein, which looked at United Church of Christ clergy leadership styles as self-reported, also found that while "there are differences in leadership style among pastors, gender is not the determining factor." Our results concur with Lehman and Klein and are supported by Ruth Wallace's study of women pastors in priestless Roman Catholic parishes. All pastoral leaders in the 1990s tend to have more of an inclusive, democratic leadership style than a directive, autocratic style. These three studies use somewhat different indicators to measure clergy perceptions of how they lead, but all three arrive at similar findings.[9]

In considering the question of gendered leadership styles within professions, it is good to keep in mind that different kinds of occupations attract different personalities, and that gatekeepers for occupations tend to select persons with particular styles and values. Personality tests and inventories given to seminary students consistently show that men and women preparing for ordained ministry or already serving as clergy differ from men and women in the general population. Usually, men entering the ordained ministry exhibit more "feminine" personality characteristics than do men in the population at large. Furthermore, a study of Anglican clergy in Great Britain found that not only were the personality profiles of men and women entering the ordained ministry different from those for the general populace, but "implicitly or explicitly the selection procedures seem to value feminine personality characteristics in male clergy and to value masculine personality characteristics in female clergy."[10] Some of the perceived differences in leadership styles reported by male and female clergy are no doubt being sustained by the conscious and unconscious screening of candidates for ordination by seminaries, judicatories, and denominations.

HOW DENOMINATION AND AGE AFFECT LEADERSHIP STYLES

The differences between clergy women and clergy men in the leadership style they say they most often use are minimal. Some differences do appear, however, among clergy women and clergy men when denomination and age are taken into consideration.

For example, clergy women in the Spirit-centered denominations are less likely than the majority of clergy women in other denominations to believe that women share power more than men do. Furthermore, they are also less inclined than the majority of other clergy women to view their own leadership style as "democratic." In fact, neither female nor male clergy in Spirit-centered denominations view their leadership style as democratic. It is evident that the ideal of "power with" leadership has less impact on how clergy women in the Spirit-centered denominations view their own leadership style than it does on clergy women in other denominations.

In contrast, Unitarian-Universalist clergy women could be expected to have the least reason for believing that women have a more democratic leadership style than men, because of all clergy men in our study, Unitarian-Universalist clergy men think that they are the most democratic. In fact, all Unitarian-Universalist clergy have a strong bias for using a "power with" leadership style.

No such unified view of the ideal leadership style is evident among Southern Baptist ordained men and women. Not only do considerably more Southern Baptist clergy women than clergy men believe that women share power more than men, but

Southern Baptist clergy women are 20 percent more likely than clergy men in their denomination to see themselves as *very* democratic in leadership style. This substantial difference between the self-defined leadership style in Southern Baptist ordained women and ordained men reflects a similar gap in their understandings of ministry. These clergy women are also far more likely than Southern Baptist clergy men to endorse the position that lay women and clergy women should share equally with men in local and national church leadership, and that worship services should sometimes use female images of God. Since these more feminist positions are generally linked by clergy in this study with greater value and the use of a power *with* leadership style, this suggests that clergy women have a more inclusive, less hierarchical concept of ministerial leadership than Southern Baptist clergy men. (See Appendix 3.2, "Clergy Self-Perceived Leadership Styles and Views of How Women Clergy Share Power by Gender and Denomination.")

We looked to see if other characteristics of clergy, in addition to denominational identity, combine with gender to influence preferred styles of ministerial leadership. We wondered if age would make a difference. We also asked if the decade in which an ordained person attended seminary might shape lifetime attitudes about leadership.

As we have already noted, in the twentieth century leadership expectations have shifted from a power *over,* or asymmetrical, clergy-laity authority pattern to a power *with,* or symmetrical, authority model reflecting more egalitarian societal norms. According to Jackson Carroll, as society has come to prefer increasingly egalitarian patterns of authority, clergy of both genders have become more democratic than directive in their leadership style. Furthermore, younger clergy and clergy who have recently graduated from seminary are more inclined to adopt democratic leadership styles than are older clergy who went to seminary long ago.[11]

Unfortunately, when we compare the leadership preferences of younger clergy women and clergy men, the picture is not so simple. Edward Lehman's study of clergy women who graduated from seminary prior to 1971, before the women's movement and feminist ideals swept colleges, graduate schools, and seminaries, shows that pioneer clergy women used a directive leadership style. At that time, they were similar to men in their values about ministry and in their leadership style. Younger women, however, are different. Among more recent seminary graduates, Lehman reports a distinct gender difference. Whereas recently seminary-educated clergy women are apt to use an inclusive leadership style, recently seminary-educated clergy men tend to go the opposite way and become more directive.

Lehman attributes this difference to the fact that female and male seminarians had different experiences in seminary in the late 1970s and the 1980s. Women students were involved in a lively feminist subculture and, concomitantly, were more inclined to use a democratic leadership style, whereas men during the same period either were avoiding the feminist subculture or, perhaps in retaliation, were becoming more interested in exerting their authority as clergy.[12]

Our sample is primarily of clergy women who attended seminary in the 1980s, where they were invariably exposed to a feminist subculture. Consistent with Lehman's findings, the clergy women in our sample—those who graduated after 1981—prefer a very democratic leadership style. This is true only of the women, however. Consistent with Lehman's findings, recently graduated clergy men in our sample are somewhat less likely than the women to adopt a very democratic leadership style.

When we look at the chronological age, rather than the era of seminary attendance, of all clergy in our sample—men and women—it turns out that age gives the most reliable prediction regarding the kind of leadership style preferred by clergy. The younger a person is in ordained ministry, the less likely that person is to believe that he or she has a very democratic leadership style. This is especially true for clergy men. Whether this is due to inexperience and a lack of self-confidence or whether it speaks to a rising desire for more directive leadership in the contemporary church and society is not clear. Younger men now entering ordained ministry may be drawn to this career because they believe that clergy have, or should have, authority. Or it may be that only after years of work in the church do clergy, especially clergy men, see the benefits of a more democratic leadership style for effective ministry.[13]

Consistently, as we have already noted, the clergy women in the Spirit-centered denominations tend to be less democratic in leadership style. As a group they are older, but how old they are has no linear relationship to their leadership style. Among clergy women in the congregation-centered denominations, the situation is reversed. Clergy women in this denominational cluster tend to have a democratic leadership style, regardless of their age. With the institution-centered denominations, the picture is more complicated. Among clergy women in the institution-centered denominations, the younger the clergy woman, the less likely she is to use a very democratic leadership style. This pattern is similar to that of the younger clergy men, mentioned above.

What does this mean? Are younger clergy women in the institution-centered denominations feeling particularly pressured to act more like the younger men to get ahead? If so, it is hard to tell if using a more directive leadership style will actually help these younger women (and men) in their church careers. If it is true that contemporary society is becoming increasingly appreciative of egalitarian leadership, choosing a directive leadership style could backfire—further marginalizing the church and clergy leaders. (See Appendix 3.3, "Clergy Leadership Style by Seminary Cohort, Age, and Denominational Cluster.")

MINISTERIAL POSITION
AND LEADERSHIP STYLES

Part of the answer to whether adopting a directive or a democratic leadership style is a good strategy for career success depends on ministerial position. A clergy woman or clergy man may be an assistant or associate pastor, a sole pastor, or the senior minister in a multistaffed congregation. Senior ministers, who supervise other clergy and professional staff, have the freedom to use a different leadership style from that of clergy who have no one to delegate work to or who must respond to the desires and leadership style of a senior minister colleague. In our sample, although slightly less than half of the clergy women and clergy men in parish work serve congregations as sole pastors, relatively few clergy women are senior pastors and relatively few clergy men are assistant or associate pastors.

Table 3.2
Ministerial Positions of Clergy Serving Local Churches (by Gender)

	Women (1,405)	Men (1,419)
Ministerial Position		
Senior pastor	8%	28%
Sole pastor	47%	55%
Co-pastor	11%	3%
Assistant/Associate pastor	28%	11%
Interim position	6%	3%
	100%	100%

Lehman suggests that position directly affects leadership style; however, he found that female senior ministers dealt with leadership styles quite differently than male senior ministers. Whereas women in senior pastor positions appear more interested in empowering the congregation than do women in lesser pastoral positions the reverse is true for men. According to Lehman, male senior pastors are less likely to care about trying to empower the congregation and more interested in directing it than are males in either co-pastorates or sole pastoral positions.[14]

In our study, we do not find that the pastoral position held by clergy of either gender has any consistent effect on the leadership styles clergy employ. Some of this lack of difference is no doubt due to the power of denominational expectations—which consistently have more influence than pastoral position or clergy gender. Theologically and socially liberal Unitarian-Universalist clergy adopt a very democratic leadership style, regardless of gender or position on a church staff. Female clergy in the other congregation-centered denominations are more likely than male clergy to adopt a democratic leadership style. We have already noted that the theologically and socially more conservative Spirit-centered clergy use a somewhat directive leadership style, regardless of gender or position.

However, we do find interesting differences in leadership styles between women and men in various pastoral positions within the institution-centered denominational cluster, although because there are few women senior pastors in this cluster (both in our sample and in reality), findings must be interpreted with caution. Presbyterian and

United Methodist women who achieve the level of senior pastor use a more democratic leadership style than do ordained women in these denominations who are not
senior pastors. By contrast, the level of parish position does not appear to distinguish
the leadership style of clergy men in these denominations. The difference that status
makes for women senior pastors may be, as Lehman postulates,[15] that these women
are no longer fettered by the need to achieve status through following male leadership models; they are finally able to delegate much of the pastoral drudge work, and
they are freer to follow their inclination to use a more democratic, inclusive leadership style than they were as sole or assistant pastors.

Yet for women in the more hierarchical Episcopal and Lutheran denominations, the relationship between position and leadership style is reversed. In these
denominations, the level of pastoral position does not affect the leadership styles
of clergy men. Women senior pastors in these two denominations, however, are 19
percent less likely to use a very democratic leadership style than are women in sole
or assistant pastoral positions. In fact, Episcopal and Lutheran women who are senior pastors are less likely to use a very democratic leadership style than are clergy
women or men in any position in all of the other denominations, even in the Spirit-
centered cluster. The fact that these two institution-centered denominations were
the last to ordain women and did so only in the 1970s suggests that women clergy
in these denominations, particularly the female senior pastors, are serving under
pressures that other women do not face. Women senior pastors in Episcopal and
Lutheran churches may feel scrutinized and circumscribed to lead in ways historically appropriate for senior pastors in their denominations. As a consequence,
they seem to be adapting their own style to fit how they *believe* male senior pastors act. (See Appendix 3.4, "Ministerial Position and Self-Perceived Leadership
Style.")

LAY ATTITUDES
TOWARD CLERGY LEADERSHIP

Lay leaders may form their own perceptions of how inclusive or dictatorial
their pastor is, depending as much (or more) on their own stereotypes as on what
pastors actually do:

> People make assumptions about men's and women's leadership styles and personal-
> ity. I am sure my first congregation called me because they believed that I was a "nice
> girl" whom they could easily control; my predecessor, a man, had been very con-
> trolling. While I am not controlling, I am assertive. They were surprised; and it took
> me years to figure out why, if I was doing my job, they were so offended. The stereo-
> types about women and men play out in subtle and insidious ways. When a man is
> assertive, he is a strong leader to be respected and honorably reckoned with. An as-
> sertive woman is bitchy, controlling, and power hungry, a force to be managed and

curtailed. The knife cuts the other direction as well: people expect women to be empathetic and men to be critical. When the reverse occurs, men are considered sensitive, to be protected/supported, and women are considered cold, without need of support or care.

(Unitarian-Universalist clergy woman)

According to Lehman, the gender both of lay leaders and of their pastor affects how laity view their pastor's leadership style. The gender of the lay leaders, however, is of particular importance; lay men see their pastors as exhibiting more directive, "masculine" ministerial styles, while lay women see their pastors as using more inclusive, "feminine" ministerial styles—in both cases, regardless of whether their pastor is a woman or a man.[16] In our study, however, lay women and men do not differ significantly in how democratic they perceive their senior or sole pastor's leadership style to be, regardless of whether this pastor is a man or a woman.

Table 3.3

Clergy Leadership Style by Gender of Pastor and Lay Leader

% = % who say pastor is "very democratic" in leadership style

Lay Leader is	Senior/Sole Pastor is		Assoc./Assist. Pastor is	
	Woman	Man	Woman	Man
Woman	42%	42%	40%	39%
Man	39%	42%	39%	65%

As we can see, lay men differ from lay women in how they view the leadership style of an associate or assistant minister, if their church has one. Lay men are more likely than lay women to view the associate or assistant minister as very democratic if this minister is male. It may be that lay men expect directive leadership from men, and when a male associate or assistant minister takes orders from a senior minister, they view this clergy man as more "democratic" than they would a woman acting the same way in the associate or assistant position. Generally, clergy men in the associate or assistant position are viewed as more democratic than clergy women in the same position in both the congregation-centered and in the Spirit-centered denominational clusters. Lay leaders in the institution-centered denominations see both female and male associate or assistant pastors as predominantly using democratic leadership styles and certainly as more democratic than senior or sole pastors. This is particularly true of those clergy who are female in the institution-centered denominations.

Table 3.4

Lay Leader Perceptions of Clergy Leadership Style by
Gender of Pastor and Denominational Cluster

% = % who say pastor is "very democratic" in leadership style

Lay Leaders' Denomination Cluster	Senior/Sole Pastor is		Assoc./Assist. Pastor is	
	Woman	Man	Woman	Man
Congregation-centered	45%	45%	26%	47%
Institution-centered	28%	41%	52%	54%
Spirit-centered	54%	52%	31%	67%

What laity think of clergy is extremely important to clergy job satisfaction and career. Clergy are called, trained, and ordained to serve the church. Their work is all-consuming in their lives. How well they are judged by denominational leaders and by local laity, who control clergy job opportunities, is extremely important.

Fortunately for women clergy, overall opinions about the effectiveness of ordained women are generally positive. This is true even with denominational and lay leaders who are initially wary about how well clergy women will be able to minister to theologically or socially conservative laity. Lehman's extensive studies of women clergy in the United States, England, and Australia[17] document the ways in which most church members eventually come to accept the ministry of women pastors, even when the laity are apprehensive to begin with. Unfortunately, resistance to clergy women increases with "higher," more prestigious church positions and salaries.

When we compare the knowledge and attitudes of lay leaders from the seven mainline denominations interviewed in the 1980–81 *Women of the Cloth* study with those of lay leaders in the same denominations in our 1993–94 research, it is clear that many more women are in pastoral ministry in the 1990s than were in the 1980s, and these women are held in high regard. Laity in the 1990s are about 25 percent more likely than laity in the 1980s to be in communities where other churches are served by ordained women. Laity, especially lay men, have dramatically increased their knowledge about women clergy and are more likely to believe that lay and clergy women *do* hold positions or have influence comparable to lay and clergy men of their denomination in their area. (See Appendix 3.5, "Lay Leader Attitudes about Clergy, 1980–1981 and 1993–1994.")

Now that laity in contemporary society see that women do enjoy more equality in the church than was true in the early 1980s, many lay leaders are not as eager as they were at that time to want their own congregation to appoint an equal number of lay women and lay men to their parish governing board or even to ordain more women to full ministerial status in their denominations. However, lay leaders in the 1990s feel that more women should be regional and national church executives—recognizing that most of these top positions are still male-dominated.

Both surveys indicate that the interest of laity in inclusive language referring to humans has changed little since the early 1980s, with less than half of lay leaders agreeing that such language should be used in church services. Although, today, lay leaders do not believe that the ordained ministry is given the stature and prestige it had in the early 1980s, high proportions of female and male lay leaders in both the 1980s and the 1990s have indicated they would be happy if they had a daughter who was ordained. Finally, less than one-third of the lay leaders in these mainline denominations agree that if a ministerial vacancy occurs in their local church, the search committee should "actively seek a woman candidate." Clergy women are more prevalent, more visible, and doubtless more acceptable to a majority of laity in the 1990s, but this very visibility has led lay leaders in some of the churches to feel that it is no longer necessary to work to get more women into lay and pastoral leadership positions.

In congregation-centered denominations, having direct experience with a woman pastor leads to positive views about having another woman pastor, about using inclusive language in church services, and about increasing the number of women clergy in those denominations (where it is already quite high). Lay leaders in institution-centered denominations who presently have a woman pastor are more favorably inclined than those lay leaders who belong to congregations without a woman pastor toward more women in leadership within their denominations and toward using inclusive language in church services—although the differences are less pronounced.

By contrast, lay leaders in Spirit-centered denominations who have a woman as pastor, if they are influenced by this at all, appear to be less favorable than those without a woman pastor toward more women serving in executive staff positions in their denominations. They are particularly negative about the use of inclusive language in church services.

It is ironic, from the standpoint of history, that significantly more lay leaders in the Spirit-centered denominations than in the other two denominational clusters are ambivalent or opposed to ordaining more women in their denominations. These laity actively resist seeking a woman pastor to fill a vacancy, using inclusive language, and appointing equal numbers of lay women and lay men on their church governing boards. Interestingly, having a woman pastor as an assistant or part-time pastor (which is often the case in these Spirit-centered denominations) does little or nothing to lessen the lay resistance to women clergy. In most of the other denominational clusters, exposure to a woman pastor has been a positive experience and has predisposed laity to receive women pastors more easily. (See Appendix 3.6, "Attitudes of Laity Who Have a Woman Pastor.")

Over the decades from the 1970s through the 1990s, the number of women pastors has grown exponentially. An even larger increase is apparent in the number of church members who have seen and heard a woman pastor—if not in their congregation or in a congregation they visited, than in some other public setting. All evidence points to the fact that increased exposure to the presence of clergy women has accelerated their acceptance as effective leaders of congregations.

LEADERSHIP EFFECTIVENESS OF CLERGY

Whatever leadership style clergy use, and no matter what laity think of them, how effective are they as leaders in their own estimation? Research shows that the degree to which clergy, or the practitioners of any occupation, think of themselves as competent in their professional work is influenced by past performance. In addition, the professional self-concept of the clergy woman or man has a direct effect on the future ability of clergy to perform competently and retain commitment to their chosen profession.[18] With this in mind, we have analyzed a group of responses to related questions on our survey and created the Clergy Professional Self-Concept Index. Recent research on Christian Church (Disciples of Christ) clergy men,[19] Lutheran clergy women,[20] and Episcopal clergy women and men,[21] using various indexes measuring clergy self-confidence and self-esteem in carrying out the ministerial role, have been found to predict satisfaction and commitment to the clergy career.

Index 3.1
Clergy Professional Self-Concept Index
Items scored from 1, "usually true," to 4, "usually false"

---

1. I felt accepted, liked, and appreciated by most in my church or ministry position.
2. I felt I was really accomplishing things in my ministry.
3. I (did not) feel bored and constrained by the limits of this church position, resources, or people.
4. I have been successful in overcoming difficulties and obstacles in my ministry.

---

standardized item alpha: clergy women .61; clergy men .64

Do clergy women on the average feel more or less competent than clergy men? Women often have a more difficult time than men in being accepted initially and in carrying out their ministries, which might weaken their self-concept as competent clergy.[22] By contrast, in their efforts to become clergy, many women have had to overcome numerous obstacles and survive difficult experiences and hard knocks, leading to greater self-confidence as women who know who they are and who feel good about themselves.

On the whole, clergy think quite well of their abilities, as measured by the Clergy Professional Self-Concept Index, and clergy women as a group do not differ significantly from men in their feelings of professional competence.

Table 3.5
Responses on the
Clergy Professional Self-Concept Index by Gender

	Women (2,263)	Men (2,026)
Very strong, good (scores 4–5)	37%	36%
Quite strong (scores 6–7)	34%	34%
Moderate, fair (scores 8–10)	25%	26%
Low, weak self-concept (11–16)	4%	4%
	100%	100%

Difference between women and men −.01, not significant

Do clergy who use a directive leadership style feel more competent professionally than those who use a democratic leadership style? We found no relationship for either clergy women or clergy men between how democratic they perceive their leadership style to be and how effective they assessed themselves to be in carrying out their job. As many of the clergy told us, even though clergy use a leadership style that they hope will be effective, the realities of a particular parish sometimes drive them to feel that they have failed to lead the congregation effectively.

When clergy feel they have made a positive change in the life of their congregation, their self-assessment as professionally competent rises. If a congregation changes under pastoral guidance from one of declining to increased membership, from being a church where members are apathetic or in conflict to being one where the members are enthusiastic and optimistic about their church's future, and from being in financial jeopardy to enjoying financial security, then it is very likely that the pastor will feel very good about herself or himself as an effective leader. If the congregation declines in these ways during the pastorate, the pastor's perception of his or her pastoral effectiveness similarly plummets. Because high proportions of clergy women and clergy men in our study believe they have been instrumental in shepherding their congregations to better health in membership, morale, and financial stability, their professional self-concepts are relatively strong.

Clergy vary in what areas of congregational life they see as most apt to change during their pastorate. In our sample, approximately one-third or more said that when they started their ministry in the congregation in which they now serve, it was a congregation with declining membership. Two-fifths of these pastors were pleased to report that, since their arrival, the membership of their congregation has grown. In addition, most of these pastors reported that the morale of their congregation has improved, as evidenced by increased optimism and enthusiasm among a majority of their congregation during their years there. In the area of financial health, they are less optimistic. In fact, between one-quarter and one-third of the pastors in our study reported that the financial situation of their congregation has worsened.

Women pastors are more pessimistic than men about the financial realities, yet clergy women appear to interpret a financial decline less personally than do the men when they have not been able to do much about improving the financial situation of their congregation. Worsening financial health of the congregation does not affect the professional self-concept of clergy women as adversely as it does the professional self-concept of clergy men. Thirty-four percent of clergy women who think that the finances of their congregations have worsened still hold a high professional self-concept, as opposed to only 25 percent of clergy men with similar assessments of their congregational situations. (See Appendix 3.7, "Professional Self-Concept and Changes in the Congregation since the Pastor First Came.")

A majority of ordained women and men in parish ministry like to think that most persons and groups they minister to and with recognize their pastoral leadership abilities at least "fairly well." At the same time, they perceive differences in the degree of esteem in which different kinds of people hold their leadership abilities. For example, pastors of both genders believe that professionals and educators in their congregations consider them better leaders than do business executives, and that women over age seventy respect their leadership more than do youth. In the total sample, women and men pastors do not differ in how well they believe various groups of people evaluate them as leaders, with one exception: although there is no difference between women and men in how well they believe other clergy men view them as leaders, ordained women are somewhat more likely than ordained men to believe that other clergy women evaluate their leadership positively. As might be expected, clergy men are less confident than clergy women that ordained women see them as good leaders—with some justification. Interestingly, clergy men who see themselves as using a very democratic pastoral leadership style are slightly more likely than clergy men who are directive in their leadership to believe that clergy women admire their leadership abilities.

Age and experience are often factors in the ways in which people assess effective leadership. On balance, however, years of living are more important than years of experience after ordination in how well pastors believe others evaluate them as leaders. Older pastors are more likely than younger pastors to believe that older laity recognize their leadership abilities positively—especially laity of their own gender. Older clergy of both genders in pastoral ministry are also more apt than younger clergy to feel that their judicatory executives and other clergy, regardless of gender, respect them as leaders. Older male pastors are particularly likely to believe that other ordained men esteem their leadership. Mature clergy men, especially those over fifty-five, are consistently very secure in their leadership. This confirms the importance of what some observers call the "old boys' club" in creating job satisfaction among older male clergy.

The degree to which pastors believe that others judge them as effective leaders also varies by denominational cluster. The least gender difference among clergy in how well they think different groups view their leadership abilities appears in the institution-centered denominations, and the most gender difference appears in the Spirit-centered denominations. Female pastors in the Spirit-centered denominations feel different groups of people respect them as leaders more than any other clergy in this study, especially more than male pastors in the Spirit-centered denominations. Clergy women in the Spirit-centered denominations seem convinced that what they are doing is appreciated by most of those with and to whom they minister. Although this is actually not a fully realistic assessment, it does explain why these clergy women are so content. (See Appendix 3.8, "Recognition of Leadership Abilities of Parish Clergy.")

Taken together, these findings underscore the fact that women pastors believe they are seen and they see themselves as effective pastors. Their views are comparable to those of clergy men. Furthermore, a four-fifths majority of all the ordained women and men in our sample of pastors indicate it is at least "somewhat" true, and two-fifths indicate it is "usually" true, that during the last year they got "joy and satisfaction" from their work in ministry in a local congregation.

This greater acceptance, however, does not mean that gender has ceased to be a factor in clergy careers. Larger congregations continue to call men over women for higher-paying positions. Although important steps have been taken to enable women to carry out traditional ministry and to create new forms of ministry, ongoing challenges must be met before ordained ministry for women ceases to be an uphill calling. Placement discrimination, salary inequities, and dead-end careers indicate that problems persist. The obstacles increase when church leaders rest on a belief that clergy women in the 1990s have gained equal access to the careers they feel called to and that therefore no special efforts are needed to ensure that qualified women are given equal consideration in filling all of the positions that are sought by clergy men.

4

A JOB

Job satisfaction in ordained ministry is more than just feeling appreciated as an effective pastor. It also requires getting enough money to live on. Repeatedly, we were told in our survey that clergy women suffer from financial discrimination as professionals in the workplace. When we examine the facts, we discover that clergy women do seem to be disadvantaged in relation to clergy men, even when the women have the same level of education, type of training, years of experience, and hold the same type of clergy job in a similarly sized church within the same denomination.

Clergy women also develop career paths that look substantially different from those of their male counterparts. For example, clergy women are more likely than clergy men to take part-time work and interim, secular, and co-pastor positions. These positions offer less pay, fewer benefits, and fewer opportunities to move into better-paying jobs.

Our research suggests that in spite of the progress that has been made in providing opportunities for women as ordained clergy, ordained women still suffer from a high degree of discrimination in their profession. Interviews indicate that women regularly encounter hostility and prejudice from colleagues, supervisors, and parishioners in the church. Sadly, many of our denominations have yet to achieve a norm of equal opportunity and appreciation for clergy women.

Using statistics from the general population, which includes Roman Catholics and other religious groups that do not ordain women, the 1990 United States occupational census reports that roughly 11 percent of all clergy are women. The same census also reports that 21 percent of all doctors are women and 25 percent of all lawyers are women.[1]

A major reason for the relatively low percentage of women in the clergy workforce is that the constitutional separation of church and state in the United States exempts religious institutions from having to comply with the Civil Rights Act of 1964, which outlaws discrimination on the basis of sex or race. It is perfectly legal for churches to bar women from attaining full ordination to the ministry. A recent study by Mark Chaves[2] reports that approximately half of all denominations in the United States currently do not ordain women. However, this fact does not entirely account for the lower participation rate of women in the ordained ministry. In our sample, which includes the largest Protestant denominations that grant full-status ordination for women, the percentage of clergy women ranges from 1 percent to 30 percent, averaging 10 percent. (See Appendix 4.1, "Percentage of Clergy Women in Major Protestant Denominations [1994].")

The low proportion of clergy women in the general population is likely to surprise many people. They see the rising numbers of women enrolled in seminaries, the dramatic increases in the number of women being ordained, the greater visibility of women clergy in the churches, and the majority of lay women in the pews, and they conclude that we are moving toward a time when male clergy will be in the minority. Our findings suggest that this time remains quite distant, for two reasons: first, while the numbers of women in the ministerial profession have been rising, they have risen more slowly than have the numbers of women in other professions; second, while the rate of female ordination is increasing, it is not increasing as quickly as it once did. The rate of increase in the numbers of women clergy in those denominations that have been most open to ordained women has slowed over the last ten years, especially when compared to the period between 1977 and 1986.

This leads us to ask, "Why is the proportion of women clergy so low?" A number of explanations are possible. Women may be more likely to leave the ministry after ordination because of discrimination and few employment opportunities. Women may be discouraged from entering ordained ministry because of perceptions of discrimination. The average age of women entering ordained ministry tends to be somewhat higher than that of men, although, as we have already noted, the average age of both clergy women and clergy men has increased over the 1980s and 1990s. Women therefore may have shorter work careers than men. Women who find themselves called to ordained ministry may eventually switch to other helping professions because of greater opportunities, higher wages, and the legal protections against discrimination that secular organizations are able to offer. Finally, fewer women may be attracted to this profession because they interpret the Bible as prohibiting women from seeking ordination.

EARNINGS DIFFERENCES BETWEEN MALE AND FEMALE CLERGY

One way of looking at discrimination between male and female clergy is to analyze differences in the earnings of both genders. By examining a large number of cases, we are able to determine whether many of the standard explanations people use to answer why female pastors are paid less than their male colleagues are true. It is said that women as a group tend to have less experience than men, are concentrated in part-time work, prefer to serve in lower-paying positions (co-pastorates or associate or assistant pastorates), serve in smaller churches, or have less-impressive educational credentials than men. Our large sample allows us to adjust for each of these factors in order to see how they affect salaries generally and whether an earnings difference still exists between male and female clergy after all these factors are accounted for.

Salary inequity is one of the most tangible and symbolic forms of discrimination. Earnings send an important message about how an organization or social group values the relative worth of its personnel. If women are earning less than similarly qualified men, the message is plain: the organization values them less. When salaries are tied to jobs, as they are for the majority of church positions, and men are given first preference for the most desirable jobs, the men get the highest salaries.

Women clergy consistently report that they feel discrimination because they are not paid well:

> Pay is very inequitable. In a recent study done in my conference comparing men's and women's salaries, the discrepancies between men and women are increasing. Men are consistently getting higher salaries at the same level of experience, and often for similar church positions. At one church in town, the senior minister is given $61,000 in cash salary (not counting housing and other benefits) while the assistant minister's cash salary is $28,000. . . . We *just* want [adequate] salaries!
>
> (United Methodist clergy woman)

> The "glass ceiling" still exists for women, not so much in appointments as in *salary*. In this conference the glass ceiling is around $30,000. Only three women out of one hundred are making more than $32,000, whereas men with similar experience, between sixty and ninety men, are making more than that. . . . The old rule of pay your dues and wait your time is clearly a rule for boys only.
>
> (United Methodist clergy woman)

The Methodist system makes the discrimination more visible because salaries are public, but there is evidence that salary discrimination occurs widely across denominations. The reported average annual earnings of male and female clergy for the denominations in our sample in 1993–94 ranged from a high of slightly under $50,000 to a low of approximately $20,000. These figures include both cash salary and the self-reported value of benefits.[3] (See Appendix 4.2, "Average Earnings of Full-Time Clergy Ranked by Women's Salaries.")

To understand the differences between the average compensation packages of clergy women and clergy men, it is important to consider all of the non-gender-related factors that can possibly explain such differences.[4] For example, it is often argued that age, experience, and educational achievement make a difference in what people earn. Such characteristics are presumably unrelated to gender. In addition, certain structural and organizational factors, such as the rank a clergy person holds or the kind of clergy position (e.g., senior pastors earn more than associates and assistants), can also explain differences in earnings. Much of the literature suggests that one way women experience discrimination is by being systematically tracked into lower-paying and less-powerful positions and career patterns. We recognize this as a possible pattern and adjust for clergy rank in our analysis. Our findings show, however, that even when male and female clergy hold the same kind of position within comparable churches, the woman will still be paid less for doing the same job.

To weigh these factors in our analysis, we have estimated salary differences for eight types of positions held by clergy: senior pastor, sole pastor, assistant or associate pastor, interim pastor, co-pastor, regional staff, national staff, and secular employment unrelated to the church. Recognizing that the size of a church budget often determines salaries as much as the experience of the ordained person or the denomination of a particular congregation, we also adjust for the size of a congregation in our analysis.[5] Finally, we have considered denominational affiliation, since salary levels vary from denomination to denomination. All of these factors can lead to differences in salaries that have nothing to do with gender.

After making adjustments for each of these factors, it is possible to state what portion of the differences between the earnings of clergy men and clergy women are directly related to gender. *Even discounting all of these factors, we find a 9 percent difference between the salaries of clergy women and clergy men.* Put another way, women earn only 91 percent of the salaries of men for working the same hours in the same types of jobs, within the same denomination, in the same size church, after adjusting for differences in age, experience, and education. When compared to salary discrimination in other occupations as charted in recent studies, the size of this gap seems wide. A recent study of the salaries of men and women in service industries shows a much narrower gap. When adjustments are made for firm and occupation, the gender gap between men's and women's earnings in the service industries was roughly 2 to 3 percent.[6]

Our finding of a 9 percent gap between male and female clergy earnings, from a broad sample of denominations, lends compelling weight to the stories of discrimination and prejudice we have heard in our interviews. Indeed, the persistence of this gender wage gap suggests that the problem goes far beyond the individual stories we have collected. Job discrimination experienced by women clergy is a systematic problem that needs to be addressed at an institutional level. The gender wage gap cannot be explained by differences in education, experience, position, and denomination. (See Appendix 4.3, "Denominations Ranked by Average Adjusted Earnings for Full-Time Clergy Women.")

It seems ironic that religious denominations, committed to values of justice and equality, would practice such overt discrimination toward women. Many of our interviews suggest that male clergy believe women have an equal right to be ordained and practice ministry. What, then, accounts for the persistence of discrimination?

Ed Lehman has done important research on the congregational sources of discrimination against women clergy.[7] He argues that even when a majority of members in a congregation feel a woman is equally qualified as a man to serve as a pastor, these same members may also perceive that hiring a female pastor would cause conflict among some members of their congregation. Hiring committees seek to avoid conflict when choosing a pastor and are therefore likely to choose a man over an equally qualified woman in order to preserve organizational harmony, even if their personal preference may be for a female candidate.

We speculate that another structural source of discriminatory practices stems from the ambiguity and isolation surrounding clergy work. One way in which clergy receive promotions into higher-paying jobs is through positive evaluations of their work performance. However, our research shows that the ambiguity and isolation surrounding clergy work make it inherently difficult to assess the performance of many clergy. We believe that when performance is difficult to evaluate through objective criteria, subjective judgments come into play, and these judgments tend to use the "measure of a man" as the standard against which women are judged.

The ambiguity of clergy work and the fuzzy spheres of responsibility and authority cause a great deal of stress for many clergy. As one pastor put it:

> One problem with clergy work is that there is no clear standard for what it means to be a "good pastor." One way to deal with the uncertainty is to work harder and harder until you are working sixty to seventy hours a week and then you burn out because there is still so much more you could do.
>
> (United Methodist clergy woman)

When we examine the job expected of clergy, performance expectations and job descriptions tend to be vague and unspecified. Parishioners see clergy on Sundays or occasionally during the week and evaluate the pastor according to the preaching and organization of the service, his or her personality, and some elusive perceptions of "character." Many of the tasks of the "clergy job," such as preparing the sermon, setting up for coffee, balancing the budget, or preparing announcements, are largely unsupervised and unmonitored by any one person. When a pastor is the only ordained person on the staff of a church, and sometimes the only paid employee of the church, he or she is "supervised" by lay volunteers or "accountable" in some distant fashion to a wider denominational executive. Information about pastors' performance under these conditions is often gathered unsystematically from many sources.

Arthur L. Stinchcombe's research on the use of information within organizations explains how uncertainty surrounding employment can cause problems.[8] When someone is first hired, employers are often uncertain about what they are getting. This ambiguity continues for a time after the person begins work, but eventually, it dissipates with observation and productivity. With jobs such as ministry, however, it is more difficult to reduce uncertainty, because there is very little opportunity to observe all that a pastor does and productivity is difficult to define. Stinchcombe finds that when supervisors cannot measure performance clearly, they use a very general assessment of "character" and "background," combined with seniority, to allocate rewards. By contrast, when supervisors can measure the productivity of a worker, "character" and "background" play a small role in determining rewards.

What we learn from Stinchcombe's research is that when work performance is difficult to judge, as it is in clergy work, employers (denominational judicatory staff and local congregational leadership) will evaluate employees (clergy) on the basis of perceived character, background, and seniority. This makes all clergy employment difficult to support with appropriate rewards and feedback, and it makes the work of clergy women especially vulnerable. When evaluations are made on the basis of perceived character, background, and seniority, clergy women tend to be in a disadvantaged position simply because implicit comparisons are more likely to be made with the dominant image associated with clergy, which is male.

This fits with the stories we have heard from women about "feeling" that no matter how they meet objective criteria, no matter how experienced they are, and no matter how well they do on the job, they still lack something. Clergy women lack the "male character" that has been so deeply connected to ordained ministry throughout the centuries. Gender is still an ascriptive trait associated with the character of clergy.

Historically, masculinity—that is, being male—has been constructed as a component of clergy character. It is present in the patriarchal language of the liturgy, in the symbols, in the rituals, and in the texts. In our interviews with clergy and laity, some still express a belief that women may not legitimately be ordained as clergy. It should not be surprising, then, that maleness becomes part of the character associated with a "good pastor."

This judgment of character is likely to occur on a preconscious level, for structural reasons. Ninety percent of the present clergy labor force is comprised of men. This means that nine out of ten times, the previous pastor in any job was a man, and the next candidates will be evaluated by his standard. Within the lifetime of any hiring committee, its members are collectively likely to have had their views of clergy shaped by male clergy. Supervisors tend to be men and tend to be attracted to candidates with similar characteristics. Even when supervisors are women, they may share a preference for or similarity with "male" characteristics. Women clergy often bring a different charisma from men, a different style of leadership, and different communication styles in their interactions with parishioners. Even when ordained women display "masculine" traits, these traits will be interpreted differently when displayed by a woman. Women are less likely to fit the family profile of male clergy because they are less likely to have the equivalent of a "clergy wife" to provide unpaid support staff to the church (although this profile is becoming less frequent for men as well). They are less likely to be perceived (when married) as the primary "breadwinner" of the family, and churches may thus feel justified in paying female clergy less than men. In sum, women have ascribed characteristics that are inherently incongruent with the "character" of the historical ordained clergy model. This, combined with the structure of clergy work and the ambiguity that surrounds performance assessment, makes women more vulnerable to subjective evaluations of their performance.

What can be done to change this situation?

A clue can be found in a recent study comparing pairs of male and female engineers whose careers were followed through six organizations. In this research, women were able to advance most quickly in firms in *turbulent markets* and in firms where work tasks were structured in *flexible networks*. In flexible network settings, when work was done by personnel organized in egalitarian teams and when communication and decision making tended to be horizontal rather than vertical, men and women tended to be evaluated on the basis of qualifications and skills rather than gender. The chief characteristic of these work settings was that different ways of thinking, different values, and different opinions were considered *resources* for working out solutions to existing problems. On those teams, female engineers, with their different points of view, were seen as a resource for the organization rather than a problem. In addition, the egalitarian nature of the work team enabled team members to get to know one another very well, valuing one another's qualifications and strengths unrelated to gender. On these egalitarian teams, "the women become visible as professionals for their colleagues and superiors, instead of invisible as professionals and overly visible as women."[9]

This research found that, in contrast, women do less well than men in bureaucratic organizations that seek to ensure a "continual reproduction of the culture." In such bureaucratic organizations, women become professionally *invisible,* while men, who demonstrate the same characteristics as the employers, are hired and promoted, reproducing group similarities. The research also found that women experienced no particular advantages in organizations with formal affirmative action and equal employment policies.

Based on these findings, it is easy to see how the male-oriented, patriarchal traditions of the church with their hierarchical structures of authority, the isolation of clergy work, and the loose oversight of pastors make the ministry difficult for clergy women. The very structure of the clergy labor market maintains patterns of sex discrimination, because no one is in a very good position to evaluate the real and positive contributions women bring to their ministry. Because all clergy carry out their ministries in isolated task environments and with uneven oversight and hierarchical habits, "the measure of a man" is still the standard against which all clergy are evaluated. This is why the clergy women in our study continue to report that they are perceived as "unsuited" for clergy work, in spite of the fact that ordained ministry requires nurturant skills generally associated with women.

FINDING A JOB

Another source of discrimination occurs in the job-seeking process. The kinds of jobs women get are affected by the ways in which denominations handle the process of matching clergy with jobs. In the early history of Protestantism, clergy placement was not a problem. Young men trained for ordained leadership academically and practically. After college or seminary, aspiring clergy lived with a seasoned pastor to "read divinity" and to learn "on the job." In those denominational traditions where formal education was not essential, patterns of apprenticeship enabled seasoned pastors to mentor the next generation of leadership. Sons followed in the footsteps of their fathers, and many pastors served one congregation for their entire life.

With the increase in formal theological education and the expansion of church life on the western frontier, clergy careers changed. Pastors became more mobile, serving small congregations and then moving on (or "up") to larger congregations or into wider settings of ministry. Getting each new job depended on personal networks and how church leaders evaluated their effectiveness in ministry. It also, in most cases, required that laity extend an invitation, or "call," when they hired a new pastor. Methodists modified this "call system" by ordaining pastors to *itinerant* ministry, whereby once clergy are called and ordained to full-status membership in a Methodist conference, they are moved from job to job under the direction of a bishop.[10] This is often referred to as an "appointment system."

Today, getting a job as an ordained man or woman has become extremely complicated. Clergy need not only to respond to God's call to preach, teach, and administer sacraments but to find a concrete opportunity, either by call or appointment, to serve in a specific setting for ministry.

The characteristics of a good job vary for each individual. In general, a "good job" is seen as employment in a congregation that is stable and fairly compatible with the outlook of the pastor, one that offers a livable wage, one that provides challenges for its pastors to learn and build skills that allow them to advance in their career, and one that is geographically located in an area in which it is desirable to live. A less-than-ideal job might be in a conflict-ridden congregation or in a congregation that is hostile to the pastor's outlook and views; it might be a congregation that does not or cannot pay enough to support a pastor or that requires the pastor to assume responsibilities for more than one congregation or take secular employment to supplement his or her income; it might be in a congregation that offers few opportunities for professional growth or is located in an isolated area, far from social amenities.

Any denomination will have a number of desirable and undesirable jobs, as measured by the characteristics listed above. The kinds of jobs women get are affected by the ways in which denominations handle the process of matching clergy with jobs.

In the denominations in our study, we identify three organizational features that address this issue: we look at the effect of centralized employment information systems, affirmative action staffing, and managed denominational appointment systems on placing clergy women and clergy men. By examining the effects these characteristics have on reducing the gender wage gap, we look at whether the presence of these organizational procedures facilitates the equal placement and promotion of clergy women.

We use salary to measure the desirability of clergy positions. In doing so, we assume that salaries are attached to positions rather than to people. In other words, earnings tend to increase when people move to better positions rather than because people receive raises. If this is true, then how persons get jobs has an indirect effect on how clergy men and clergy women are paid. When organizational procedures offer equal advantages to clergy men and clergy women who are searching for jobs, it should be possible to explain all earnings differences by referring to the individual characteristics noted above—age, experience, education, denomination, church size, and so forth.

We know that earnings differences in our study are not fully explained in that way; therefore, we ask whether certain organizational procedures might reduce the gender wage gap. If they do, we can assume that these procedures will help promote the equal access of men and women to similar jobs. However, if they increase the gender wage gap, we assume that such procedures reduce the access of qualified clergy women to the jobs that clergy men are getting. Our goal is to identify the denominational practices and characteristics that provide the best institutional arrangements for promoting earnings equality among male and female clergy.

Denominations in our sample vary widely in the ways in which they organize their labor markets. At one extreme, illustrated by the Southern Baptists, the clergy labor market resembles an open, competitive market, that is, all jobs are open to all applicants. Classical economic theory argues that this is the most efficient allocation of people to jobs. The assumption is that a totally free market will optimize costs and benefits so that people will find jobs that match their qualifications.

Unfortunately, this perspective makes a number of unrealistic assumptions. First, it assumes that people are perfectly mobile, that is, that they can move to wherever the best job is located. Second, it assumes that clergy and their employers have perfect information about the job market and their options. Third, it assumes that people will behave rationally. In reality, job seeking and finding is often erratic. Searches occur in narrowly defined geographical areas, and information is often limited. Positions are not widely advertised, and decisions are heavily dependent on existing contacts. Since existing contacts usually develop among people with similar traits, congregations are more likely to hire persons who are similar to themselves with regard to gender, race, education, and income. This pattern is not helpful to women and tends to preserve the status quo by maintaining homogeneity.

Contemporary research on the ways in which social inequality is reproduced, particularly in hiring situations, shows that no change is possible until the inherent biases of such closed social networks are seen as a problem. In other words, only when congregations or denominational leaders get beyond their insider mindset do changes in hiring patterns occur.

Denominational Employment Information Systems. Some denominations recognize that churches rely on closed social networks for information about candidates when they are seeking to hire a new pastor. To promote the hiring of women and minorities, they have adopted centralized systems to provide better information about prospective candidates than what is generally available on "the grapevine." Information in the central office varies, but it may include a standardized candidate dossier, letters of recommendation, supervisor evaluations, grades, placement scores on general exams, preferences as to the kind of position sought, and desired geographic locations. The purpose of this centralized procedure is to provide congregations seeking pastors with the most complete information on all qualified clergy. It is an attempt to overcome the "good old boy network" by insisting that congregations collect information about a wider pool of applicants that includes women and minorities.

Once information on every available candidate is stored in a centralized location (electronically or otherwise), any local congregation and any clergy person looking for a job has equal access. In a perfect world, this system will match qualified candidates with the needs of particular churches. Congregations with access to the best information should be able to make considered judgments about prospective candidates and reduce their reliance on informal networks. Clergy looking for new jobs should be able to find more places for ministry that match their talents and desires. However, such denomination-wide information systems for clergy placement never work perfectly. One reason is that the full list of qualified candidates may be screened at the regional level and only selected candidates passed on to a congregation. Nevertheless, our analysis shows that such information systems do make it easier for women and minorities to be hired, because they facilitate decision making based on relatively objective criteria instead of on uneven informal networks of information.

When we examine the earnings of clergy women and clergy men in denominations that use a centralized, denomination-wide employment information system for clergy placement, the gender wage gap narrows to 6 percent, whereas in denominations that do not use such an employment information system, the gender wage gap is 12 percent.[11]

We conclude, therefore, that one reason for the inequity between the earnings of clergy women and those of clergy men is that employers do not always have the best information about qualified clergy women. Our findings indicate that inequities can be partially addressed by improving the distribution of information about qualified job candidates. This finding also supports our earlier interpretation about how ambiguity or lack of information regarding women's work performances may be a structural source of discrimination.

Denominational Staff Positions. Another way in which denominations have sought to promote the careers of female clergy is to provide staff positions in top denominational offices that are devoted to supporting "women in ministry." These "women's desks" or "advocates," as they are sometimes called, make an institutional statement that the denomination is serious about supporting women. These staff are actively engaged in helping women clergy develop networks, disseminating and collecting information about the status of women clergy, and raising the consciousness of denominational officials and grassroots members about the needs of clergy women. We ask whether the presence of such a women's advocate reduces sex discrimination as measured by the gender wage gap.

In the 1970s and 1980s, national denominational staff positions that advocated for women clergy did raise the consciousness of churches about women. In the 1990s, however, there is no difference in the gender wage gap in denominations with or without these denominational staff advocates. In many cases, budget constraints and staff downsizing have actually diminished the capacity of denominational staff positions to support women clergy. Unfortunately, from our research it appears that staff positions do not affect the gender wage gap one way or another, although they may do some important work in support of clergy women.

National staff positions symbolize an institutional commitment to women clergy, but they are often too far removed from local congregational and regional decision makers to make a difference. These denominational staff positions signal the denomination's commitment to women's leadership in the larger political environment. Denominational women's advocates are regularly found in most of the congregation-centered and many of the institution-centered denominations. Their impact is probably more important in the institution-centered denominations because these denominations have the greatest need to symbolize visibly their commitment to female clergy, given the fact that battles over women's ordination have often been strongly contested in these denominations.

Denominational Appointment Systems. The third organizational practice or characteristic that supports equality for clergy women in their search for jobs is the managed appointment system. An appointment placement system can be considered the opposite of a free market system. In fact, it bears a strong resemblance to patronage systems or a union shop.

In an appointment system, control over the allocation of clergy to jobs is focused in the hands of a few individuals who, to a large extent, match clergy with positions and control hiring patterns. The United Methodists, the Free Methodists, the Episcopal Church, and the Evangelical Lutheran Church in America employ some version of an appointment system.[12] All of these systems manage the clergy job search very directly at certain points in the clergy career, even though the four denominations differ in important ways.

Whereas employment information systems improve the flow of information, which facilitates free market processes, denominations with an appointment system rely on a closed system whereby seasoned church leaders mentor clergy and guide careers, ostensibly to maximize benefits for clergy and for the congregations. Appointment systems depend on a regional denominational official or executive (variously called a bishop, district superintendent, etc.), who consults with other ranking denominational leaders and with local congregational leadership to place or appoint individual clergy men and clergy women in their initial jobs and, in some systems, in every subsequent job. In our sample, the appointment systems used by the United Methodist Church (UMC) and the Free Methodist Church are the most closely managed systems.

Viewed from one perspective, appointment systems managed by the wrong people can easily keep women from gaining equal access to good jobs. However, once a system is sensitized to include women, it has much to be said for it.

The United Methodist Church is attractive to many women precisely because full-status ordination (membership in a United Methodist annual conference) carries with it assurances of lifetime employment. For this reason alone, the United Methodist Church has attracted a number of female clergy who have been frustrated by the poor job opportunities in other denominations.

The structural features of the United Methodist Church appointment system are also attractive to women. In our interviews, the most frequently heard career complaints in every denomination center on the inability of clergy women to get jobs. Clergy women repeatedly lament being stuck in dead-end jobs that do not permit them to acquire skills necessary to advance their careers. They tell stories about having a difficult experience in one job and finding themselves stuck with the undesirable reputation that they are "difficult to work with"—which, in an open market system, may severely limit their capacity to find another position. In a managed appointment system, clergy are more likely to have opportunities to move on from an unsuccessful appointment and thereby learn from their mistakes.

When a United Methodist clergy woman accepts her lifetime "call" to itinerant service as a member of a United Methodist conference, some of the obstacles women experience in denominations driven by a free market system disappear. In addition, salaries tend to be higher in the United Methodist system because the denomination controls the supply of clergy to the churches. This creates a monopoly situation, giving the denominational leaders greater market leverage over churches to press for higher salaries for clergy. The guarantee of employment provides job security that female clergy need to maintain a continuous and decent standard of living throughout their careers. Furthermore, the itinerancy system promotes mobility, making the "ghettoization" of women in dead-end jobs difficult. Through different appointments, clergy women have a variety of parish experiences, giving them opportunities to gather useful and marketable skills. Finally, even if a clergy woman has a bad experience, the continual rotation required by an itinerancy system gives her the opportunity to overcome that experience and have a "second chance" to renew her ministry.

It sounds as if the appointment system is the perfect solution to help women overcome the gender wage gap. Yet when we compare the denominations that have this system (namely, the United Methodists and the Free Methodists) with those that do not, we find that being in an appointment placement system has *no significant effect* on the gender wage gap. Clergy women do not fare any better in these denominations than in other denominations with regard to earnings.

Although United Methodist salary levels tend to be higher for both clergy women and clergy men than those in many of the other denominations, clergy men with similar education, experience, and rank still earn, on average, 9 percent more than clergy women. The level of inequity among the United Methodists and the Free Methodists is very similar to the level of inequity in other denominations.[13]

The Evangelical Lutheran Church in America (ELCA) and the Episcopal Church have a modified appointment system. In these denominations, the synodical bishop (ELCA) and the diocesan bishop (Episcopal Church) have a great deal of influence over where new seminary graduates are placed in their first church positions. Typically, the bishop will present one to three candidates to a local congregation and allow the church to choose among them. The church may be strongly advised to accept one of these candidates. In subsequent job moves bishops are less involved, but the judicatory influence is still considerable because Lutheran and Episcopal congregations regularly go to their bishop when they are seeking a new pastor, and the bishop may exercise a great deal of influence over whom the church interviews, if not calls (hires). In certain instances, a congregation with abundant resources may conduct an independent search for its pastor. Most of the time, however, placement is regulated in that the majority of appointments take place under a bishop's auspices, and the bishop remains the most influential party in the hiring process. Control continues to rest in the hands of a single regional executive or with the staff of a judicatory office. Obviously, in these denominations the attitude of the bishop and his or her staff toward female clergy will have a significant impact on the careers of clergy women.

When we group together all of the denominations that use some type of managed appointment system for clergy placement and compare their salary levels with those denominations that do not have such a system, we find that the gender wage gap does not narrow. Given the general assumption that appointment systems, such as that in the United Methodist Church, are better for clergy women, we find this surprising.

Ultimately, managed appointment systems are only as good as their leaders. A system that places a great deal of discretion in the hands of regional executives will benefit women only if the executives themselves become proactive in the placement of women. Unfortunately, an appointment system has no inherent feature that controls whether judicatory power will be used for or against women clergy.

Our interviews with clergy women in denominations with appointment systems support this mixed assessment of managed placement procedures. Even the most benign appointment system provides opportunities for discrimination. One United Methodist clergy woman reported how her district superintendent decided that she could work only half time because she was a woman and needed to be kept "safe." He concluded that a part-time position was appropriate because she would not have to get home too late. Unfortunately, working half time meant she would not be able to fulfill the requirements to become a fully ordained member of her conference. When she complained, her district superintendent told her he could not find a full-time position for her in the area where she currently lived. She then tried to speak to the bishop to request a full-time position. At that the district superintendent became angry and threatened that if she spoke to the bishop, he would see to it that she never obtained a position. He told her he was amazed that she had progressed so far toward ordination, since he was convinced that she did not possess a divine call to ministry. Luckily, soon after this conversation, a new district superintendent was appointed. The woman was eventually appointed to a full-time position in a small rural church. However, this church had the reputation of being a "preacher-eater," namely, a congregation that makes life so difficult for pastors that clergy end up leaving the congregation and sometimes quitting pastoral ministry altogether. We do not know what happened to this woman, but if she continues in ordained ministry, it will be in spite of, rather than because of, the appointment system.

Discrimination is not unique to any particular denomination, and no system can guarantee equal treatment. When power is concentrated in the hands of a few decision makers, as it is in managed appointment systems, the results may be positive or negative, depending on prejudices held by district superintendents or bishops, which are likely to influence the careers of clergy in appointment systems.

CLERGY CAREER PATHS

Given the variety of jobs available to clergy, it is important to look at the "clergy career." How are female clergy doing? And more important, do clergy men and clergy women differ significantly in their career paths?

Very little systematic research has been done on the career paths of clergy after ordination. However, there is reason to believe that men's and women's careers unfold differently. We know that women clergy generally make the decision to seek ordination later in life. They are more likely than men to enter the clergy profession after experiencing a divorce or to be single or married to another ordained person. There are distinct gender differences in the kinds of first jobs men and women assume in their clergy career. Clergy men are far more likely than women to move into a small sole pastorate as their first position, whereas clergy women are far more likely than men to become assistant or associate pastors as their first job. Starting in different places has ramifications for male and female career paths for many years to follow.

This suggests that different forces are shaping clergy women's career decisions. Clergy women appear to follow a more diverse pattern of career choices or opportunities. They are more likely than men to be in nonparish positions. In their first two jobs after ordination or official authorization to ministerial leadership, clergy women are more likely than men to find employment in secular jobs. For these women, however, secular work does not mean that they have left their clergy career. In fact, we have found that a small number of clergy who take secular jobs eventually move back into recognized positions of church leadership. The picture is extremely fluid, and at present, very little is known about such "intermittent clergy," that is, clergy who move in and out of church-related work throughout their careers.

Sociologists report that general patterns of men's and women's careers vary substantially. Women are more likely than men to be in lower-paying jobs and also more likely to be in part-time work. Researchers suggest that a "dual labor market" exists, with primary and secondary labor pools. Jobs in the primary labor market tend to pay better over the long run, lead to promotions, have good job security, and provide opportunities to broaden skills and gain access to more and better jobs. Jobs in the secondary labor market tend to have less security, pay less over the long run, provide fewer opportunities for learning or advancement, and be constrained by barriers that prevent easy movement into the primary labor market. It is common, in many parts of our economy, to find that men dominate the primary labor market and women inhabit the secondary labor market.

Are women trapped in the secondary labor market because of discrimination or because family situations, such as the raising of small children, pressure them to seek more flexible forms of employment? When people "voluntarily" move into the secondary labor market, as in the case of a mother or father who takes less demanding employment in order to spend more time with family, they will often remain underemployed after the children grow up, because employers are biased toward hiring persons with continuous primary labor market histories.

Generally speaking, most research on occupations and careers uses what is called cross-sectional data. In other words, researchers gather information about what a particular group of people are doing in their occupations at a particular point in time. Findings from this "snapshot" of information are then generalized into conclusions about career patterns over time. Ideally, careers are studied as a sequence of jobs held by an individual. When we look back on our careers, we see them as an evolutionary process. The first job is often important in providing the skills, resources, and networks that give access to the next job. Experiences in a sequence of jobs shape vocational attitudes. Positive experiences encourage people to choose similar kinds of work in the future, whereas negative experiences may prod people to change career directions completely. By looking at careers as a sequence of jobs, we are better able to see how men and women end up in different positions and the factors that might shape their career paths.

Our research examines the first three jobs in the career histories of male and female clergy. More than 25 percent of the clergy in our study found a job that suited them right after ordination and have never moved. In our study, 368 out of 1,416 men (26 percent) and 445 out of 1,553 women (29 percent) are currently still in their first job.

The majority of clergy, however, move frequently. Sometimes this is because their ecclesiastical system requires that they move; sometimes they feel they have completed the ministry that they were called to in a particular place; and sometimes they move seeking greater job satisfaction.

We describe the kinds of jobs clergy men and clergy women obtain immediately after graduation from seminary by using the following categories: "senior pastor" (pastors in large congregations with other clergy on staff); "large sole pastors" (sole pastors of congregations with an average weekly attendance of more than 150 people); "small sole pastors" (sole pastors in small congregations with an average weekly attendance of fewer than 150 people); "assistant or associate pastors" (one of several pastors in a large congregation); "other parish clergy" (persons with specialized responsibilities for youth, music, education, or interim ministries within congregational settings); "nonparish other" (ordained clergy working outside congregational settings—denominational executives, military or school chaplains, missionaries, evangelists, seminary professors, etc.); and "secular" (ordained clergy in non-church-related employment).

Distinct differences are apparent in the kinds of jobs clergy men and clergy women hold immediately after ordination. Men are most likely (35 percent) to become sole pastors of small congregations. Women are most likely (35 percent) to become assistant or associate pastors in a multistaffed congregation. One reason for this may be that congregations that have never had a woman pastor are more willing to "try out" a female pastor when she is not the only ordained leader in the congregation. Furthermore, having a woman as an assistant or associate pastor may feel more comfortable because it fits historical expectations that women should be in "assisting" roles. One clergy woman in our survey complained that lay members of her church sometimes see her as a "paid pastor's wife."

Denominations with appointment systems give other reasons for placing ordained women in assistant or associate positions. One district superintendent told us that he feels an "assistant" position provides good training for women before they assume the responsibilities of a sole pastor. This logic is equally applicable to men, and in fact, 32 percent of male seminary graduates (almost as many men as women) start out their careers as associate or assistant pastors.

In the overall occupational landscape for clergy, it may be appropriate to consider "parish other," "nonparish other," and "secular" work as a secondary labor market. If this is the case, then the fact that the first jobs of clergy women are far more likely (46 percent) to be in this secondary labor market than the first jobs of clergy men (23 percent) is a very significant fact. Since the first call or placement is often a good predictor of subsequent job moves, this initial distribution has a continuing impact on the career paths of clergy women.

Table 4.1

First Jobs Held after Ordination by Male and Female Clergy

	Women (1,553)	Men (1,416)
Senior Pastors	1%	4%
Large Sole Pastors (+150 avg. attendance)	2%	5%
Small Sole Pastors (−150 avg. attendance)	15%	35%
Assoc./Assist. Pastors	35%	32%
Parish Other	16%	6%
Nonparish Other	14%	6%
Secular Employment	16%	11%

When we move beyond the first job to examine the full career paths of female and male clergy, we find that sole pastor positions and assistant or associate pastor positions turn out to be "transitional" jobs. That is, they are likely to serve as stepping-stones to positions of more responsibility, particularly if the position is held by a pastor early in her or his career. It is therefore significant that two-thirds of clergy men start their clergy careers in one of these two types of positions, compared to only half of the clergy women.

MOVING INTO THE SECOND JOB

When we examine the careers of clergy men who start out as sole pastors in small churches (congregations with an average weekly attendance under 150), we find that 31 percent of these men find their next job as the sole pastor of a large church (congregations with an average weekly attendance over 150) and 29 percent become the pastor of another small church. Of the clergy women who start as pastors in a small church, however, only 26 percent take a new position as the sole pastor of a large church while 11 percent move to another small church. Interestingly, a large number of clergy women (21 percent) move from being sole pastors in small churches to some form of specialized ministry in a congregational setting ("parish other").

Of the clergy men who start as assistant or associate pastors, 25 percent move to another assistant or associate position, 24 percent become sole pastors of large churches, and 21 percent become sole pastors of small churches. Of the clergy women who start as assistants or associates, 32 percent move to another assistant or associate position, 10 percent become the sole pastors of large churches, and 7 percent become sole pastors in small churches.

Another way to think of these differences in men's and women's careers is to think of the moves as between managerial and staff positions. Senior pastorates and sole pastorates are like managerial positions, with major responsibilities for the oversight of a church and, in the case of a senior pastor, for supervising others in the operations of a church. These pastorates lead to an expansion of skills and require increasing levels of responsibility. Assistant and associate positions and various specialized ministries within a congregation ("parish other") are like staff positions. In these positions, responsibility is limited, and one is generally under the supervision of another clergy colleague.

When we look at levels of professional responsibility in relationship to clergy career paths, we see that when clergy men move from their first job to their second job, 53 percent move into managerial positions (excluding nonparish and secular jobs), but when clergy women move from their first job to their second job, only 20 percent move into managerial positions. By the third job, we can document two distinct differences between the careers of clergy women and clergy men: first, clergy women are far less likely than clergy men to be in managerial positions, and second, clergy women have much more complex and diverse career paths than clergy men.

MOVING INTO THE THIRD JOB

Clergy women reporting on their third career move gave us the following picture: 1 percent became senior pastors, 4 percent became pastors in large churches, 14 percent became pastors in small churches, 19 percent became assistant or associate pastors, 21 percent served in other congregational ministries, 20 percent found nonparish ministries, and 17 percent entered secular employment. By their third job on their career paths, nearly 80 percent of clergy women are almost equally distributed across assistant or associate pastor positions, positions in specialized ministries, nonparish ministries, and secular work. When we further distinguish between "managerial" and "staff" positions, we discover that only 19 percent of clergy women are in managerial or primary labor market positions after three job moves, whereas 49 percent of clergy men are in such positions after three job moves.

Table 4.2
Third Jobs Held after Ordination by Male and Female Clergy

	Women (753)	Men (750)
Senior Pastors	1%	9%
Large Sole Pastors (+150 avg. attendance)	4%	10%
Small Sole Pastors (−150 avg. attendance)	14%	30%
Assoc./Assist. Pastors	19%	13%
Parish Other	21%	10%
Nonparish Other	20%	9%
Secular Employment	17%	17%

Our study shows that the career paths of female clergy are dramatically different from the career paths of male clergy. Male clergy are more than twice as likely to hold positions of managerial authority. Without judging whether this difference is a sign of success or failure, we can observe that the difference is dramatic.

Furthermore, the career paths of clergy women are considerably more diverse than those of clergy men. Men seem to follow fewer options. By the time clergy men reach their third job, only 9 percent are engaged in the growing variety of ministries beyond the parish, compared to 20 percent of the women. At the same time, the numbers of clergy men and clergy women in secular employment are roughly equal.

THE IMPACT OF CHILDREN
ON CLERGY CAREER PATHS

What happens to the career histories of clergy men and clergy women who have children within five years after ordination? Does having children affect women's careers differently than it affects men's? Since women normally spend more time in child-rearing activities than men, are clergy women with children more likely than clergy men with children to occupy the secondary labor market? By examining the family and career histories of clergy women and clergy men, we can begin to answer these questions.

In our study, 361 women and 843 men had children within five years of their ordination. Why did we find so many more men than women with children, even though we had responses from approximately the same number of clergy men and women? This is the result of some significant differences between the career paths of clergy men and clergy women. Clergy men are more likely than clergy women to have a traditional career path, incorporating college, seminary, and marriage. In our study, clergy men tend to be younger and often are married, whereas the clergy women are likely to be single, either because they never married or because they married and subsequently divorced before being ordained. Furthermore, if married, the ordained woman may have chosen to delay child rearing. As a consequence, there are far fewer women than men in our study who have had children within five years after their ordination.

The existing literature on how the "mommy track" affects career choices suggests that women with small children are more likely to move into part-time work or jobs that have fewer time commitments and responsibilities—that is, the secondary labor market. Consequently, when we examined the second jobs of men and women who had a child within five years after their ordination, we anticipated that being a parent might make more of an impact on the career choices of women than of men—making the women less likely than the men to take jobs as sole or senior pastors, where they would have demanding leadership responsibilities. We also examined the career paths of male clergy, not only to compare them with those of female clergy but to see if, as fathers assume more parenting responsibilities, becoming a father has any effect on career choices.

Our comparison of clergy women with children and clergy women without children across job types (in their second job) does not show many differences. Roughly the same percentages of women occupy senior positions, large sole pastorates, small sole pastorates, and associate or assistant positions. Women with children are moderately more likely than women without children to be in "parish other" positions, such as youth pastor, music pastor, or education specialist, and slightly less likely to be in nonparish positions, such as denominational administrator, seminary teacher, or missionary.

When we look at those clergy who have moved out of their first position, we find that fatherhood seems to have a positive effect on career mobility. Clergy men with young children are more likely to be in senior or sole pastorates than clergy men without children. On the other hand, ordained men without children are slightly more likely than ordained men with families to have moved to jobs as assistants, associate pastors, specialized parish work, nonparish work, or into the secular labor market.

What accounts for the effect of young children on the careers of clergy men? Our study agrees with Paula Nesbitt's study of Episcopal priests with children, which notes that children positively affect the advancement of clergy men and minimally impact on the advancement of clergy women.[14] Nesbitt suggests that married clergy men with children are more likely than other clergy men to have a stay-at-home wife who can support and assist the husband in his ministry. It is also likely that denominational executives in appointment systems exert some influence to see that male clergy with families serve in larger churches where salaries are higher.

Whether clergy women have any children has little effect on their career paths, and when it does, it is a negative impact. Nesbitt found this to be true for Episcopal clergy. Recent studies of executives and professionals in secular organizations suggest the same thing. There is a perception in both church and society that women have a disproportionate role (compared with men) in caring for children and that therefore they will not give as much energy to their careers as will men with children.[15]

Our findings also show that clergy women take more responsibility for raising children than do clergy men. In chapter 2 we noted that among clergy in full-time ministry who have young children, ordained women are 40 percent more likely than clergy men to be primary caregiver for a child and nearly three times more likely than clergy men to report having difficulty in carrying on a full-time ministry at a time when they have children under ten years old.

It may be that clergy women who are active pastors and have young children are more at risk than clergy men for being seen as either rejecting or compromising their responsibilities as mothers or being unable to do the job for which they are being paid.

Table 4.3
Clergy with and without Children in Their Second Job

| | Women | | Men | |
	with Children (261)	without Children (847)	with Children (633)	without Children (415)
Senior Pastors	1%	1%	7%	6%
Large Sole Pastors (+150)	13%	13%	29%	23%
Small Sole Pastors (−150)	6%	4%	20%	14%
Assoc./Assist. Pastors	24%	22%	17%	19%
Parish Other	24%	17%	7%	9%
Nonparish Other	13%	18%	6%	11%
Secular	17%	19%	12%	16%

Percentages rounded up to the next highest percentage.

In spite of the fact that the female clergy in our study tend to have fewer young children than do the male clergy, laity are consistently more concerned about the family responsibilities of their female pastors than they are about the family situations of male clergy:

> I feel that as in most professions, clergy women have difficult times juggling motherhood and full-time careers. We all need to understand that raising children is the most important work anyone can do. It in itself is a full-time job.
>
> (American Baptist lay woman)

> Both my father and mother were ordained ministers. I am not against women in the ministry. I just feel that full-time pastoring demands too much from women with families and home responsibilities.
>
> (Church of the Nazarene lay man)

> As a woman with a typically male occupation (engineer) I realize that most people still view certain occupations as better suited for men. . . . I think ideally, and in God's wisdom, a woman should care for her children. Therefore a mother of young children would probably not be a good candidate for a full-time minister's position. (Unfortunately, we do not live in an ideal world yet, and some women must work full-time. I am fortunate enough to work part-time while my children are in school.)
>
> (United Church of Christ lay woman)

By comparison, lay men and lay women never mention the issue of child care if their pastor is male, unless he is a single parent. In that situation, when comments are made, they are almost universally positive, applauding a man for doing a difficult thing.

Overall, female pastors with children are seen as breaking two traditional images associated with their gender: first, they are engaged in a profession historically held by men, and second, they are allowing their careers to compete with their family responsibilities. Women with children, or even women of childbearing age, sometimes cause search committees and denominational executives doing placement to stop and think about different issues—maternity leave, reduced workloads, and, most significant, how they feel about hiring a mother with young children if they truly believe that such women should make their families their first priority. In keeping with other studies, however, we find the fact that clergy women challenge the traditional image of the clergy "man" is still more important for career placement and opportunities than whether clergy (male or female) have family responsibilities.

Even though the career patterns of clergy with children and clergy without children show moderate differences, gender is the pivotal factor in accounting for career path differences between male clergy and female clergy. Our research shows that 6 percent of clergy men overall move to senior pastor positions in their second job, but less than 1 percent of clergy women overall do so. Forty-five percent of male clergy in their second job are in sole pastorates, compared to only 18 percent of female clergy.

So where do the women go? Many are still in associate or assistant pastor positions, more so than male pastors. In addition, clergy women are more likely than clergy men to move to specialized ministries in congregations and in church-recognized settings. Clergy women are also more likely than clergy men to be in secular work, although by the third job, equal proportions of clergy, male and female, are in secular work.

When compared with the traditional careers of clergy men, the clergy job for women is both limited and open. It seems to be limited in that women's careers consistently get tracked into less powerful and influential positions. It seems to be open in that women are finding new and unconventional ways to define jobs and invite the churches to ordain them.

5

A CALLING

One of the most common practices in the history of the Christian church is the setting apart of persons for leadership through the liturgical rite, sacrament, or ordinance known as "ordination." In the Bible, Acts 6 tells of the twelve disciples calling for a division of labor between those to serve community needs and those responsible for preaching and teaching. They argued, "It is not right that we should neglect the word of God in order to wait on tables" (Acts 6:2). As a consequence, the community chose seven leaders of good standing for special service, and they stood before the apostles, "who prayed and laid their hands on them" (6:6).

This biblical story marks the beginning of a process in Christian history whereby the churches have "ordered" their ministries. The apostle Paul repeatedly suggested that the church was the "body of Christ" (1 Corinthians 12). Within the body, Paul believed, God appointed leaders to different responsibilities, to sharing various gifts and exercising diverse forms of leadership. "The gifts [God] gave were that some would be apostles, some prophets, some evangelists, some pastors and teachers, to equip the saints for the work of ministry, for building up the body of Christ" (Eph. 4:11–12). Not only was it efficient to diversify roles within the church, but it was part of God's plan. Setting apart leadership for the church was a theological obligation.

Furthermore, in ordering ministries, Christians linked ordination—the setting apart of some persons by "prayer and laying on of hands"—directly to the life and ministry of Jesus through what has become known as an "apostolic succession." Apostolic succession seeks to uphold the principle that authentic ordination is possible only when new ordinands are "set apart" through "prayer and laying on of hands" by Christian leaders previously ordained in a similar manner—thereby connecting the authority of ordained ministry to the first disciples selected by Jesus.

Throughout history, Christians have argued about how and who ought to be "ordained"—young or mature adults, well-educated or especially pious persons, married or celibate persons, males or females, heterosexuals or homosexuals. In these debates, ordination is almost always understood to be more than a functional arrangement to get the work done. Persons who are ordained (clergy) are acknowledged to be especially gifted by God. After ordination, they carry an "indelible mark" that sets them apart for life from ordinary Christians (laity). All contemporary understandings of ordained ministry are grounded in the tradition that clergy are "called" by God, as well as the church, to assume "holy" or "priestly" responsibilities, such as sharing God's message through preaching and officiating at the sacramental rites of the church (ministries of Word and sacrament). Clergy may have different responsibilities across various denominations, but in spite of great diversity, all Christians practice some rite or liturgy that sets apart church leadership by prayer and laying on of hands. Most traditions call this process "ordination." It emphasizes the fact that ordained ministry is a sacred trust.

The history of ordination is further complicated by the fact that in the development of the Christian church in western Europe, a conviction grew that ordained persons should be male and celibate. Recent research on the early church suggests that such a definition of ordination was not always the case. Ancient and medieval church records show that women have held key responsibilities for oversight, discipline, liturgy, teaching, and service at various points in Christian history. Contemporary denominations argue over this legacy, and some, such as the Roman Catholic Church, deny that women have ever had any claim to priesthood.

For Protestantism, however, the sixteenth century in western Europe brought radical changes. Reformers challenged prevailing views of ordination, arguing for married and highly educated clergy. Protestantism insisted that celibacy was actually a problem and that married clergy were needed to minister to the needs of families. Soon, Martin Luther and the other Reformers, many of whom had been celibate priests, sought wives and promoted a more holistic view of ordained ministry.

Protestantism also stressed the intellectual leadership of the clergy. Instead of focusing on priestly sacramental duties, Protestant clergy emphasized preaching and teaching. They replaced the ornate vestments of the altar with the Geneva gown of the lectern and pulpit and of the university. They demanded that clergy "know" more, and they required scholarly credentials for ordination. Ordained ministry became a "learned" profession, open only to those who completed a rigorous academic program.

Protestantism further changed the relationship between clergy and laity. Although most Protestant denominations continued to distinguish clergy through ordination, Protestant theology emphasized the "priesthood of all believers," challenging basic assumptions about the powers of clergy. Protestant ordination was not so much an objective or ontological event as a simple recognition of gifts and authorization of ministerial functions. That is, among Protestants, ordained ministers were not any more holy than the laity; they were simply viewed as persons blessed with needed talents and empowered to function religiously with and on behalf of the whole community. Protestants considered ordination a special or "holy" calling, but its holiness was connected with the actions of the whole people of God—the priesthood of all believers—rather than with the life of a particular individual. Apostolic succession, for many Protestants, consisted in the collective legacy of the Christian community keeping faith through the ages, rather than in a sequence of ceremonies (or hands) linking one ordination ritual to the next.

These changing understandings of ordination in Christian history have shaped the issue of women's ordination. Many Protestants (and some Roman Catholics) came to ask: If all persons are called to ministry by their baptism, and if there is neither Jew nor Greek, male nor female, in Christ Jesus (Gal. 3:28), then why can't women be ordained? If the entire community is a royal priesthood carrying out God's ministries, women are part of that priesthood. If all Christians need to study the Bible and teach their faith to their children, then women can and should do that as well as men.

In North America, women began asking these questions openly in the early nineteenth century. Protestant women in the United States discovered new talents, took on new roles, and sought public visibility and political power. It was natural for women from many religious traditions to challenge their churches to move beyond unexamined assumptions about the maleness of clergy. Ordination, they insisted, was for women as well as men.

Attitudes about clergy women in all denominations have changed significantly during the last quarter of the twentieth century. In spite of difficulties and inequities on the job, women pastors are serving more and more congregations, and many are being accepted. At the same time, clergy women continue to encounter resistance, simply because they are female. As clergy women claim their sense of calling, it is important to understand how, and what is supporting them in their ministry and service as ordained clergy.

> The major impact of increased numbers of women clergy here is that we will be raising generations of churchgoers now who do not see ordained ministry as something done by just one gender.
>
> (United Church of Christ clergy women)

> When I was assistant pastor in the black American Baptist Church, a young girl came up and hugged me hard, indicating that it was really important to her that a woman be a minister. In other instances when I have done chaplaincy at a retirement home, several ladies came up to me and said that it was just wonderful to see me—they had felt called to ministry too, but the time was not right.
>
> (American Baptist clergy woman)

> I have heard several older men say that they did not know whether they would want to go back to a male minister now that they have experienced a female minister. This is quite an admission for these men who have been members for a long time.
>
> (United Church of Christ lay woman)

> My church is slowly working its way from being very much of the opinion that only men make the best ministers to the belief that women can be just as good as men as ministers.
>
> (American Baptist lay woman)

Even though understandings of ordained ministry have changed since the dramatic increases in the ordination of women in the 1970s, clergy women still experience significant discrimination as professionals in the workplace. Clergy of both genders continue to find themselves in congregations that want something different from them as leaders than they were led to expect in seminary or than they were told by the congregational committee which hired them. Clergy regularly find themselves in ministry settings that are isolated, declining in membership and resources, and fraught with conflict, which foster professional burnout at a high rate. Even when things go well, the career of an ordained minister is difficult.

So why do men and women continue to feel this call, or choose this career? Historically, it has not been an easy vocation, and for ordained women, it continues to be an "uphill calling."

DISCERNING GOD'S CALL

Many clergy do not feel that they "choose" the ordained ministry; rather, it chooses them. The call to become an ordained minister is beyond their control. God chooses, and the process takes many forms.

A man or woman may have a one-time dramatic experience or vision or may simply slowly grow into the idea. Everyone agrees, however, that ordained ministry is not merely a human choice. It is a gift from God. Even as they embrace the gift, however, those who respond hope that a ministerial career will be personally rewarding. Most of those who enter the "occupation of divinity" believe that ordained ministry is not just interesting employment in a fairly high-status job but a divine treasure. Unfortunately, clergy are repeatedly disappointed when the churches are unable to accept their talents *and* provide employment with enough material resources to support them as they seek to serve church and society.

Some women and men get a flash of insight or a sudden revelation that God is calling them to ministry. They respond to a divine call in a dramatic way and prepare themselves for ordination. Others may have a similar experience but do not take it seriously until they find it confirmed and reinforced by additional experiences over a period of time. Still others do not have any particular moment in their lives when they feel a call. They simply grow into their vocation gradually—becoming convinced that God is inviting them to go into the ministry only after much soul-searching; testing through volunteer work in congregations; long talks with family, friends, and pastors; and even after enrolling in and graduating from a theological seminary.

Among the clergy in our study, about half of the men and women in each denominational cluster say that their decision to enter ordained ministry involved both a specific incident in their lives when they felt a call and a period of time during which they gradually came to believe that they were called. Clergy women overall are approximately twice as likely as clergy men in the Spirit-centered denominations to recall a special moment when they realized that God was calling them to the ordained ministry. In contrast, clergy in the congregation-centered and institution-centered denominational clusters, especially men, are more likely than clergy in the Spirit-centered denominations not to claim that at any specific time they felt a divine call to enter the ministry. These clergy report that they experienced a subtle, gradual, growing awareness that God wanted them to be ministers.

An understanding of "call" differs dramatically among our three denominational clusters. For example, clergy in the Spirit-centered denominations (men and women) are quite unlikely to become clergy in their denominations *unless* they can recall a particular moment when they became convinced that God wanted them to devote their lives to ministry. (This does not necessarily mean "ordained" ministry.) When clergy in the Spirit-centered denominations are making their vocational decisions, they are more likely than those in the other denominational clusters to cite the importance of their conviction that God wishes them to be ordained and their belief that through ordained ministry they can serve God better. Relatively few clergy (men and women) in any denomination, with marginally higher numbers in the Spirit-centered denominations, think that ordination bestows on them unique divine powers.

A majority of clergy women and clergy men in the congregation-centered and institution-centered denominations are not quite sure that God has explicitly called them to ordained ministry in order to carry out a God-given mission in the church and the world. God still figures heavily in their wrestling with the question of ordination, but they are less confident than clergy in the Spirit-centered denominations about what God wants them to do. They believe, however, that ordination will enable them to carry out more effectively whatever that is.

Table 5.1
The Decision to Enter the Ordained Ministry

	Denominational Cluster					
	Congregation-Centered		Institution-Centered		Spirit-Centered	
	Women	Men	Women	Men	Women	Men
N =	1,213	1,026	953	787	300	259
Decision to Enter the Ordained Ministry was						
Gradual	29%	32%	26%	32%	15%	13%
Both (one-time and gradual)	53%	47%	58%	51%	55%	47%
One-time	18%	21%	16%	17%	30%	40%
	100%	100%	100%	100%	100%	100%
God Was "Helpful" in the Decision to Be Ordained	86%	78%**	93%	91%	99%	96%

**There is a statistically significant difference between women and men of .00001 and better.

Not only do at least three-fourths of all clergy women and clergy men in each denominational cluster say that God was helpful in their decision to be ordained, but for the great majority of these clergy, no other source or influence on their "ordination decision" is more important. The primacy of the divine call in the decision to seek ordination dominates regardless of how suddenly or gradually these women and men make their decision to seek ordination. Furthermore, the length of time clergy take to decide to seek ordination is not related either to how old they were when they made this life choice or to when they got up the nerve to tell their denominational officials what they believed God wanted them to do with their lives. (See Appendix 5.1, "Motivations in Seeking Ordination.")

From the mid-1970s into the early 1980s, the women's movements in many mainline Protestant denominations openly encouraged women who felt called by God to enter seminary and be ordained. Women were inspired to change "the sexist nature" of a male-stereotyped occupation by actually entering it themselves. These women were proud to be called feminists and were often described by others as having a passion or "feminist fire."

Most of the clergy women whom Hartford Seminary surveyed in 1980–81, who were part of the first large wave of ordained women to become pastors, indicated that a contributing factor, although not the central reason, in their seeking ordination was to "change the sexist nature of the church."[1] Over half (56 percent) of the women pastors surveyed in 1980–81 said that changing the sexist nature of their denomination was a reason "of at least some importance" in their decision to seek ordination. (It was "quite important" for 27 percent.) Twelve years later, the situation has changed. In 1993–94, no more than about one-third (35 percent) of women pastors in the same seven denominations studied in the 1980–81 study[2] said that this was a reason of even "some importance" in their decision. (It was "quite important" for only 10 percent.) The feminist fire to change the institutional leadership of the church has clearly cooled since 1980–81.

Table 5.2
Desire of Women to Change the Sexist Nature of the Church
(parish clergy women from the seven comparable denominations)

	1980–81	1993–94
quite important	27%	10%
somewhat important	29%	25%
not important	36%	56%
does not apply, don't know, no answer	8%	9%
	100%	100%

AGE AND THE CALL
TO ORDAINED MINISTRY

Among the active clergy in our study, there is a considerable range in the ages at which they remember first thinking seriously about a career in the ordained ministry. Furthermore, God may call an individual, but if family, church, and society withhold support, it is hard for people to believe that this is what God really intends them to do with their lives. In many of the denominations in our study, women professing a call from God to enter the ordained ministry were not well received. They were scorned, told that they were overstepping their female role, and considered guilty of lying or pathetic self-delusion when they shared such an idea. This made it very difficult for many women to tell anyone what they thought God was calling them to do, especially denominational officials serving as gatekeepers to the ordination process.

Such traditional thinking about who is "eligible" to be ordained contributes to the fact that over half of the clergy men in our study decided to enter the ordained ministry by age nineteen, whereas the age of decision for half of our clergy women is twenty-three. As many as one-third of the clergy women in our study decided to become ordained at the age of thirty or older; three times more women than men made the decision about ordained ministry after age thirty. In the more theologically conservative Spirit-centered denominations, five times as many women as men first seriously considered becoming clergy at age thirty or older.

It follows that the older someone is when she or he first considers becoming an ordained minister, the older that person will be when she or he asks denominational officials about ecclesiastical requirements and seeks official approval. Clergy women in our study are about four times more likely than men to have waited until they were thirty-five years old or older before they approached denominational officials regarding ordination. As a consequence, 40 percent of the clergy women in our study were over thirty-five when they approached denominational officials, compared with 10 percent of the clergy men.

In spite of this difference between men and women, it is important to note that since 1980, the age at which both women and men first think seriously about becoming ordained and the age at which they first approach denominational officials about becoming ordained have risen. When we compare clergy ordained before 1980 with those ordained after 1985, the average age at which both men and women decide to seek ordination has risen about six years. However, even among clergy ordained after 1985, women are still more likely than men to have made the decision to enter ordained ministry at an older age.

If traditional discrimination against women clergy is the major reason that women tend to choose ministry as a career later in life than men do, then we might expect that because more women have become clergy in recent years, women ordained since 1986, for example, would have decided to seek ordination at a younger age than women ordained before 1980. It turns out, however, that the reverse is actually the case. In every denominational cluster, the more recently women have been ordained, the older they were when they first decided to become ordained. Furthermore, patterns of discrimination do not explain why clergy men are also deciding to seek ordination at increasingly older ages.

One theory is that gender discrimination, often indirect and very subtle, increases the length of time between when women first feel called to the ordained ministry and when they actually approach their denominational representatives about ordination. A lack of support from people who are important to them may cause women who feel called to ordained ministry to question their own sense of call longer or at least may increase their fears and cause them to put off approaching denominational officials longer than women (and men) who feel more acceptance for their vocational decision.

Among male and female clergy in all three of our denominational clusters, the number of years between the initial call (often thought to be direct from God) and the first approach to a denominational official about being ordained has risen. This is true for all of the men in our study and for all of the women except those in the Spirit-centered denominations. Yet, regardless of denominational cluster or ordination dates, clergy women do not take any longer than men do from the time they make a personal decision to enter the ordained ministry to the time they approach denominational officials to begin a process leading toward ordination. Both women and men are simply making these decisions later in life. (See Appendix 5.2, "Age, the Call, and Seeking Ordination.")

Women and men are making the decisions to respond to God's call, to seek ordination, to approach denominational authorities, to go to seminary—in short, to "become" clergy—later than they did a generation ago for various reasons. Some of this delay reflects the diminished status of ordained ministry in contemporary society. With less appreciation from family, higher educational costs, and less prestige in public life than might have been the case a generation ago, becoming a minister is not considered attractive or "worth it" by many young people. It seems that with age, however, the calling becomes more appealing. Some observers suggest that the trend whereby clergy make their vocational decisions later in life is actually improving the quality of ordained leadership in contemporary Protestantism.

SEMINARY AND THE CALL
TO ORDAINED MINISTRY

It is important to remember that not all clergy go to seminary. During the twentieth century, however, as increasing numbers of young people have attended college and even graduate school, educational expectations for clergy have steadily risen. Reformed Protestants have always insisted on a "learned clergy," founding colleges and seminaries to educate pastors from the colonial period to the present. In contrast, on the American frontier and in the growing cities of the late nineteenth century, revivalist religion often blessed the leadership of "uneducated" clergy in grassroots movements and did not require seminary education for ordination. Some denominations, seeking to meet the needs of burgeoning immigrant congregations, did not have the resources to insist on seminary-trained clergy. Furthermore, popular religious enthusiasm, which found expression in Holiness and Pentecostal revivals from the mid–nineteenth century into the early twentieth century, celebrated the power of the Holy Spirit to empower religious leaders without formal education.

The years since 1920 have seen a steady increase in denominational educational requirements needed for ordination. Part of this is due to the fact that being a pastor is a more complicated job than it was before the early twentieth century, requiring more training. Further, by maintaining and raising educational standards for clergy, churches seek to keep and strengthen the general understanding of ordained ministry as a "learned profession."[3] Although Holiness, Pentecostal, and some other theologically conservative denominations have been slower than the mainline denominations to require graduate degrees for ordination, overall, educational credentials are increasingly linked to the authorization of clergy. In many cases, this has actually made it more difficult for women to be ordained, because they do not have and cannot get the required education. This is ironic because higher education often creates a climate that is quite receptive to women; educated clergy are generally less influenced than "uneducated" clergy by narrow interpretations of scripture regarding women's leadership.

In our study, almost all of the clergy women and clergy men in the congregation-centered and institution-centered denominations have been to seminary. However, the situation of clergy in the Spirit-centered denominations is dramatically different. Despite a slight increase in the proportion of seminary-educated clergy women in the Spirit-centered denominations since the early 1980s, less than half of the clergy women and clergy men ordained in these denominations in the last ten years have attended seminary. Educational expectations remain low, but they are increasing. Clergy are encouraged to present educational credentials in support

Table 5.3

Percentage of Clergy Attending Seminary before Ordination

	Denominational Cluster					
	Congregation-Centered		Institution-Centered		Spirit-Centered	
	Women	Men	Women	Men	Women	Men
N =	1,183	987	929	777	270	246
Year Ordained						
before 1980	95%	95%	97%	98%	18%	42%
1980–1985	94%	96%	98%	97%	44%	45%
1986 and later	95%	93%	99%	99%	33%	45%

of their call to ordained leadership—credentials they have earned by studying privately, attending Bible colleges, or reading and working with experienced clergy to prepare themselves for the work of ministry.

Our research also shows that not all clergy who attend seminary are sure that they want to be ordained or are clear about the kind of ministry to which they feel called. Some seminarians are looking for a faith and a career, others are clear about their faith but searching for the right career, and still others come with a strong faith and career commitment. Clergy women recall being less motivated than clergy men to get a seminary education in preparation for a specific ministerial career. And as already noted, far fewer clergy women in the Spirit-centered denominations than in the other two denominational clusters have a seminary education. Those clergy women in the Spirit-centered denominations who do attend seminary, however, are more likely than clergy women in the other denominations to have entered seminary with a strong faith and a specific career in mind. This is probably because a strong career commitment is a necessary motivation for women in the theologically conservative denominations to enter seminary at all.

In all three of our denominational clusters, clergy women are consistently less likely than clergy men to report that they were sure of their commitment to a faith and a career when they entered seminary. The difference in this area between clergy women and clergy men is smallest among recent seminary graduates. In fact, the more recently clergy women and clergy men have gone through seminary, the more apt they are to recall that on entering, they were already committed to a faith and a career.

One reason for this greater vocational certainty among recent graduates is that they are considerably older than those who entered seminary before 1985. Before 1980, 61 percent of the women and 77 percent of the men entered seminary at age twenty-five or younger. Between 1980 and 1985, only 36 percent of the women and 47 percent of the men were that young. By 1985, the twenty-five-year-old group had dropped to 22 percent of the women and 38 percent of the men. In contrast, among clergy who entered seminary before 1980, only 15 percent of the women and 4 percent of the men were over thirty-five years old, and among clergy who started seminary after 1985, 47 percent of the women and 27 percent of the men were older than thirty-five.

Seminarians who enter their studies in their thirties and forties are more mature than younger seminarians and more likely to be denominationally and vocationally committed before enrolling in a professional program leading to a Master of Divinity degree. For example, among all those who answered the questionnaire, only 36 percent of the women and 54 percent of the men who began seminary at age twenty-five or younger recall that they were committed to a faith and a career. Fifty-five percent of the women and 71 percent of the men older than thirty-five years of age on entering seminary recall themselves as committed to a faith and a career.

Table 5.4
Motivations on First Entering Seminary

	N =	Congregation-Centered		Institution-Centered		Spirit-Centered	
		Women 1,144	Men 957	Women 936	Men 773	Women 95	Men 119
Looking for a faith and/or career		20%	21%	17%	17%	9%	8%
Have faith, undecided on kind of career		33%	23%	38%	21%	32%	16%
Committed to faith and career		47%	56%	45%	62%	59%	76%
		100%	100%	100%	100%	100%	100%
		sig.	.002	sig.	.00001	sig.	02

Table 5.5
Vocational Commitment among Seminarians
by Year They Entered Seminary

Year Began Seminary	% = Committed to a Faith and Career on Entering Seminary	
	Clergy Women	Clergy Men
Before 1980	40%	56%
1980–1985	43%	58%
1986 on	54%	68%

Although women are still not as sure as men about what kind of career will be possible for them after seminary, in recent years they seem to be increasingly secure on entering seminary in their conviction that they are called to ordained ministry and that they can be ordained.

One reason for the new certainty that women feel about their call to ordained ministry is probably partly related to the increasing numbers of women in seminary classes and on seminary faculties. For example, female clergy in our study who went to seminary before 1980 recall that no more than 25 percent of their entering class was female, and sometimes less than that. Since 1980, the presence of women in seminaries has risen steadily. Clergy women and clergy men who started seminary in 1986 and later report (on average) that their entering class was over 40 percent female.

When we ask the clergy in our study about other benefits from their seminary education, they report great appreciation for instruction in basic skills for ministry, especially in preaching and counseling, and for the ways in which the seminary actually strengthened their faith. In retrospect, they note that they could have used more skills in parish administration. All in all, a majority of the clergy in our study, especially those in institution-centered denominations, tell us that their seminary education was helpful as they prepared for ordination. In addition, about half of these clergy (slightly more women than men) value the fact that their seminary experience gave them networks that continue to provide them with informal but important friendships and support long after they have left seminary.

Unfortunately, clergy women and clergy men are far less positive about the value of their seminary years in readying them for some of the unpleasant realities they face as clergy—such as sexism, racism, and class differences. In fact, very few of the clergy women or clergy men in our study see their seminary experience as offering any real help in helping them survive and find satisfaction in their difficult and sometimes lonely lives as clergy.

It has been hypothesized that clergy women are shaped as feminists during their seminary education. Yet when we asked the clergy women in our study about their course work in seminary, fewer than one-fifth of them say they took any courses dealing primarily with the roles, problems, or experiences of women in ministry. Furthermore, regardless of whether they took such courses, no more than one-fifth of these women clergy think that their seminary education did anything to help them understand issues that face women in ministry.

For the clergy in our study, seminary was a mixed blessing. It provided some important tools and experiences, but it did not prepare the clergy women, especially, for the difficulties they encountered after graduation. (See Appendix 5.3, "The Value of Seminary.")

GETTING ORDAINED

In its attempts to "order" and regulate clergy leadership, every denomination has some process whereby it determines those it will ordain as clergy. There are probationary procedures, educational requirements, examinations, internships, psychological and theological reviews, and face-to-face assessments. Denominational gatekeepers may be other clergy (bishops or committees) or responsible lay people.

In our study, we asked clergy about the process leading to their authorization to full status as clergy in their denomination. Generally speaking, for all but the women in the institution-centered denominations, less than one-third of the clergy women and clergy men said that they had difficulty getting ordained. This is obviously due to the fact that institution-centered denominations often have formal and complex ordination procedures. One clergy woman in an institution-centered denomination shared her frustration:

> The ordination process of the Episcopal Church needs reforming. It is brutal to some, harrowing to some, never easy to any. It is too long and every step of the way, someone can say "No," even though all the other steps say "Yes." There must be a better, more God-centered way.

(Episcopal clergy woman)

Another major reason that women often have greater difficulty getting ordained in institution-centered denominations than in other denominations is that these are the denominations most likely to require that candidates for ordination have a specific job opportunity or "call" from a congregation before they can be ordained. Getting through seminary and passing examinations is often easier than convincing a congregation to call a woman as its pastor.

One would think that as more congregations experience and accept women pastors, it would become easier for women to be ordained. Unfortunately, this does not appear to be the case. Our research shows no decline in difficulty reported by women in institution-centered denominations from the mid-1980s into the 1990s, and the congregation-centered and Spirit-centered denominations show an actual increase between the 1970s and 1990s in the proportion of clergy women reporting difficulties getting ordained. Clearly, an increase in the numbers of women does not automatically result in greater ease for women entering or staying in a ministerial career.

Table 5.6
Difficulty Getting Ordained

N =	Congregation-Centered		Institution-Centered		Spirit-Centered	
	Women	Men	Women	Men	Women	Men
	1,183	987	929	777	270	246
Quite easy	46%	52%	31%	39%	43%	36%
Somewhat easy	30%	30%	30%	33%	29%	30%
Difficult	24%	18%	39%	28%	28%	34%
	100%	100%	100%	100%	100%	100%
Those Reporting "Difficult," by Year Ordained						
Before 1980	16%	12%	42%	22%	18%	24%
1980–1985	21%	26%	32%	36%	29%	38%
1986–1989	27%	25%	44%	32%	25%	47%
1990–1993	35%	35%	40%	33%	53%	49%

Paula Nesbitt's study of Episcopal and Unitarian-Universalist clergy women suggests that when the percentage of women to men in church institutions reaches 30 percent, a backlash develops against women, which intensifies as the number of women increases further.[4] This backlash, it may be hypothesized, is aggravated further when men begin experiencing some difficulties in getting ordained—which they sometimes interpret as a result of competition from women. Our study shows that with fewer positions available than has been the case in many denominations, clergy men as well as clergy women in the congregation-centered and Spirit-centered denominations are reporting more difficulty getting ordained in the 1990s than they did in the 1970s and early 1980s:

> Basically, it seems that "God calls and the church stalls" when it comes to women in ministry. My denomination is very good about ordaining women. However, finding a church placement is difficult in many parts of the country. About the best one can generally hope for is to find an associate position, and even that is not easy. I know of a large number of clergy women who have no parish assignment. They work in either church-related agencies, or social service agencies, or secular positions. It saddens me that all of these ministerial gifts are going to waste. It is frustrating as well.
>
> (Disciples of Christ clergy woman)

> As a member of the Wesleyan Church we have a solid historical stance for supporting the ordinations of women. However, very few have "braved the currents" and trudged into the ordained "male waters." As ours is a traditional denomination, perhaps the ordination of women is more of a pragmatic, cultural hurdle to overcome. Very few males are willing to be change agents in that regard, thus keeping potential ordained females at arm's length.
>
> (Wesleyan Church clergy man)

Getting through the ordination process is increasingly complicated for all clergy. For most clergy, doing so requires three years of graduate-level academic work, six months to a year of internship, and a concrete job offer in some setting needing ordained leadership. Regardless of these difficulties, a strong majority of both clergy women and clergy men in all three denominational clusters said that if they had it to do over again, they would—in spite of the time, expense, and hassle. These clergy men and clergy women feel that they are "called of God." Yet as one clergy woman put it, "I know God called me. I like my vocation. But it is an unbalancing act. Not as much opportunity for less pay."

Being ordained is a calling, not just a job. It is a sacred trust. On the one hand, ordination is a holy blessing, bestowing on clergy objective or ontological power and privilege from God. On the other hand, ordination is a credential to regulate the functional and spiritual life of Christians, conferred by human organizations called churches. In this study of clergy women, we have sought to examine how the influx of women into ordained leadership is changing things—not merely changing

the numbers of female and male leaders, not merely changing the stresses and bless-
ings of the job, but changing the very ways in which clergy women and clergy men
understand their ministry and ordination.

Using the denominational clusters developed in our analysis, we note that
congregation-centered denominations were the earliest to make room in their thinking and practice for women clergy. Congregation-centered denominations make decisions in local congregations and often do not require regional or national permission
to ordain. The Congregationalists (now the United Church of Christ), the Unitarian-
Universalists, the Christian Church (Disciples of Christ), and the Northern Baptists
(now American Baptists) all began ordaining women in the nineteenth century.

The fact is, however, that not all congregation-centered denominations have
supported women's ordination. The Church of the Brethren exhibits a deep informal resistance to clergy women. Southern Baptists have taken a strong biblical and
theological stand against the ordination of women, even as a small number of local Baptist congregations have exercised their freedom to ordain women.

In our institution-centered denominations, the struggle for the ordination of
women has been theological and practical. Because these denominations have a
"high" view of ordination, the ordination of women has required a fundamental
rethinking of church tradition and practice in the Episcopal, Lutheran, Presbyterian, and United Methodist denominations.

And finally, the Spirit-centered denominations, which initially had no prohibitions against the ordination of women, have shown a growing apprehension about
clergy women. The Church of God (Anderson, Indiana), the Church of the
Nazarene, the Free Methodists, and the Wesleyan Church sometimes embrace a
theological fundamentalism that is inconsistent with their roots. In the twentieth
century, these denominations have given mixed messages regarding the issue of
women's ordination.

CLERGY UNDERSTANDINGS
OF ORDINATION

To determine what clergy women and clergy men are actually thinking about
ordination in the midst of their ministries, we have examined their responses to
several key questions: Is ordination needed to maintain the quality of the church's
ministry? Does ordination create a barrier between clergy and lay people? In the
ideal church, will a time ever come when there will no longer be a need for ordained ministry? Are clergy women changing the meaning of ordination? In addition, we have looked closely at general perceptions about ministry, asking clergy
if they believe that ordained ministry still carries a prestige and dignity that no
other profession shares, whether they agree that more women should be ordained
to full ministerial status in their denomination, and whether they think that increased numbers of clergy women are lowering the prestige of the ordained min-

istry. Finally, in asking women about their motivations to seek ordination, we are able to document how these motivations have changed since the 1980s.

Are women changing the meaning of ordination? This is a difficult question. Many clergy admit that as more women are ordained, the *practice* of ministry is changing, but they refuse to say that the *meaning* of ordination is changing. Others concede that ordination itself is being transformed. Clergy women are significantly more likely than men to agree that women are changing the meaning of ordination.

Table 5.7
Responses to Statement about Meaning of Ordination (by Gender)
Agree: "Women are changing the meaning of ordination."

	Clergy Women	Clergy Men
agree	36%	14%
feelings mixed	27%	19%
disagree	37%	67%
	100%	100%

Looking at this question by denomination, we see the largest difference between the answers of clergy women and of clergy men is among the United Methodists, where 45 percent of the clergy women but only 12 percent of the clergy men agree. The differences are almost as great in the Church of the Brethren, where 43 percent of the clergy women, compared to 13 percent of the clergy men, agree. Clergy in the Spirit-centered denominations show little difference between women and men, and only 10 percent of all clergy in the Spirit-centered denominations agree that clergy women are changing the meaning of ordination.

Some clergy women are not sure whether women are changing the meaning of ordination, but they recognize that things are different. One United Church of Christ clergy woman wrote, "I feel there are many seeking ordination for the wrong reasons. When asked about their 'call to ministry' some have no idea what it means!" Yet she continued, "I realize this may also be true of men." A Unitarian-Universalist clergy woman worried, "It [ordination] is becoming more like another administrative hoop to jump through and less like a God-instilled gift or recognition of extraordinary religious favor or privilege."

Other clergy women, however, feel that women are actually changing the tradition and reshaping the meaning of ordained ministry:

I think women in ministry are changing the understanding of power in relation to ordination. Rather than something conferred upon them women are using ordination as a means to claim their power and gifts and use them in service with others. I think it is a subtle shift from power over to power claimed and shared.

(Church of the Brethren clergy woman)

I believe that women see themselves as "set in the midst" for ministry. Not set apart.
I believe women affirm the importance of teaching and are wary of a definition of
ministry that relies on patterns of dependency.

(Christian Church [Disciples of Christ] clergy woman)

Many of the clergy men disagreed that women are changing the meaning of
ordination, making a distinction between ministry and ordination. As one American Baptist clergy man put it, "They may be changing the definition of ministry
but not ordination." A Lutheran clergy man wrote, "Individual women may add
various new dimensions of pastoral 'style' but the meaning of ordination does not
change." And a few, such as this Wesleyan clergy man, totally rejected the legitimacy of ordination for women: "I don't think that it is God's place for women
to be in leadership positions. But they are every bit as capable of meeting ordination qualifications as men. Capability is not the issue." Another Wesleyan
clergy man also disagreed with the statement, but for different reasons: "The
meaning of ordination has less to do with demographics and more to do with spiritual qualifications. Hence, the cure for a patriarchal church, which is what we
have, is not in the raising of quotas, but in the discovery and development of more
women who are already qualified." Finally, a number of clergy men refused to
make any judgment:

No generalization can be made. Some [women] change the meaning simply because
historically women were not ordained and now they are. Others seem to be re-
mythologizing Christianity, subordinating faith to the ultimate goal of legitimatizing
and glorifying a feministry.

(United Church of Christ clergy man)

Should more women be ordained? Not surprisingly, most clergy women agree
with this statement.

Table 5.8
Responses to Statement about Increasing Women's Ordinations (by Gender)
Agree: "More women should be ordained to
full ministerial status in my denomination."

	Clergy Women	Clergy Men
agree	72%	49%
feelings mixed	21%	30%
disagree	7%	21%
	100%	100%

When we compare the responses to the two questions about whether women are changing the meaning of ordination and whether more women should be ordained, clergy women, especially in the institution-centered denominations, who agree that women are changing the meaning of ordination are more likely than those who disagree about the meaning of ordination to agree that more women should be ordained in their denominations.

An exception to this is found among the Unitarian-Universalists, where men and women alike do not feel the need for more women to be ordained in their denomination. This is probably because there are plenty of Unitarian-Universalist clergy women, and therefore clergy in that denomination feel little need to change things. In the Church of the Brethren and the Southern Baptist denominations, clergy men and clergy women agree that women are changing the meaning of ordination; however, the men are more likely than the women to disagree that more women should be ordained in their denominations. It appears that when clergy women see change, they want more women to be part of the change, but when the men see change (which, in some denominations, men do not like), they do not want more change (particularly if it means more clergy women).

Perhaps some clergy are ambivalent about the need for more women being ordained because they do not see a strong need for ordained clergy of any gender in the church of the future. Women, with less interest in hierarchy, are also less concerned with ordination. Clergy women are somewhat less likely than clergy men to believe that the ideal church requires ordained clergy, although, not surprisingly, the majority of clergy of both genders continue to value ordination. To determine if that was the case, we tested agreement and disagreement with the statement "In the ideal church, there will no longer be a need for ordained ministry." We conjectured that some clergy might consider ordination less important or even unnecessary in the church of the future. As we predicted, clergy women are more open than clergy men to an ideal church where ordained ministry is not needed. But most clergy, of both genders, continue to value ordination.

Table 5.9
Responses to Statement about Ideal Church (by Gender)
Agree: "In the ideal church, there will no longer be a need
for ordained ministry."

	Clergy Women (2,485)	Clergy Men (2,116)
agree	22%	19%
feelings mixed	33%	23%
disagree	45%	58%
	100%	100%

Logically, we thought that clergy in the congregation-centered denominations, especially Unitarian-Universalist clergy, would be the most likely to agree with this question because of their high lay involvement and their more functional theologies of ordination. We thought that clergy in the institution-centered denominations would be the most likely to disagree with this statement because ordained leadership is so crucial for their sacramental life. But the results were surprising. While many of the clergy in the congregation-centered denominations agree with the statement, almost two-thirds of the Unitarian-Universalist clergy disagree that ordination will no longer be necessary in the ideal church. Furthermore, clergy women in the Church of the Brethren and Southern Baptist churches (perhaps an unlikely group) turn out to be the most willing to envision the church without ordination, even as they have the highest percentages of clergy (especially women clergy) who believe that more women should be ordained in their denominations. It appears that these women want more women to be ordained as long as the church is ordaining anyone, but they are not so sure that ordination is that important in the ideal church. On the ideal church and ordination question, the Unitarian-Universalist clergy and all of the clergy in the Spirit-centered denominations, but not clergy in the institution-centered denominations, are the least willing to let go of ordained ministry.

Two explanations may interpret these findings. First, although the Unitarian-Universalists view ordination from a very pragmatic and even secular perspective that might allow them to see ordination as expendable, they recognize that the church as an institutional or organizational system requires authorized ministry. Almost two-thirds of the Unitarian-Universalist (60 percent of the clergy women and 66 percent of the clergy men) clergy disagree that in the ideal church there will no longer be a need for the ordained ministry.

Second, the Unitarian-Universalists may exhibit what can be called a "third-generation" pattern in their attitudes toward ordination. Their denomination has been ordaining women and living with female clergy for over 130 years. They have gone through that period of change which rejects past practices (a second-generation characteristic), and they are reclaiming the importance of ordination and the sacredness of religious leadership. They are like the grandchildren of immigrants (the third generation) who move beyond their parents to reclaim the language and culture that the second generation tried to forget.

When we compare responses to the question of whether ordination will be needed in the ideal church with responses to the question of whether the respondents think more women should be ordained in their denominations, we find that those few clergy men who believe that more women should be ordained (especially clergy men in the Church of the Brethren and among the Southern Baptists) are also very likely to believe that in the ideal church, there will no longer be a need for ordination.

An even more interesting finding comes when we compare answers to the ideal church question with clergy feelings about whether women are changing the meaning of ordination. Those clergy women who want more women ordained in their denominations (this is most of the clergy women in our sample, with the exception of the Unitarian-Universalists) are slightly more likely than those clergy women who are ambivalent or disagree that more clergy women should be ordained to believe that "in the ideal church there will no longer be a need for ordained ministry," and that "women are changing the meaning of ordination." This is true for clergy men also, although the connections between the three statements are not as clear for men as for women.

Comparing responses to these three statements,[5] we can make several observations. Denominational affiliation is crucial. With these statements, the denominational clusters used in other parts of this study break down. In the congregation-centered denominations, Unitarian-Universalists and the Church of the Brethren and the Southern Baptists differ from the rest of the cluster. Twice as many clergy women as clergy men (85 percent to 40 percent) in the Church of the Brethren and Southern Baptist churches believe that more women should be ordained in their denominations. Only 25 percent of these women, however, believe that the ideal church will need ordination. The contrasts between clergy men and clergy women among the Brethren and the Baptists are dramatic.

Overall, both male and female clergy in the Spirit-centered denominations are the most resistant to change. Not surprisingly, clergy women in the congregation-centered denominations are the most receptive to change. This can be interpreted both positively and negatively. It could be that clergy in the Spirit-centered denominations are clear about the importance of ordination and its relationship to the gifts of the Holy Spirit. It also could be that in the congregation-centered denominations, clergy men are feeling seriously threatened by the increasing numbers of ordained women. (See Appendix 5.4, "Attitudes about Ordination.")

When we look at these statements in relationship to the year of ordination, responses from clergy women show no clear patterns. However, among clergy men, how long they have been ordained does affect their attitude about the meaning of ordination. In the congregation-centered and Spirit-centered denominations, clergy men ordained before 1975 are most likely to disagree that women are changing the meaning of ordination, whereas clergy men in the same denominational clusters who were ordained after 1975 are increasingly convinced that women are changing the meaning of ordination. At the same time, 60 percent of the clergy men in the institution-centered denominations consistently disagree with this statement, regardless of their year of ordination.

IT DEPENDS ON
HOW YOU LOOK AT IT

Many women are deeply committed to their call to ordained ministry. Yet gender discrimination remains a serious and ongoing problem. Unfortunately, in spite of greater numbers and some sincere systematic efforts at change in many of the

denominations, women embarking on a ministerial career in the 1990s may actually be less capable of coping with sexism than women clergy who entered ordained ministry in the 1970s.

Sociologist Joy Charlton interviewed women seminarians in the 1970s at two
seminaries and then interviewed the same women fifteen years later. She finds that
clergy women who attended seminary in the 1970s consciously identify themselves as "pioneers" and have developed particular strengths and coping strategies.
They attended seminary during an exciting time, when women had a keen awareness of the structural sexism inherent in the church. These women knew that as
women pastors they would be "going first" into congregations—breaking new
trails for later women to follow. Although these pioneer women had a hard time
being first, because they saw themselves as pioneers they were ready to deal with
problems. To this day, they remain highly motivated to continue in their careers
as clergy.[6]

Among clergy women ordained in the late 1980s and the 1990s, the battles that
early women clergy fought are barely remembered, and their accomplishments are
taken for granted. New graduates expect to be recognized and rewarded on the basis of their skills, experience, and training. Furthermore, because women preparing for ordained ministry honestly believe that the worst forms of discrimination
are over, they do not always recognize when situations are biased against them because of their gender.

This difference in awareness suggests that clergy women ordained in the late
1970s think about ministry differently than those who entered active ministerial
service in the late 1980s and the 1990s. Women in the earlier era had a clear sense
of what they were up against. Discrimination was glaring, and the struggles of
women for ordination became public events reported on the evening news. For example, when eleven Episcopal women were "irregularly" ordained against ecclesiastical law in 1974, the "Philadelphia Eleven" became symbols of the struggle
for equal rights within the church. Women were able to mobilize around these
symbols, find solidarity, and build a sense of community—even as they dealt in-
dividually with resistance from denominational offices and local congregations.

For recent seminary graduates, this is history. A sense that the barriers are down
and that clergy women no longer need to be pioneers, blazing a trail for other
women to follow, is prevalent among these graduates. Women seminary graduates
in recent years may be more apt than their predecessors to feel that their progress
and success is dependent much more on individual merit and effort than on sys-
temic change. While many clergy women are aware that women face different and
perhaps more taxing career challenges than men, recently ordained women may
see their struggles only in individual terms, thinking that they must cope with ministry and personal lifestyle issues such as family, finances, burnout, and stress on
their own. If this is what is going on, then women clergy may be less likely to find
common cause with other ordained women and thus find themselves without any
sense of shared struggles as they deal with institutionalized problems.

Recently ordained women who know little about the earlier struggles of women clergy may be more likely than their predecessors ordained in the 1970s to blame themselves for their failure to succeed in their jobs or their inability to earn a living wage. They may be less likely than their pioneer counterparts to see their problems as the result of discrimination and may have only vague ideas about how institutions might be changed to become supportive of female clergy. Unfortunately, the professional isolation endemic to the clergy career tends to exacerbate the personalization of problems and failure when clergy fail to see their difficulties as part of any broader pattern.

6

AN EXPANDING MINISTRY

The movement of women into ordained leadership in contemporary Protestantism continues. Clergy women are living complex lives as religious leaders. They are getting jobs, but their career paths are following new patterns. Clergy women are responding to God's call to ordained service, but it is still an "uphill calling." In one sense, this is just another story of discrimination and injustice. Clergy women do not yet have equality in the church.

Equality, however, is not the only value in this story. As we have analyzed our research findings and interviewed dozens of clergy women, we are intrigued by what we find. Our research suggests that although ordained ministry is still an uphill calling for clergy women when measured by past patterns of success and satisfaction, something new is going on. Clergy women are reshaping or reinventing definitions of ordained leadership in contemporary Protestantism.

Change is evident, first of all, when we examine the relationship of clergy women to parish ministries—especially to senior and sole pastorates. As we have already noted, clergy women are more likely than clergy men to hold jobs as assistant or associate pastors, as interim pastors, and in various nonparish ministries. Unfortunately, an assumption in much of Protestantism has been that when clergy do not "serve" in a local congregation—except for those in denominational leadership positions on a judicatory or national level—they are not "real clergy." Some people think that women and men in specialized or nonparish ministries have literally "left the ministry."

Increasingly, however, we are finding that clergy, and especially women clergy, are choosing nonparish ministries *instead of* parish work. Some of the reasons are circumstantial and some are personal. First, a chaplaincy, interim work, or specialized ministry in a social agency is attractive because the ordained man or woman believes that his or her gifts are better suited to a specialized ministry than to ministry in the parish. Second, in nonparish ministries, clergy are often better able to maintain boundaries between work and private life than in parish ministry. Third, certain clergy discover that they really do not like parish ministry and that they can earn more money outside the parish than as local pastors.[1] Fourth, some clergy in nonparish ministries are there because they literally cannot get a call to local parish ministry.

For example, the Southern Baptist Convention has gone on record against the ordination of women. Among Southern Baptists, however, "Baptist freedom" and local commitment to liberty of conscience mean that some Southern Baptist congregations have ordained women. Not surprisingly, these women have very limited career options. If they leave the local congregations that ordain them, they often move into nonparish positions because they are simply unable to obtain a call to serve in another local Southern Baptist church. Some Southern Baptists are willing to recognize clergy women as long as they do not aspire to be local pastors.

Whatever other people think about ordained women and men who work in church-recognized settings beyond local congregations, we were interested in how these clergy felt about their own situation. Did the clergy in these nonparish, church-related positions feel less competent as professionals in ministry than those who worked as parish ministers?

For clergy women, the answer to this question is no. Our research shows no different self-perceptions between clergy women who are serving in parish ministry and clergy women who do various specialized ministries. Clergy men who work outside the parish, however, have a slightly higher professional self-concept than those in parish ministry, possibly because male clergy outside parish settings tend to hold executive-level denominational positions. (See Appendix 6.1, "Professional Self-Concept and Employment Status.")

That increasing numbers of women carry out their calling to ministry in nonparish church-recognized and even so-called secular jobs raises some important questions about the nature of ordained ministry. What kinds of service or activities call for ordination? If a person ceases to work in a ministry recognized by the church, does he or she give up "ordained status"?

In one sense, ordination is like baptism; it is a unique, one-time event. Once you are baptized, you cannot get "unbaptized," and once you are ordained, it is impossible to get "unordained." Ordination is a gift for life, which the ancient church understood to convey an "indelible mark."

In practice, however, it is possible to cease "being" an ordained leader, authorized or recognized by the church. Sometimes clergy fail to keep the promises they made at ordination or betray a professional code of ministerial ethics and are relieved of their responsibilities by ecclesiastical authorities. Such "defrocking" is difficult, but it does occur. At other times, clergy women and clergy men come to a realization that they do not want to continue "in the ministry." For various reasons, they decide to leave.

Denominations are not always clear about who is "in" and who is "out" of recognized or authorized ministry. Yet every ecclesiastical body has some process whereby it is possible to leave "recognized ordained ministry," to lose "ministerial standing," to cease to be "on the roster," not to be "retained on the role," or no longer to be considered "canonically resident." Ending ministerial status may be justified for one of several reasons: (1) because of some unprofessional action or misconduct, (2) because clergy are no longer working in settings "requiring ordination," or (3) because the clergy themselves ask to leave or let their credentials lapse.

It is possible to divide our sample into five categories of clergy. First, at the center of all understandings of ordained ministry, is the local pastor. This man or woman has general oversight over the life of a congregation as a senior or sole pastor.

Second are assistant, associate, or specialized ministers, who have special responsibilities for some aspect of ministry within a local parish. They are ministers of education, youth ministers, ministers of music, ministers of parish calling, and so forth. These clergy work within the local congregations but focus their talents in specialized ways.

Third are clergy who serve in ministries habitually recognized or sponsored by the churches. Seminary faculty are usually ordained. Missionaries who serve in medical and educational work also are often ordained clergy. Certainly, chaplains—hospital, prison, and military—are authorized by the churches and considered clergy, even though they do not serve in a local parish. Increasingly, some clergy are trained and ordained to be pastoral counselors, doing a ministry of spiritual guidance and psychological services. These are church-recognized nonparish ministries.

Fourth are clergy who may start out in parish ministry but soon move beyond the local congregation and even beyond the nonparish jobs where ordination has been common. They work for health and human services organizations, they do community organizing, they run a rape hotline or a shelter for battered women, or they administer various youth programs. Many of the clergy in these "unconventional" jobs are paid by secular organizations, but they insist that their job is a ministry. In some cases, where they are already ordained, denominational systems recognize and bless these clergy and allow them to remain in the denomination as ordained clergy. Although many of these jobs do not require the ministries of Word and sacrament traditionally associated with ordination, churches affirm what is technically secular work as outreach and mission.

Fifth are those who are in secular employment, who do not consider themselves to be clergy and who are not recognized as clergy by their denomination.

Although women are found in all five categories of clergy, our research suggests that clergy women are found in significant numbers in recognized and semisecular nonparish ministries. It may be that clergy women are simply attracted to these positions because of their flexibility and availability. However, clergy women may be ending up in alternative ministries because doors to traditional clergy jobs are still very difficult for women to open.

Whatever the reason, clergy women are increasingly suggesting that narrow historical understandings of ordination must be changed. They argue that ordination to ministries in community organizing, human services, and other forms of secular labor are legitimate expressions of their calling. Although these women by one definition are no longer in the employ of the church, many insist that they have not "left the ministry." They see themselves called to an expanding ministry that builds on the historical traditions of ordained ministry in local congregations but explores new frontiers of ministry on behalf of the wider church.

CLERGY IN NONPARISH
FULLY ORDAINED MINISTRIES

Denominations have authorized and credentialed their ministries in various ways in the history of the church. Although ordination stands at the center of ecclesiastical practice, churches also consecrate, commission, and license in order to recognize and regulate other, more specialized or less prestigious religious leadership. Sometimes when women have been denied full-status ordination, they have been consecrated, commissioned, licensed, or given a lesser "ordination" to empower them for needed specialized ministries in the church.

Increasingly, however, it is possible to speak about fully ordained clergy in specialized ministries outside the parish. As we have already noted, there are two types of nonparish specialized ministers: those in nonparish, nonparochial, church-related settings and those in alternative jobs of a semisecular character.

Clergy in nonparish church-related ministries are often specifically ordained to their "special calling." They are chaplains in hospitals, in the military service, and in prisons. They are missionaries sponsored by their denominations to serve human needs and to share their convictions about Christianity at home and abroad. In recent years, a new form of specialized ministry has developed—"interim ministry," consisting of those clergy who intentionally train to serve in congregations during the interim when a congregation is without a regular pastor. Although ordination is most commonly sought to authorize general pastoral leadership for congregations, all denominations have some way to recognize and ordain some clergy to service beyond local congregations.

Our research indicates that a higher percentage of clergy women than clergy men enter these specialized ministries. Although the majority of both women and men in our study are local pastors with wide responsibilities for all aspects of parish life, clergy women are 16 percent less likely than clergy men (59 percent to 75 percent) to be in parish ministry. For some observers, this is viewed as a problem; for others, this is a development that holds great promise.

Church leaders who are troubled by the trend toward specialized ministries often speak of non-parish-based clergy as "parish dropouts." They assume that these are clergy who start out in parish ministry but, after a few years, leave employment in local congregations because they cannot do the job or do not value the job. This is not always the case. Yet critics of clergy women commonly complain that women are chronic parish dropouts. They argue that the frequency of this pattern among women clergy is proof that women "cannot keep up with the demands of parish ministry," or that "congregations are not ready for women pastors," or that women should not be ordained because "they do not have what it takes to do real ministry" (e.g., parish ministry). Some even say that women "hate" the parish.

These judgments are unfair. Many women are literally "forced" to become parish dropouts because they cannot get parish jobs in their denominational or geographic situation. Other women become parish dropouts because they have terrible experiences in the parish as women. Still others end up as parish dropouts because their family responsibilities and relationships make it impossible for them to take parish jobs that require them to relocate their families. Large numbers of women, however, choose specialized ministries because they believe that God has called them to these expanding forms of ministry. They bring creativity and energy to the work of ministry "outside the ecclesiastical box."

Clergy women are 8 percent more likely than clergy men (12 percent to 20 percent) to be in church-recognized nonparish ministries—serving in interim ministry, chaplaincies, education, or other recognized alternative forms of ministry. Women are about equal with men (around 4 percent each) in their service as denominational staff. However, clergy women not serving in local congregations are twice as likely as men (16 percent to 8 percent) to be in secular or semisecular positions. Among those who report that they are in secular work, some are between clergy jobs and looking for a call, whereas others are out of the clergy labor force by choice.

When we cluster the denominations and look only at clergy women and clergy men in nonparish ministries and denominational staff appointments, the differences between women and men are not significant except in the congregation-centered denominations. This is probably because these denominations are more flexible about ordination for ministries beyond the parish and do not have as disciplined a system for parish ministry placement as do the institution-centered denominations.

The most prevalent reason clergy women and clergy men give for working in ministries outside the parish is that they feel their gifts are "better suited to this kind of ministry"; the second is that ministry not based in a local congregation gives them more flexibility to schedule family and personal time. More than two-thirds of the clergy women and clergy men in these ministries said that one or both of these reasons is at least "somewhat accurate" in addressing why they are not in parish ministry. Furthermore, clergy women and clergy men do not differ significantly in this response. The strongest difference between clergy women and clergy men in their reasons for being in nonparish ministries is seen in the fact that clergy women are more likely to say that "I could not get a parish position in this area and I am not geographically mobile." (Thirty-two percent of the clergy women to 14 percent of the clergy men said this was at least "somewhat accurate.")

Regardless of their reasons, it is a fact that more clergy women than clergy men are engaged in ordained ministries outside local parish settings. This situation can be viewed as a problem or as a blessing. Whichever way it is seen, the increasing numbers of clergy of both genders preparing for nonparish ministries or leaving parish ministry for specialized ministries challenge basic assumptions about ordination. Regardless of whether clergy women are doing this intentionally, the large numbers of clergy women in nonparish settings are stretching church practices and policies in new directions.

For example, in some denominations, nonparish ministries are not considered worthy of ordination in and of themselves. That is, clergy who want to be chaplains or counselors are required to spend a certain number of years in local parish ministry (for which they are ordained) before they can "specialize." In fact, if some of the clergy now in nonparish ministries were not already ordained, they would be denied ordination for the ministries that they presently do. Denominations argue that ordination is only for "ministries of Word and sacrament," and if a person does not need authorization to preach and teach God's word or to administer the sacraments in order to "do" a specialized ministry, then she or he should do that work in the name of the church without ordination. Clergy in nonparish ministries object. They insist that the symbolic presence of clergy in nonsacramental roles is an important witness, regardless of whether they are formally preaching or exercising liturgical leadership. Just by their presence, these clergy in nonparish ministries, many of whom are women, question long-standing assumptions about ordination and invite the churches to imagine new ways to empower leadership for the contemporary church.

LEAVING MINISTERIAL WORK

Getting churches to change is not easy. Clergy get discouraged, and sometimes they simply give up. When we asked clergy why they continue in ordained ministry, their answers varied widely: fear of what family, friends, and admired church leaders would say if they were to leave for secular work; fear of not being able to find any other paying position; and reluctance to let go of the power over others that goes with a ministerial position. The reasons given by clergy who think about leaving or actually drop out of paid ministry are mixed. Clergy leave the ministry because of basic incompetence, substance abuse, sexual misconduct, borderline psychosis, loss of faith, desire for more money or power, and distaste for ministering to and with persons who differ from themselves in race, social status, or gender. When clergy leave ordained ministry of their own volition, realizing that they are not up to the demands of the job or that they cannot keep the promises they made at ordination, they deserve a certain amount of respect for their wisdom in quitting. In certain cases, clergy leave ordained ministry because they question the meaning of ordination itself:

> Quite frankly, the ordained ministry seems like rather a useless pursuit to me. I do not see where ordination of people in ministry is making a contribution to society as a whole. . . . I do not feel their personal compassion, but rather sense their personal agendas being propagated over concern for the person. Isn't it all a power play? That is what experience has shown me. My faith says it should be caring for one another, loving one another. I do not see it.
>
> (clergy woman)

Questioning the value of ordination obviously leads to disenchantment with working in a church position. However, the sequence can also go the other way.

Clergy who cannot get church work, who are fired, or who are unhappy in their present position handle the pain of their situation by denigrating the value of ordination. Either way, it is clear that the devaluing of ordination and the desire to get out of church employment reinforce each other, leading some clergy to quit.

Clergy who question the value of ordination for ministry in a future, "ideal" church are more apt to wonder if they themselves should leave the church than are clergy who see ordination as always important for maintaining good ministry. The relationship between wanting to leave church employment and a belief that ordination is not essential for good ministry, however, is the same among both clergy women and clergy men.

Of course, not all clergy who leave authorized ministry want to depart; some of them are fired, sometimes unfairly and sometimes for good reason. In recent years, greater awareness of clergy ethics and sexual improprieties has led to more public discipline of clergy and involuntary removal of ministerial status.

The great majority of ordained women and men who work as clergy in some capacity for their denominations, however, do not want to leave and are not asked to forfeit their standing as clergy. They are committed to the ordained ministry and feel fulfilled by and appreciated in their ministerial work. Those clergy who do seriously consider leaving the ordained ministry or actually decide to quit a church career rarely do so because they have lost their faith or because they are incompetent, morally reprehensible, greedy, prejudiced, or frivolous. Rather, they leave or consider leaving generally because they care deeply about carrying out a faithful and effective ministry and, for various reasons, feel that they are unable to continue.

In fact, many of the reasons clergy give for working in ministries outside local congregations turn out to be the same reasons that lead other clergy to consider leaving ministry altogether. Research on clergy dropouts, either from parish ministry or from all paid, church-recognized ministry, shows that the experience is similar to what happens to anyone who leaves a profession or goes through religious disaffiliation. Leaving may be precipitated by a single crisis in one's personal life or in the ministry setting, or it may be the result of a more gradual realization that parish ministry—or even some other kind of ministerial career— is not for that person.[2] We know from comparable research that when persons decide to change their vocational status, several stages occur in the process of leaving, involving serious thought over an extended period of time.[3] We presume, then, that clergy who give fairly sustained thought to the possibility of leaving paid, church-recognized ministry are more apt to do so than those who seldom or never think about doing something else. A recent longitudinal study of Roman Catholic priests shows that when clergy give serious consideration to dropping out of ordained ministry, they often do leave the priesthood.[4] When Protestant clergy are thinking seriously about leaving paid, church-recognized work, therefore, it is quite likely that they may actually leave.

Our study contains responses from a sample of active Protestant clergy surveyed at one point in time. When we define those who have left ministry as those under sixty-eight years of age who have no paid church-recognized work, we find that this is 13 percent of the clergy women and 8 percent of the clergy men in our sample. Most of these clergy are now working in some form of secular work, but some (men and women) are not working at all, because they are caring for home and family while their spouse works, because they are full-time students, or because they say they need a rest from ministerial work.

Roughly one-fourth to one-third of the clergy (32 percent of the women and 28 percent of the men) have at least "sometime during the last year" seriously considered leaving ministry as a paid vocation. Significantly more of those who reported thinking about leaving paid church-related work, when compared with those who have seldom or never seriously considered leaving a career in the church, had actually done so at the time that they answered the survey.[5] (See Appendix 6.2, "Clergy Who Have Thoughts of Leaving Paid Church-Recognized Ministry and Clergy Actually Leaving Paid Church-Recognized Ministry [by Gender and Denomination].")

Table 6.1

Extent That It Was Clear during the Last Year That
Clergy Gave Serious Consideration to Leaving Ministry

	Clergy Women (2,318)	Clergy Men (2,038)
Usually true	12%	11%
Sometimes true	20%	17%
Sometimes false	11%	14%
Usually false	57%	58%
	100%	100%

If such a large number of clergy are actually thinking about leaving active (paid) ministry, this raises additional questions: (1) What factors in the personal lives or vocational situations of clergy affect how often they consider leaving active (paid) ministry? and (2) Even when clergy are somewhat unhappy in their ministry, what factors in their personal or professional lives enable them to remain in active (paid) ministry?

In seeking answers to these questions, we examined the characteristics that other research studies on clergy dropouts have found important. According to these studies, clergy who leave active ministry often have difficulty setting boundaries between church and home, become disappointed when reality does not fit their expectations of what being a minister would be "like," are unable or unwilling to handle conflict in their ministry, feel inept in accomplishing core clergy tasks, sense that church employers are underpaying or unjustly treating them, believe that they are unappreciated and unsupported by other clergy and denominational executives, or are experiencing an emotional or physical breakdown, often called burnout. One or more of these reasons, especially when combined with a lack of hope that it is possible to get a better church job in the foreseeable future and with the perception that more personally or financially rewarding work is available in secular employment, lead clergy to become increasingly serious about wanting to leave church-related work.

Most of these factors were tested in our survey. In addition, we conducted depth interviews with twelve clergy (nine women and three men) who told us on their surveys that they "had left the ministry" and indicated a willingness to be interviewed.

Looking at this situation positively, an analysis of our survey results shows that clergy women and clergy men with a strong professional self-concept; who are in good overall spiritual, physical, and mental health; who are able to set boundaries between church work and private life and manage these effectively; who feel they are fairly compensated for their ministerial work; who are respected by denominational executives; who believe it will be fairly easy to get a somewhat better church position in the future; and who participate in a clergy support group are very unlikely to consider leaving church-related work.

When we take all of these factors together and ask which of these characteristics are the most important in predicting the capacity of clergy to stay in ministry, it turns out that clergy with good overall health and a strong professional self-concept can sustain their commitment to a ministerial vocation even when faced with very difficult church situations, a lack of money, or minimal support from significant others who influence their careers. Furthermore, we found that age on entering seminary seems to have an important relationship to the commitment of clergy women to remain in ministry but has no relationship to the commitment of clergy men. Clergy women who are older when they enter seminary appear better able than younger clergy women to sustain their commitment to a church career. It may be that younger clergy women are more apt than older clergy women to be disappointed when what they actually find in a ministerial career is not what they thought it would be. Many younger clergy women have not spent years in the church as laity before becoming ordained. These younger clergy women may also be more susceptible to sexual harassment or simply more likely to be overwhelmed by the complexity of family responsibilities in relation to ministry than are older clergy women. It is important to note, however, that younger clergy women may *think* about leaving active (paid) ministry more often, but they do not *actually* drop out of church employment any more frequently than older clergy women.[6]

Clergy women consider leaving active (paid) ministry when their church situation is unpleasant and when they are not being paid enough for what they are doing. As stress takes its toll on their overall health, they begin to question their fitness for ministry. But even when clergy women seriously contemplate earning their living outside the church, they often remain in ministerial employment if they see a possibility of moving to a better church job, if they have the support of a denominational executive, and if they have the support of a group of clergy. (See Appendix 6.3, "Factors Influencing Clergy Giving Serious Consideration to Leaving Ordained Ministry and No Longer Serving in Any Paid Church Work.")

Denominational differences also affect whether clergy women—stay in active (paid) ministry. More clergy women in the Southern Baptist and United Methodist denominations (around 40 percent), in contrast with other denominations, are likely to have considered leaving church-related ministry—but probably for different reasons. Southern Baptist clergy women continue to face overt resistance from men and women in their churches and have real difficulty getting church-related employment. United Methodist clergy women, especially if they have families, have problems balancing family and career concerns with the expectations of the itinerancy system that they move to a new congregation every three or four years.

In contrast, less than 25 percent of clergy women who are Unitarian-Universalists and clergy women from the Spirit-centered denominations have considered leaving church-related work, but also probably for different reasons. Even though a salary inequity still prevails among Unitarian-Universalists, clergy women feel relatively well supported in their career in ministry in this denomination, whereas clergy women in the Spirit-centered denominations may be staying with ordained ministry out of their theological conviction that God wants them to do this work, regardless of their work experiences or family situation. Remember that clergy women in the Spirit-centered denominations are the most highly motivated to seek ordination for theological reasons. (See Appendix 6.2, "Clergy Who Have Thoughts of Leaving Paid Church-Recognized Ministry and Clergy Actually Leaving Paid Church-Recognized Ministry [by Gender and Denomination].")

Dissatisfaction with an active ministerial career is expressed through a combination of factors. In our interviews, we learned that "the little things" sometimes combine in individual situations to escalate dissatisfaction. Earning enough money to live on may seem a minor factor at first, when the big challenge is getting a call to a full-time church position at all. Initially, most clergy women have no intention of leaving the ministry, even if they are forced to get secular work to pay their bills. Gradually, however, they find themselves enjoying the secular job more than their church employment and resenting the low remuneration from the church. As one former clergy woman told us, "Since I couldn't get called to a full-time ministry position after four years of 'searching' in the United Church of Christ, I left church work." She is very happy as a special education teacher. Several other women, surviving on part-time ministry jobs and still hopeful for full-time church employment, wonder about "giving up." One of them told us, "It is disconcerting in my part-time church positions to realize that I am making less now with three advanced degrees than I was in my first year of college. It does raise some questions. . . . Yes, I think about dropping out of ministry from day to day, moment to moment—but I am still determined . . . to try for a full-time position."

One of the problems in small-town and rural congregations, other than the social isolation that clergy suffer (as described in chapter 2), is that clergy salaries in those situations are very modest. Furthermore, in those areas a clergy spouse (if there is one) has little opportunity to find employment or earn a decent wage. This becomes another reason that clergy find ministry in rural and small-town settings unappealing. After a time in these ministries, clergy may start moonlighting in some part-time secular work to pay the bills, and before long, the job satisfactions of the secular job may lead them completely out of active (paid) ministry.

In our interviews, we talked with a clergy man, with a wife and child, who was serving in a small-town church and having trouble making ends meet. His wife was a substitute teacher in the local school system. Soon he decided also to do some substitute teaching on a moonlighting basis while holding down his church job. As he became unhappy with the local congregational leaders who were criticizing everything he was doing, he found his work teaching in the junior high school increasingly appealing. Finally, when he was offered a full-time job in the school system, he left the church with no plans to return.

In another situation, a single clergy woman who could not make ends meet in her rural parish commuted to a nearby college town to work part-time in an administrative position. As time passed, she decided that not only was the money better in the college position but she liked the work better and was not so lonely. In time, she gave up her parish to become a full-time college administrator.

Have these clergy left ministry? Yes. But then again, maybe not. In our interviews, these clergy wistfully talk about how difficult it is to meet expectations. The members of congregations and the regional denominational leaders, they say, are totally unrealistic about what is possible in certain ministry settings. All of the clergy who have "left" local church service underscore a common pattern: they are extremely frustrated by church conflicts and crises *and* their denominational executives seem uncaring about what the situation is or as lazy and devious as some of the lay leaders:

> I sometimes wonder if this is really what I was called to do. A lot of clergy men and clergy women go though a period of questioning what they are doing with their lives after pastoring certain congregations for a while. The "nit-picking and whining" get to you, as does the demand that the pastor get the congregation to grow in numbers (even though the population in the area is declining), as does the conference executive's allowing congregations to do anything they want for fear of losing their support.
>
> (clergy man)

A clergy man who once served on a seminary committee to decide whether seminarians should be recommended for ordination told of hearing and verifying a story that one of the women seminarians had been given poor evaluations by her clergy supervisor because she rejected his sexual advances. The denominational executives admitted that the charge was probably true, but in light of the fact that the clergy supervisor and his congregation were big contributors to the seminary, they did not feel they could do anything about it.

We heard another story about a divorced clergy woman with young children who was working hard to impress the married senior minister. He was impressed all right, telling her that he found her ankles "so sexy during worship, he could not concentrate on leading the prayers." She told him not to say such things, but he continued. One day while she was at the copy machine, he backed into her, throwing her down over the copier. This time she was sufficiently scared and angry to go directly to the judicatory executive and the elected lay leaders of the congregation. They did nothing. The senior minister became very hostile, and she finally resigned for her own health and that of her family. She told us that although she tries to be understanding and forgiving, she does not want "to serve as a member of the clergy for this denomination in any capacity, any more . . . at all." The sole reason she has not yet totally given up her standing or clergy status is financial; she reasons that if she loses her secular job or her children need more money, she can still work as an interim or supply minister to augment her income.

How do clergy attitudes toward feminism influence decisions to stay in or leave authorized ministries? Very slightly. The degree to which ordained men advocate or oppose any feminist agenda has no relationship to whether they have thought seriously during the last year about leaving ministry. The ordained women who most strongly advocate structural or spiritual feminism, as measured by our feminism indexes in chapter 1, are only somewhat (about 10 percent) more likely than those who are lukewarm or opposed to feminist values to entertain thoughts about leaving church work altogether. It appears that feminist values are of minimal or no importance when compared with other influences on clergy thinking about leaving paid church work. One probable reason for feminist values not having a direct effect on clergy women's thoughts of about leaving is that some feminist clergy women stay in the church to fight for its transformation, while other feminist clergy women become so angry and disappointed that they leave.

Church crises, however, are the major precipitating events leading ordained women and men to consider leaving authorized ministry. Those who do leave usually have many stories to share about their last parish or church agency position, detailing the horrible ways in which they were treated by senior pastors, old-guard lay leaders, and others. After hearing some of these stories, we understand why these clergy leave church service never wanting to return to ministerial employment. In contrast, however, we also talked with clergy who go through "hell" in their parish, denominational, or chaplaincy positions and yet stay connected to church employment as valuable "tentmakers," or nonstipendiary clergy earning their living outside of the church.

In the final analysis, it seems that two pivotal factors determine whether clergy who leave formal employment in the church will stay connected to their vocation as clergy or become totally secularized: (1) whether denominational executives recognize and value the contributions of these clergy to the ministries of their congregations and judicatories and (2) whether these clergy are commended and supported by a group of clergy colleagues with whom they meet frequently.

Without these supports, the probability is high that clergy earning their living in secular jobs or who are not presently employed will completely disappear from church circles.

Clergy who formally consider removing themselves from a church career because the reality of ministry is so dissonant with what they anticipated, who find sexism too pervasive and equity too elusive, or who are nearing burnout from overwork or church conflicts are able to sustain their sense of calling and service as clergy if they are able to remain hopeful and if they receive support from other ordained leaders.

SECULAR WORK

Historically, clergy in secular work have technically left the ministry. Our research, however, challenges this assumption. Increasingly, we find that it is possible to identify a sizable group of clergy, men and women, who consider themselves actively in ordained ministry despite the fact that they are employed in a secular job. In fact, across all the denominations in our study, roughly 6 percent of ordained clergy report working in secular, non-church-related occupations. What is the "ministry" of these clergy, and why do they still consider themselves clergy? How do their denominations keep them accountable to the profession?

When we examine the job transitions of male and female clergy holding secular employment in their first, second, or third jobs after becoming ordained, we come up with revealing results. More than half of the clergy in secular work do not stay in secular work but actually move back into one of the recognized ministries of the church.

One explanation is that some seminary graduates are taking secular positions after ordination but prior to receiving a call or being placed in a pastorate. They are holding an interim secular job while waiting for a call from a church. Secular jobs at this stage in a career do not necessarily have any negative influence on clergy careers. In fact, we find that 25 percent of clergy men whose first position was a secular job moved to a sole pastorate in a large church in their second position. Eleven percent of clergy women in secular employment did the same. By the transition from the second to the third job, however, the probability of easily moving back into church-related ministry diminishes, suggesting that continuing in secular work eventually limits career options. From a second secular job, 2 percent of both clergy men and clergy women move into sole pastorates of large churches. And after the third secular job, only 2 percent of the clergy women and 8 percent of the clergy men make the move to large pastorates.

If a clergy man or clergy woman is open to returning to parish ministry as an assistant or associate pastor, the chances of moving back into parish ministry are quite good, regardless of gender or when the move is made. Thirteen percent of clergy women and 19 percent of clergy men surveyed who have secular jobs after ordination subsequently move to assistant or associate positions. Sixteen percent of clergy women and clergy men move to assistant or associate positions from a second secular job. And 15 percent of clergy women and 13 percent of clergy men are still able to move from their third secular position into responsibilities as an assistant or associate pastor.

When we look at the patterns of movement among clergy women and clergy men from secular employment into sole pastorates in small churches, we discover a curious picture. The percentage moving from secular work in the first job to a small church pastorate in the second job is small—1 percent for clergy women and 5 percent for clergy men. However, in the second job, the chance of moving from secular work into the sole pastorate of a small church increases to roughly 13 percent for both clergy women and clergy men. One interpretation is that churches recognize that clergy are gaining management skills in their secular work. When such skills are combined with some form of intermittent work in local congregations, they become recognized as preparation enabling clergy to assume positions of greater responsibility in small local churches by their second or third job—even after a spell in secular work.

As for moves from secular work into specialized ministries in local congregations and in recognized nonparish positions, between 4 and 10 percent of clergy men move from secular work into specialized *parish* positions between their first and third jobs, as do between 14 and 16 percent of clergy women. This type of career move seems more likely for women than for men. With *nonparish* positions, the situation is the same: between 5 and 7 percent of clergy men move from secular work to recognized nonparish positions between their first and third jobs, compared with between 8 and 14 percent of clergy women.

Movement from secular employment to a senior pastorate is extremely unusual. Less than 1 percent of all clergy, male or female, move from a secular position to become senior pastors. The only exception to this pattern is found among a small group of clergy men who move from their third job, which is secular, into a senior pastorate. These men may be sought by large churches who go outside the denominational placement and appointment systems to get a senior pastor with the management experience needed to lead a large, multistaffed congregation. (See Appendixes 6.4 and 6.5, "Job Transitions of Clergy Women and Clergy Men in Secular Employment in Their First, Second, and Third Jobs.")

As noted earlier, 6 percent of the clergy in our study indicated that they were employed in secular jobs. This is a relatively small group. Yet the patterns revealed in this analysis give us important clues about how clergy career paths are changing, especially among women. From our interviews, we know that some clergy working in secular employment describe themselves as tentmakers, people holding secular jobs and carrying out additional, part-time ministries in churches for little or no salary. These clergy are able to support themselves financially with their secular job and render important services to the churches on a volunteer basis. Such clergy women and clergy men do not think they have left the ordained ministry at all; rather, they remain deeply motivated by their ordination and believe that what they are doing is vocationally responsible to God and to the church. Their denominations variously recognize and affirm them as nonstipendiary clergy, dual-role clergy, bivocational clergy, self-supporting ministers, free ministers, or voluntary ministers. Many of them spend weekends and evenings in small rural churches or small neighborhood churches in urban areas, while holding down secular jobs the rest of the week.

A closer look at tentmaker clergy suggests that the motivations for this form of ministry are varied. A good number of these clergy are women and men who find full-time employment as a pastor or in some recognized church-related ministry to be unfulfilling or impractical, either because it is too stressful or because it is impossible for them to manage pastoral ministry alongside the other parts of their lives. Some of these clergy women and clergy men truly feel called to more than one vocation. They consider their tentmaking to be a special and chosen vocation and have very little desire to move into full-time church-related jobs. In our interviews, we spoke with a farmer, a town clerk, a labor mediator, a university professor, and a nurse who embrace long-term tentmaking ordained ministry enthusiastically.

A second type of tentmaker clergy consists of those who are in secular employment as a temporary measure. They are "volunteering" their ministries as a way of preparing themselves for a paid, full-time clergy position. It appears that this approach works. Churches who "employ tentmakers" are generally under less budget stress than others, and their lay leadership is very active, relieving clergy of responsibilities normally handled by a full-time pastor. The partnership is often a successful one, providing the part-time pastor with good skills and references that lead eventually to full-time employment in a church position.

Denominational officials respond to tentmakers in various ways. Some officials welcome these people, encouraging them and supporting them in order to provide needed clergy leadership in settings where congregations cannot afford a full-time pastor. But clergy in secular employment who move into ministry without going through regular channels are sometimes seen as a threat. They appear to be going around the system, and because money is not at stake, their accountability to the wider church is minimal. This sometimes can lead denominational executives to view tentmakers with suspicion, questioning their vocational commitment to ministry and their denominational loyalty.

A third group of clergy in secular employment are not really tentmakers. They have semisecular jobs, challenging churches to see their work in the secular world as a form of ministry worthy of ordination. For example, a clergy woman working in a rape crisis center or in a secular social service agency for the homeless may view what she is doing as an ordained "ministry." In spite of the fact that she is presently in a "secular job" and that her denomination initially classifies her work as secular, she challenges church leaders to expand their definitions of ordained ministry. Sometimes she convinces ecclesiastical authorities that hers is a new kind of recognized ministry. Even if she does not, she feels no need to justify her identity as clergy by also "volunteering" her services in a local congregation. Clergy in secular work who think they are doing ministry are more likely than those in traditional nonparish ministries to believe that the kind of ministry they are presently doing is more "important to the world" than parish ministry.

Table 6.2
Clergy Who Do Not Earn Their Living from
Church-Related Work (Under 68 Years of Age)
% = % saying "accurate" and "somewhat accurate"

	Women (117)	Men (62)
a. My gifts are better suited to this kind of ministry.	79%	85%
b. I believe this kind of ministry is more important to the world.	56%	49%
c. I have more flexibility to schedule family and personal time.	82%	71%
d. I have better salary and benefits in this position.	47%	57%
e. I could not get a parish position in this area and I am not geographically mobile.	41%	30%
f. I could not get a parish position in this area because my denominational offices or leaders did not support me.	30%	24%
g. I do not like parish ministry.	48%	45%

Regardless of whether the 6 percent of the clergy in our study who are not in paid church-related employment are contributing "ministerial services" to a local congregation, many of them insist that they have not "dropped out" or "left ordained ministry." Their career paths move in and out of traditional clergy roles, suggesting that definitions of ordained ministry in contemporary Protestantism are expanding. Although we have not considered these career paths in a historical perspective, we suspect that the frequency of such career paths is increasing as denominational demographics shift to smaller churches. Numerous ordained persons who hold secular jobs regularly take on temporary assignments within local congregations, fill in for vacationing pastors, perform sacramental duties such as funerals and weddings "as needed"; or, even more radical, they interpret aspects of their secular job as a ministry.[7] As churches and society change, the need is growing for forms of ministry that do not fit traditional models of full-time, lifelong service. It appears that the career paths of women are a portent of things to come.

REINVENTING ORDAINED MINISTRY

The experiences of both clergy women and clergy men in contemporary Protestantism are changing. Our survey and interviews show how clergy women especially are living extremely complex lives—balancing home, family, and their desire to serve God and the church. They do not always do things "the same old way," but they are effective leaders. Laity and the clergy themselves have generally positive experiences with the leadership of ordained women. And as the numbers increase, clergy women are proving to be extremely effective ministers.

However, significant differences in the job experiences of clergy women and clergy men remain. On the one hand, the different career patterns of clergy women suggest that women are creatively claiming new ways to "be clergy." On the other hand, clergy women earn 9 percent less than clergy men, even after adjustments are made for such factors as age, position, denomination, and experience.

We have noted that clergy women continue to have more difficulty than clergy men in finding a job because denominational deployment procedures consistently place women at a disadvantage. Even recent changes in denominational practices designed to develop more gender-neutral systems, advocates, and appointment patterns have not eliminated discrimination. Evidence suggests that women regularly find themselves in positions with less occupational status and promise (at least, by past standards of measurement) than those held by men. And although family responsibilities and children are often given as reasons for career differences between women and men, it turns out that children are not a major factor in the inequities experienced by clergy women.

We also recognize that ordained ministry is not "just another job." Clergy women and clergy men seek ordination because they have a sense of call and a conviction that God has a plan for their lives. They accept their ministry as a gift from God, believing that God and the church have called them to serve.

For clergy women, this spiritual or divine dimension to their profession is extremely important. It sustains them in the face of difficulties and discrimination. It informs their understanding of ministry and the world. And it is transforming common expectations of all ordained ministry.

Yet clergy women continue to have difficulties, even when they are within institutional structures that ought to offer them opportunities for advancement. What is needed is greater attention to the need to change ecclesiastical systems. If denominational leaders are actively hostile or insensitive to finding the right ministry settings for women, female clergy get discouraged. When this happens, it is important to remember that these women are not failures—rather, the system is failing women.

Ongoing patterns of passive hostility persist against women clergy, and without broader information and support networks, some clergy women identify their problems as personal failures rather than the limitations of the social or institutional systems in which they are located. If clergy women can overcome the isolation created by the personalization of their "failures" and gain an understanding that their problems are system-based rather than individual or situational, they may be able to mobilize and make significant new contributions to the churches and their ministries by expanding definitions of ordained ministry and—literally—taking the church into the world.

When we examine the careers of clergy women and clergy men, represented by the sequence of transitions made in their first three jobs, we can see that the career paths of clergy women differ from clergy men's. Although having children during the first five years after ordination makes some difference in the career paths of clergy women and clergy men, gender is a more significant factor than family situation. An analysis of the actual sequences of jobs held by clergy women and clergy men shows that men are likely to occupy "managerial-type" positions and women are likely to occupy "staff-type" positions. As a consequence, women are frequently "tracked" into employment in secondary labor markets—holding jobs that have less organizational power, lower salaries, less responsibility, and fewer benefits than those that men hold.

One reason often given for this discrepancy is that women choose to take less demanding jobs so that they can spend more time raising their families. Yet when we compare the distribution of clergy women and clergy men across clergy positions, the evidence does not support this interpretation. Childless clergy women as well as clergy women with children are consistently more likely than clergy men to be serving in staff-type positions. Our comparison of the career paths of clergy women and clergy men shows that the largest career path differences are not between parents and nonparents but between women and men. Clergy men are more likely than women to occupy jobs with higher salaries and greater professional responsibilities. Clergy women, in contrast, are paid less than men and consistently hold less responsible jobs. Clergy men tend to be stuck in traditional and conventional congregational jobs, whereas clergy women regularly pursue mixed, flexible, and diverse career paths. It is a mixed blessing. On the one hand, clergy women do not yet have equity in the job market; on the other hand, clergy women have incredible freedom to push the edges of ministry beyond historical habits.

We have highlighted the difference between the career paths of clergy women and clergy men by noting the role of secular work, or those times when they are not employed in church-related ministries. Some clergy women, especially those who hold secular positions without leaving the ministry (at least in their thinking), are not following the rules. Rather, they are expanding traditional assumptions about ordained ministry beyond the image of an ecclesiastically paid, full-time, lifelong pastor.

At the same time, we note that many recently ordained women seem to have a weaker sense of political solidarity with other clergy women than their predecessors had, which may lead them to interpret their problems in individualist rather than institutional ways. When this happens, some clergy women blame themselves for their difficulties rather than recognizing that existing ecclesiastical systems may be at fault. Perhaps when contemporary clergy women shift their perspective from seeing their individual failings as the problem and recognize that institutional systems are still frustrating their careers, they will be able to help various denominational systems become more hospitable to women.

THE VIEW NEAR THE SUMMIT

Most clergy women have a strong sense of call. At the end of the twentieth century, they have come a long way. But their journey is still uphill. Yet as clergy women move into a profession historically dominated by men, they are pushing the edges of expectation and definition. The 1990s have seen a number of studies, articles, and books on clergy women, documenting their contemporary experience and placing it in historical context. Much of this research suggests that old patterns of clergy leadership are undergoing significant change.

Observers and participants in this new situation embrace four or five different perspectives or agendas to explain and predict the future of clergy women. First are those who think that the increasing numbers of clergy women will force the church and the powers that have historically controlled the churches to change and become more egalitarian. They argue that the numbers alone will overwhelm the present structures and bring about true leadership equality in contemporary Protestantism. They quote scripture and insist that in Christ Jesus there is no longer male or female, and they await a new day. Unfortunately, studies of occupational change show no evidence that sheer numbers correct inequities and overwhelm past assumptions or that the promise of the scriptures is any nearer to fulfillment than it was two thousand years ago.

Second are those who look at the growing numbers of women in ordained ministry and predict a reactionary backlash. They associate clergy women with the liberal modern agenda, and they see Protestant strength moving away from mainline liberal religion. Fundamentalist and conservative Christian bodies are growing, and in many of those communities, clergy women are not welcome. There is a growing pessimism about the capacity of the churches to embrace the leadership of women in truly equitable ways. Male clergy, they note, will not relinquish power easily, and clergy women, even if ordained, will eventually be co-opted and limited by hierarchical traditions deeply embedded in the history of ordained ministry. This analysis says that things are going to get worse before they get better.

Third are those who recognize that although clergy women seem to be "taking over" the ordained ministry within mainline Protestantism, it will be a hollow victory. By the time substantial numbers of women gain access to ordained ministry, the occupation will have lost its prestige (if it has not already), and women will find themselves in a devalued vocation keeping dying denominational systems afloat. This is what has happened in other recently feminized secular occupations, and it will happen to clergy women.

Fourth are those who applaud the ways in which women have made great "advances" in religious leadership but suggest extreme caution. Change is exceedingly complex. Without a major retooling and rethinking of the assumptions and symbols surrounding ordained ministry, ecclesiastical cultures will continue to track women into second-class leadership options. Women dare not be naive and overly optimistic about what it takes to redeem entrenched habits from the past. As Paula Nesbitt puts it in her study of Unitarian-Universalist and Episcopal clergy women, the future will be "increasingly crowded with female colleagues in lower to mid-level placements," and although some women will attain positions of religious leadership, "it is doubtful that it will increase beyond a token level in either numbers or influence. . . . In short, women will continue to labor in the vineyard while the masters reap the fruits of their harvest."[8]

Finally, it is possible to agree with this sobering and realistic judgment but insist that the glass is half full rather than half empty. Looking closely at the wonderful ministries of clergy women since 1970, we submit that women are expanding expectations and definitions of religious leadership for the whole church.

Although parish ministry will continue to be an important leadership pattern at the center of Christian understandings of church and society, in the future, fewer local clergy will be full-time, lifetime, paid pastors. The careers of clergy women already point to a day when more clergy will work in church-related ministries outside the parish or for several congregations; when clergy will move in and out of secular employment, blurring historical distinctions between clergy and laity; when clergy will be authorized by and accountable to several ecclesiastical bodies; when clergy may be paid for work done in secular institutions yet be empowered to do that work as an agent of the Christian church. Clergy will live between their commitments to the church and to the world, insisting that both commitments be called and recognized as "ministry."

The experience and sense of calling among clergy women in the 1990s show that clergy women are not merely survivors; nor are they breaking down old barriers simply to get into a vocation shaped and still dominated by male perspectives. Rather, clergy women are reinventing ministry for the future, refusing the old definitions and expectations. Clergy women are expanding the very essence of Christian ministry and guiding the whole church to rethink and renew its leadership and membership.

Statistical Appendixes

Appendix 1.1
Number of Respondents in the Hartford Seminary Study
by Gender and Denomination (1994)

(15 denominations, alphabetical)

	Clergy Women	Clergy Men
American Baptist Churches	227	183
Assemblies of God	41	14
Christian Church (Disciples of Christ)	265	204
Church of God (Anderson, Indiana)	67	58
Church of the Brethren	86	61
Church of the Nazarene	128	109
Episcopal Church	236	191
Evangelical Lutheran Church in America	254	220
Free Methodist Church	11	4
Presbyterian Church (U.S.A.)	252	179
Southern Baptist Convention	116	107
Unitarian-Universalist Association	236	242
United Church of Christ	283	229
United Methodist Church	211	197
Wesleyan Church	53	74
Other, no affiliation given	19	44
TOTAL (4,601)	2,485	2,116

Appendix 1.2
Changing Numbers of Clergy in Major Protestant Denominations*

	1977 Women	1977 Men	1986 Women	1986 Men	1994 Women	1994 Men
American Baptist Churches	157	5,163	429	3,676	712	5,046
Assemblies of God	1,572	12,356	1,588	15,667	1,574	16,996
Christian Church (Disciples of Christ)	388	3,712	743	3,328	988	4,481
Church of God (Anderson, Indiana)	272		275		296	2,659
Church of the Brethren	27	797	120	1,988	142	1,021
Church of the Nazarene	426		355		377	3,036
Episcopal Church	94	12,099	796	13,009	1,394	9,920
Evangelical Lutheran Church in America	73		790		1,519	11,706
Free Methodist Church	11		69		24	1,854
Presbyterian Church (U.S.A.)[1]	350	13,555	1,524	18,084	2,705	11,873
Southern Baptist Convention					1,130	34,000
Unitarian-Universalist Association	39	571	81	723	376	860
United Church of Christ	400	4,746	1,460	3,649	1,843	5,454
United Methodist Church	319	19,916	1,891	18,991	3,003	17,614
Wesleyan Church	384		255		238	1,952

*Blanks indicate that statistical information is not available.

[1]For the PC (USA) 1977 data are from the former northern Presbyterian church and 1986 and 1994 data are from the reunited Presbyterian church.

(*Note:* Some of the 1977 and 1986 data from the National Council of Churches was collected by Constant Jacquet Jr.; other statistics and 1994 data were collected by Hartford Seminary. These statistics sometimes differ from totals published by denominational offices. This is because we have used the same definitions for inclusion (i.e., active and fully ordained) across time periods and denominations. See Appendix 4.1 for the latest reported totals of women clergy in the denominations studied by Hartford Seminary.)

Appendix 1.3

Change in Number of Clergy Women
as Percent of Total Clergy

1977   1986   1994

ABC   COB   CH (DOC)   EC   PC (USA)   UCC   UMC   RCA

Appendix 1.4
Ordained Women and Men in the Hartford Seminary Study (1994)
(15 Denominations Clustered)

	Women	Men	Total
Congregation-Centered			
American Baptist Churches	227	183	410
Christian Church (Disciples of Christ)	265	204	469
Church of the Brethren	86	61	147
Southern Baptist Convention	116	107	223
Unitarian-Universalist Association	236	242	478
United Church of Christ	283	229	512
Total congregation-centered	1,213	1,026	2,239
Institution-Centered			
Episcopal Church	236	191	427
Evangelical Lutheran Church in America	254	220	474
Presbyterian Church (U.S.A.)	252	179	431
United Methodist Church	211	197	408
Total institution-centered	953	787	1,740
Spirit-Centered			
Church of God (Anderson, Indiana)	67	58	125
Church of the Nazarene	128	109	237
Other "Spirit-centered" (Free Methodists/Wesleyan/ Assemblies of God)	105	92	197
Total Spirit-centered	300	259	559
Total other, or not coded	19	44	63
TOTALS	2,485	2,116	4,601

Appendix 1.5
Responses on Feminist Indexes by Gender and Denomination

% = % scoring in the top fourth (roughly) of the indexes
or "very to quite strong" structural feminist score
or "very strong" spiritual feminist score

	Structural Feminism		Spiritual Feminism	
	Women	Men	Women	Men
Congregation-Centered				
American Baptist Churches (w = 227, m = 183)	66%	29%	50%	24%
Christian Church (Disc.) (w = 265, m = 204)	61%	25%	63%	31%
Church of the Brethren (w = 86 m = 61)	51%	33%	55%	18%
Southern Baptist Convention (w = 116, m = 107)	59%	6%	56%	2%
Unitarian-Universalist Association (w = 236, m = 242)	44%	29%	80%	70%
United Church of Christ (w = 283, m = 229)	54%	26%	66%	40%
Institution-Centered				
Episcopal Church (w = 236, m = 191)	52%	21%	59%	30%
Evan. Lutheran (ELCA) (w = 254, m = 220)	57%	29%	71%	29%
Presbyterian Ch. (U.S.A.) (w = 252, m = 179)	58%	28%	60%	32%
United Methodist Church (w = 211, m = 192)	68%	26%	69%	28%
Spirit-Centered				
Church of God (Anderson) (w = 67, m = 58)	16%	10%	15%	4%
Church of the Nazarene (w = 128, m = 109)	18%	4%	6%	1%
Other Holiness (Free Meth. and Wesleyan) (w = 64, m = 78)	11%	1%	2%	1%
Assemblies of God (w = 41, m = 14)	10%	14%	6%	8%

Appendix 2.1
Lesbian and Gay Clergy in Committed Relationships

	N =	In Committed Relationships		Other	
		Lesbians (147)	Gays (64)	Women (2,338)	Men (2,052)
1. Employment Location					
congregation		46%	78%	58%	75%
nonparish ministry		24%	8%	17%	11%
secular employment		19%	12%	15%	8%
2. Ease of Getting Another Church Position Slightly Better Than the One You Have Now					
difficult (somewhat to very)		75%	63%	68%	56%
3. Gave Some Serious Thought to Leaving Ordained Ministry		43%	37%	31%	28%
4. Are over Age 55		16%	9%	25%	24%
5. Boundary Maintenance Ability					
Very high, good (scores 4–7)		21%	18%	21%	25%
Low, poor ability (scores 12–16)		31%	35%	31%	29%

Appendix 2.2
Ever-Divorced Clergy by Gender and Denomination

	Clergy Women		Clergy Men	
	Total N	% Divorced	Total N	% Divorced
American Baptist Churches	227	19% (43)	183	13% (24)
Christian Church (Disc. of Christ)	265	26% (70)	204	24% (48)
Church of the Brethren	86	15% (13)	61	12% (7)
Southern Baptist Convention	116	17% (20)	107	4% (4)
Unitarian-Universalist Association	236	47% (111)	242	44% (107)
United Church of Christ	283	26% (74)	229	20% (47)
Congregation-Centered Denominations	1,213	27% (331)	1,026	23% (237)
Evan. Lutheran Church in Am. (ELCA)	254	19% (48)	220	9% (20)
Episcopal Church	236	30% (72)	191	25% (47)
Presbyterian Church (U.S.A.)	252	25% (63)	179	19% (34)
United Methodist Church	211	26% (56)	197	19% (37)
Institution-Centered Denominations	953	25% (239)	787	18% (138)
Spirit-Centered Denominations (Ch. of God, Naz., Free Meth., Wes., Assemblies of God)	300	4% (13)	259	4% (11)
TOTAL (answering)	2,466	24% (583)	2,072	19% (386)

Appendix 2.3
The Most Satisfying Aspects of Ministry

	Parish-Based Clergy					
	Congregation-Centered Denom.		Institution-Centered Denom.		Spirit-Centered Denom.	
% = % saying one of the three most satisfying	Women (708)	Men (761)	Women (625)	Men (608)	Women (92)	Men (210)
a. Personal salvation of individuals	12%	28%	11%	20%	72%	81%
b. Conducting worship, admin. sacra.	47%	31%	68%	53%	23%	24%
c. Crisis counseling	36%	30%	34%	27%	26%	13%
d. Pastoral care	18%	20%	18%	16%	12%	21%
e. Ministry of administ.	17%	11%	19%	12%	18%	9%
f. Preaching	51%	68%	60%	74%	48%	73%
g. Teaching	36%	44%	36%	46%	48%	37%
h. Community outreach and service	15%	17%	11%	12%	13%	13%
i. Min. to/with ethnic groups	2%	2%	2%	1%	4%	3%
j. Helping women who are needy or abused	3%	>1%	4%	>1%	5%	>1%
k. Social action advocacy	5%	8%	2%	3%	1%	1%
i. Providing a model for youth	27%	10%	23%	11%	27%	10%
j. Changing trad. images of the church	24%	17%	14%	14%	10%	15%

Appendix 3.1
Clergy Self-Perceived Leadership Styles, 1980–1981 and 1993–1994

Scored: 1 = "directive" to 10 = "democratic"

1. Comparisons of clergy in pastorates only (1980–1981 and 1993–1994) in the
seven denominations surveyed in both studies[1]

	1980–1981		1993–1994	
	Women (635)	Men (739)	Women (1,026)	Men (1,025)
1–4 (directive)	14%	19%	15%	20%
5 (midpoint)	11%	16%	19%	16%
6–7 (somewhat democr.)	32%	29%	24%	31%
8+ (very democr.)	43%	36%	42%	33%
	100%	100%	100%	100%

2. Comparisons of pastors and those not in pastorates (1993–1994)

	Pastors		Not in Pastorates	
	Women (1,375)	Men (1,545)	Women (841)	Men (449)
1–4 (directive)	15%	20%	14%	21%
5 (midpoint)	18%	16%	17%	18%
6–7 (somewhat democr.)	25%	30%	23%	24%
8+ (very democr.)	42%	34%	46%	37%
	100%	100%	100%	100%

cor.   −.08, sig. .0001
cor.   −.11, sig. .0001

[1]American Baptist Churches, Christian Church (Disciples of Christ), Evangelical Lutheran Church in America (a merger of two Lutheran denominations), Episcopal Church, Presbyterian Church (U.S.A.) (a merger of two Presbyterian denominations), United Methodist Church, United Church of Christ.

Appendix 3.2
Clergy Self-Perceived Leadership Styles and Views of How Women Clergy
Share Power by Gender and Denomination

	% who agree that women share power more		Self-Perceived Leadership Styles			
			Very Direc. (1–4)	Very Demo. (8–10)	Very Direc. (1–4)	Very Demo. (8–10)
	Women	Men	Women		Men	
Congregation-Centered Denomin.						
Am. Baptist Churches (w = 98, m = 118)	70%	23%	13%	51%	18%	34%
Christian Ch. (Disc.) (w = 140, m = 131)	63%	20%	21%	39%	24%	34%
Ch. of the Brethren (w = 51, m = 40)	62%	13%	16%	39%	18%	43%
Southern Baptist Conv. (w = 36, m = 86)	71%	11%	6%	53%	20%	31%
Unitarian-Universal. A. (w = 168, m = 167)	66%	29%	9%	50%	10%	52%
United Ch. of Christ (w = 189, m = 180)	68%	22%	8%	49%	16%	33%
Institution-Centered Denomin.						
Episcopal Church (w = 152, m = 140)	73%	15%	13%	40%	17%	30%
Evang. Lutheran Ch. (w = 152, m = 164)	61%	17%	19%	33%	30%	30%
Presbyterian Ch. (U.S.A.) (w = 149, m = 149)	67%	15%	11%	42%	19%	36%
United Methodist Ch. (w = 108, m = 137)	69%	16%	21%	40%	17%	33%
Spirit-Centered Denominations						
Church of God (w = 30, m = 36)	55%	19%	33%	33%	36%	29%
Ch. of the Nazarene (w = 26, m = 93)	47%	9%	23%	31%	26%	24%

Other denomina.[1]	28%	10%	33%	33%	35%	23%
(w = 27, m = 75)						

[1]The following denominations are represented by too few clergy in this sample to treat separately and are put together here: Assemblies of God, Free Methodist, Wesleyan.

Appendix 3.3
Clergy Leadership Style by Seminary Cohort, Age, and Denominational Cluster

% = % very democratic in leadership style

	Women	Men
A. Seminary Cohort (graduated)		
Before 1981	43%	44%
1981–1988	42%	32%
1989–1994	41%	33%
B. Age (currently)		
over age 55	45%	42%
age 44–55	46%	36%
age 35–43	43%	29%
under age 35	37%	24%

C. Age and Denominational Clusters

	Congregation-Centered Denomin.		Institution-Centered Denomin.		Spirit-Centered Denom.	
	Women	Men	Women	Men	Women	Men
Age						
over 55	50%	45%	47%	40%	26%	32%
44–55	48%	39%	47%	33%	31%	31%
35–43	47%	35%	38%	27%	35%	19%
under 35	46%	28%	27%	24%	29%	18%

Appendix 3.4
Ministerial Position and Self-Perceived Leadership Style

| | Women | | Men | |
	Very Direc. (1–4)	Very Democr. (8–10)	Very Direc. (1–4)	Very Democr. (8–10)
Senior pastor	16%	39%	24%	30%
Sole pastor	16%	41%	18%	35%
Co-pastor	19%	37%	23%	32%
Assist./assoc. pastor	13%	44%	27%	30%

Self-Perceived Leadership Styles of Senior Pastors
Compared with other Ministerial Positions[1]

| | Women | | Men | |
Percent = % very democratic	Senior Pastors	Other	Senior Pastors	Other
American Baptist Churches Christian Church (Disciples) United Church of Christ (sen. p.: w = 40, m = 99)	40%	47%	34%	34%
Church of the Brethren Southern Baptist Convention (sen. p.: w = 1, m = 33)	(only 1 wm.)	45%	27%	38%
Unitarian-Universalist Association (sen. p.: w = 13, m = 30)	54%	50%	50%	53%
Presbyterian Church (U.S.A.) United Methodist Church (sen. p.: w = 12, m = 53)	67%	40%	34%	34%
Episcopal Church Evangelical Lutheran Church (sen. p.: w = 17, m = 64)	18%	37%	27%	31%
Spirit-Centered Denominations (sen. p.: w = 12, m = 75)	25%	33%	20%	26%

[1]In denominations and denominational clusters where there are enough female senior pastors to make comparisons.

Appendix 3.5
Lay Leader Attitudes about Clergy, 1980–1981 and 1993–1994[1]

	1980–1981		1993–1994	
	Women	Men	Women	Men
I. Acquaintance with clergy women other than as own pastor				
A. Are there any women ministers at other churches in this community? % "Yes"	47%	45%	74%	70%
B. Have you been acquainted with women ministers in other churches or communities where you were previously? % "Yes"	36%	29%	62%	47%
II. Percent in agreement with these statements				
A. Women, whether lay or clergy, do not hold position or influence in this area comparable to lay and clergy men of my denomination.	43%	41%	24%	28%
B. My congregation should appoint an equal number of lay women to lay men on the parish governing board.	64%	61%	40%	39%
C. If a ministerial vacancy should occur in my congregation (or finances permit an additional minister to be hired), the search committee should actively seek a woman candidate.	34%	20%	31%	29%
D. Inclusive language (referring to humans) should be used in church services.	44%	36%	41%	31%
E. More women should be ordained to full ministerial status in my denomination.	71%	62%	53%	47%

F. There should be more women in
    executive staff positions in
    regional and national offices of
    my denomination.   58%   48%   54%   39%

G. The ordained ministry still carries
    a prestige and dignity that no
    other profession shares.   64%   56%   49%   48%

H. I would be pleased if I had a
    daughter who wanted to be a
    parish minister.   73%   69%   77%   69%

---

[1]American Baptist Churches, Christian Church (Disciples of Christ), Episcopal Church, Evangelical Lutheran Church in America, Presbyterian Church (U.S.A.), United Methodist Church, United Church of Christ.

Appendix 3.6
Attitudes of Laity Who Have a Woman Pastor

	Congreg.-Centered		Institut.-Centered		Spirit-Centered	
N = lay leaders	141w/130m		114w/142m		24w/11m	
	W	M	W	M	W	M
I. Acquaintance with clergy women other than as own pastor						
A. Are there any women ministers at other churches in this community? % "Yes"	82%	72%	74%	70%	58%	78%
B. Have you been acquainted with women ministers in other churches or communities where you were previously? % "Yes"	51%	54%	47%	65%	46%	82%
II. Percent in agreement with these statements						
A. Women, whether lay or clergy, do not hold position or influence in this area comparable to lay and clergy men of my denomination.	21%	33%	25%	27%	50%	64%
B. My congregation should appoint an equal number of lay women to lay men on the parish governing board.	43%	34%	42%	37%	12%	18%
C. If a ministerial vacancy should occur in my congregation (or finances permit an additional minister to be hired), the search committee should actively seek a woman candidate.	41%	20%	27%	25%	4%	0%

D.1.	Inclusive language (referring to humans) should be used in church services.	51%	29%	45%	35%	12%	54%
D.2.	There should be more hymns and prayers using female imagery and names for God.	22%	38%	31%	35%	38%	45%
E.	More women should be ordained to full ministry status in my denomination.	60%	30%	58%	47%	35%	36%
F.	There should be more women in executive staff positions in regional and national offices of my denomination.	60%	31%	54%	45%	26%	46%
G.	The ordained ministry still carries a prestige and dignity that no other profession shares.	38%	52%	49%	54%	54%	45%
H.	I would be pleased if I had a daughter who wanted to be a parish minister.	79%	61%	79%	70%	71%	82%

Appendix 3.7
Professional Self-Concept and
Changes in the Congregation since the Pastor First Came

% = % Very High/Strong Professional Self-Concept

	Improved	Stayed the Same	Worsened
1. Membership of the congregation			
Clergy women	43%	35%	14%
Clergy men	40%	34%	15%
2. Optimism about the church			
Clergy women	43%	24%	24%
Clergy men	41%	34%	20%
3. Finances of church			
Clergy women	38%	27%	34%
Clergy men	40%	36%	25%

Appendix 3.8
Recognition of Leadership Abilities of Parish Clergy

% = % of parish clergy who say their leadership abilities are recognized
"very well" by each of the following

	Denominational Clusters					
	Congregation-Centered		Institution-Centered		Spirit-Centered	
	Women 682	Men 714	Women 600	Men 591	Women 90	Men 202
1. Regional denomin. executive	49%	40%	36%	34%	43%	34%
2. Youth	30%	22%	26%	22%	39%	25%
3. Single adults (20–35 yrs)	34%	25%	30%	26%	53%	31%
4. Parents of young children	50%	35%	42%	35%	52%	42%
5. Professionals	53%	40%	42%	41%	54%	29%
6. Business exec.	26%	26%	25%	27%	38%	23%
7. Women not working outside the home	41%	30%	35%	28%	51%	27%
8. Men age 70 plus	37%	38%	33%	36%	40%	30%
9. Women age 70 plus	48%	44%	43%	41%	53%	32%
10. Clergy women	55%	35%	45%	28%	49%	24%
11. Clergy men	38%	41%	30%	31%	39%	38%

Appendix 4.1
Percentage of Clergy Women in Major Protestant Denominations (1994)

	Clergy Women		Clergy Men
American Baptist Churches	712	(12%)	5,046
Assemblies of God	1,574	(8%)	16,996
Christian Church (Disciples of Christ)	988	(18%)	4,481
Church of God (Anderson, Ind.)	296	(10%)	2,659
Church of the Brethren	142	(12%)	1,021
Church of the Nazarene	377	(11%)	3,036
Episcopal Church	1,394	(12%)	9,920
Evangelical Lutheran Church in America	1,519	(11%)	11,706
Free Methodist Church	24	(1%)	1,854
Presbyterian Church (U.S.A.)	2,705	(19%)	11,873
Southern Baptist Convention	1,130	(4%)	34,000
Unitarian-Universalist Association	376	(30%)	860
United Church of Christ	1,843	(25%)	5,454
United Methodist Church	3,003	(15%)	17,614
Wesleyan Church	238	(11%)	1,952

NOTES ON APPENDIX 4.1

Statistical Sources for the Presbyterian Church (U.S.A.)

Deborah Bruce and John Marcum, Research Services, Presbyterian Church (U.S.A.), Louisville, Kentucky, "Comparing Female and Male Pastors in the Pres-byterian Church (U.S.A.)" (paper presented at the annual meetings of the Society for the Scientific Study of Religion and the Religious Research Association (St. Louis, October 1995): In 1994, "there are currently about 15,000 active (i.e., not retired) ministers serving the Presbyterian Church (U.S.A.); 18.6% of these are women. This percentage has increased from 7.8% in 1984."

See also the *Presbyterian Clergywoman Survey: Final Report* (Louisville, Ky.: Research Services, Presbyterian Church (U.S.A.), October 1993): "In the spring of 1993, all 2,447 ordained women on the mailing list of the Women's Ministry Unit were surveyed."

Statistical Sources for the Southern Baptist Convention

Carolyn DeArmond Blevins, "Women and the Baptist Experience," in Catherine Wessinger, ed., *Religious Institutions and Women's Leadership* (Columbia: University of South Carolina, 1996), pp. 158–79. Blevins made a telephone call on April 27, 1995, to Sarah Frances Anders, who keeps records of the number of ordained women in the Southern Baptist Convention (see p. 179 n. 36 in Blevins) and was told, "Southern Baptists in 1995 had 1,130 ordained women" (p. 173).

Appendix 4.2
Average Earnings of Full-Time Clergy Ranked by Women's Salaries

Denomination	Gender	Mean Salary	Std. Dev.
Unitarian-Universalist Association	Women	$40,976	15.699
	Men	47,276	17.409
Episcopal Church	Women	40,489	14.318
	Men	47,173	15.188
United Methodist Church	Women	38,016	14.586
	Men	45,536	17.489
Southern Baptist Convention	Women	35,022	12.033
	Men	48,476	10.446
United Church of Christ	Women	34,564	10.662
	Men	39,242	12.092
Presbyterian Church (U.S.A.)	Women	34,268	12.266
	Men	37,923	12.461
American Baptist Churches	Women	34,099	14.816
	Men	39,175	15.045
Evang. Lutheran Ch. in Am.	Women	33,362	11.163
	Men	40,152	11.525
Assemblies of God	Women	32,750	13.937
	Men	47,666	25.106
Christian Church (DOC)	Women	32,459	11.851
	Men	36,817	15.275
Church of the Brethren	Women	30,096	8.215
	Men	34,652	10.806
Free Methodist	Women	28,500	20.041
	Men	32,000	.000
Church of God (Anderson)	Women	24,818	12.0815
	Men	37,333	11.7392
Church of the Nazarene	Women	20,231	11.6987
	Men	27,114	10.2803
Wesleyan	Women	20,000	6.0000
	Men	31,550	9.0987

For comparison purposes, the figures in this table exclude part-time workers and those who work fewer than thirty hours a week—thereby excluding about 11 percent of the sample. Five percent of the men and 17 percent of the women report part-time employment in their current position. To include them, however, would artificially lower the salaries earned by women, since more women than men are part-time workers and part-time workers tend to earn less than those who work full-time. Nonetheless, it is relevant that women are more likely to work part-time. This may be because they have chosen to work part-time voluntarily in response to other family or personal responsibilities or because they are unable to find full-time work.

Appendix 4.3
Denominations Ranked by Average Adjusted Earnings
for Full-Time Clergy Women

 1. Episcopal Church
 2. Unitarian-Universalist Association
 3. Evangelical Lutheran Church in America
 4. Presbyterian Church (U.S.A.)
 5. United Church of Christ
 6. United Methodist Church
 7. Southern Baptist Convention
 8. Church of the Brethren
 9. American Baptist Churches
10. Assemblies of God
11. Christian Church (Disciples of Christ)
12. Church of God (Anderson, Indiana)
13. Church of the Nazarene
14. Wesleyan Church

Free Methodists are not included because of the small number of usable cases.

Appendix 5.1
Motivations in Seeking Ordination

Percentage answering "quite important"

	Denominational Cluster					
	Congregation-Centered		Institution-Centered		Spirit-Centered	
	Women	Men	Women	Men	Women	Men
N =	1,213	1,026	953	787	300	259
a. Desire to serve God better	68%	63%	69%	70%	82%	79%
b. Conviction that God wished you ordained	58%	47%**	64%	62%	76%	77%
c. Official church legitimacy	47%	33%**	24%	18%**	60%	46%**
d. Desire to administer the sacraments	36%	17%**	50%	32%**	32%	26%
e. Change the sexist nature of the church	16%	2%	11%	1%	5%	0%
f. Needed ordination to get a paying job	27%	19%**	14%	8%	10%	4%
g. Encouragement from others	46%	36%*	44%	38%	30%	22%
h. To receive special power from God	5%	4%	5%	8%	16%	11%

Significant differences between men and women are as follows:
** = sig. .00001 and better
* = sig. .001 to .0002

Appendix 5.2
Age, the Call, and Seeking Ordination

Age at which first felt called	Denominational Clusters					
	Congregation-Centered		Institution-Centered		Spirit-Centered	
	Women	Men	Women	Men	Women	Men
N =	1,201	1,013	937	780	287	257
Age						
17 and younger	23%	37%	26%	40%	25%	42%
18 to 21	17%	29%	18%	34%	24%	32%
22 to 29	25%	23%	24%	16%	18%	20%
30 and older	35%	11%	32%	10%	33%	6%
	100%	100%	100%	100%	100%	100%
		**		**		**
Age at which first felt called by year ordained						
before 1980	23.0	19.2	21.8	18.3	21.5	17.7
1980–1985	26.6	21.0	23.9	21.0	25.5	21.4
1986 and later	28.0	23.5	26.1	20.7	30.0	19.1
Age at which first approached officials						
21 and younger	10%	30%	17%	46%	16%	35%
22 to 25	22%	34%	23%	26%	19%	29%
26 to 34	28%	25%	29%	20%	25%	27%
35 and older	40%	11%	31%	8%	40%	9%
	100%	100%	100%	100%	100%	100%
		**		**		**
Age at which first approached officials by year ordained						
before 1980	28.0	23.6	26.5	21.9	28.4	23.3
1980–1985	32.4	26.4	28.9	25.5	32.8	26.1
1986 and later	34.7	30.0	32.2	26.9	36.3	26.5

**Difference significant at .00001 or better.

Appendix 5.3
The Value of Seminary

	Denominational Cluster					
	Congregation-Centered		Institution-Centered		Spirit-Centered	
	Women	Men	Women	Men	Women	Men
N =	1,144	957	936	773	95	119
Percent saying "valuable" for						
a. strengthening faith	65%	62%	55%	58%	76%	72%
b. passing ordin. exams	57%	57%	78%	72%	68%	51%
c. being a good preacher	62%	61%	62%	65%	75%	75%
d. being good counselor	52%	52%	39%	45%	59%	48%
e. administrative skills	18%	18%	8%	13%	34%	29%
f. understanding issues facing women in ministry	23%	21%	21%	19%	16%	7%
Coping with/Confronting						
g. sexism	25%	25%	24%	22%	17%	11%
h. racism	24%	41%	24%	35%	17%	26%
i. class(ism)	16%	29%	16%	27%	19%	23%
j. preventing burnout in ministry	9%	9%	7%	7%	16%	22%
k. building a friendship network	50%	40%	46%	34%	49%	46%

Appendix 5.4
Attitudes about Ordination

	Disagree	Disagree	Agree
	"Women are changing the meaning of ordination."	"In the ideal church, there will no longer be a need for ordained ministry."	"More women should be ordained to full ministerial status in my denomination."

Congregation-Centered
Denominations

American Baptist Churches, Christian Ch. (DOC), United Ch. of Christ

women	34%	36%	72%
men	71%	53%	52%

Unitarian-Universalist Association

women	25%	60%	45%
men	65%	66%	48%

Church of the Brethren, Southern Baptist Convention

women	38%	25%	85%
men	57%	48%	40%

Institution-
Centered
Denominations

women	31%	48%	72%
men	63%	64%	46%

Spirit-
Centered
Denominations

women	74%	75%	70%
men	79%	69%	48%

Appendix 6.1
Professional Self-Concept and Employment Status

	Congregation-Centered Denominations		Institution-Centered Denominations		Spirit-Centered Denominations	
	Women	Men	Women	Men	Women	Men
Now over age 55	.17	.15	.13	.18	.17	.12
Year ordained (longer time ordained)	.08	.04	n.s.	n.s.	n.s.	.15
Works in congregation	n.s.	n.s.	n.s.	n.s.	n.s.	n.s.
Nonparish recognized work	n.s.	.13	n.s.	n.s.	n.s.	.17
Family Income (high to low)	.11	.14	.15	.11	.10	.15
Has thought seriously about leaving church job	−.38	−.39	−.38	−.39	−.36	−.39
Is not church-employed	−.13	−.11	−.12	−.12	−.14	−.11

All correlations given significant at .001 level.

Appendix 6.2
Clergy Who Have Thoughts of Leaving Paid Church-Recognized
Ministry and Clergy Actually Leaving Paid
Church-Recognized Ministry (by Gender and Denomination)

	Last year, sometimes or usually thought about leaving church-recognized ministry		Under 68 years old without paid church-recognized ministry	
	Women	Men	Women	Men
Congregation-Centered Denominations				
American Baptist Churches (w = 227, m = 183)	33%	30%	16%	7%
Christian Church (DOC) (w = 265, m = 204)	36%	27%	11%	7%
Church of the Brethren (w = 86, m = 61)	33%	21%	9%	15%
Southern Baptist Convention (w = 116, m = 107)	40%	24%	21%	4%
Unitarian-Universalist Association (w = 236, m = 242)	23%	26%	6%	12%
United Church of Christ (w = 283, m = 229)	38%	31%	12%	7%
Institution-Centered Denominations				
Episcopal Church (w = 236, m = 191)	23%	25%	11%	9%
Evangelical Lutheran Church in America (w = 254, m = 220)	31%	34%	7%	5%
Presbyterian Church (U.S.A.) (w = 252, m = 179)	31%	31%	12%	9%
U. Methodist Church (w = 211, m = 197)	44%	23%	14%	6%
Spirit-Centered Denominations				
Assemblies of God (w = 41, m = 14)	10%	21%	29%	0%

Church of God (Anderson, Ind.) (w = 67, m = 58)	18%	28%	25%	12%
Church of Nazarene (w = 128, m = 109)	23%	31%	19%	3%
Other Holiness (Free Meth., Wesleyan) (w = 64, m = 78)	15%	25%	8%	8%

Appendix 6.3

A. Factors Influencing Clergy Giving Serious Consideration to Leaving Ordained Ministry[1]

Clergy Women	Clergy Men
1. Poor overall health	1. Poor overall health
2. Weak professional self-concept	2. Weak professional self-concept
3. Younger on entering seminary	— —not significant— —
4. Do not feel sufficiently paid for ministerial work	3. Do not feel sufficiently paid for ministerial work
5. Not a member of a clergy support group	4. Not a member of a clergy support group
6. Do not believe it will be easy to get a better church position	— —not significant— —
7. Feel denominational executive does not recognize abilities	5. Feel denominational executive does not recognize abilities

B. Factors Influencing Clergy Who Are No Longer Serving in Any Paid Church Work

Clergy Women	Clergy Men
1. Not part of a clergy support group	1. Not part of a clergy support group
2. Seriously considered leaving ministry	2. Seriously considered leaving ministry
3. Do not believe it will be easy to get a better position	3. Do not believe it will be easy to get a better position
4. Feel the denominational executive does not recognize their abilities[2]	4. Feel the denominational executive does not recognize their abilities

[1]Appendix 6.3 is a regression analysis. Factors are listed in descending order of importance of each influence, considering the relative importance of other factors influencing clergy considering leaving paid ministry (A) or actually having left paid ministry (B). Factors are listed in descending order by strength of significant beta coefficients.

[2]The multiple r squared is .06 for women and .05 for men.

Appendix 6.4

Job Transitions of Clergy Women in Secular Employment in Their First, Second, and Third Jobs

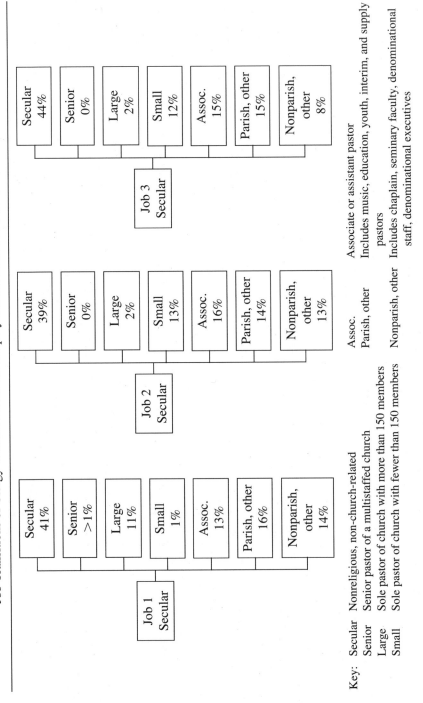

Key:
Secular	Nonreligious, non-church-related	
Senior	Senior pastor of a multistaffed church	
Large	Sole pastor of church with more than 150 members	
Small	Sole pastor of church with fewer than 150 members	
Assoc.	Associate or assistant pastor	
Parish, other	Includes music, education, youth, interim, and supply pastors	
Nonparish, other	Includes chaplain, seminary faculty, denominational staff, denominational executives	

Job 1 Secular
- Secular 41%
- Senior >1%
- Large 11%
- Small 1%
- Assoc. 13%
- Parish, other 16%
- Nonparish, other 14%

Job 2 Secular
- Secular 39%
- Senior 0%
- Large 2%
- Small 13%
- Assoc. 16%
- Parish, other 14%
- Nonparish, other 13%

Job 3 Secular
- Secular 44%
- Senior 0%
- Large 2%
- Small 12%
- Assoc. 15%
- Parish, other 15%
- Nonparish, other 8%

Appendix 6.5

Job Transitions of Clergy Men in Secular Employment in Their First, Second, and Third Jobs

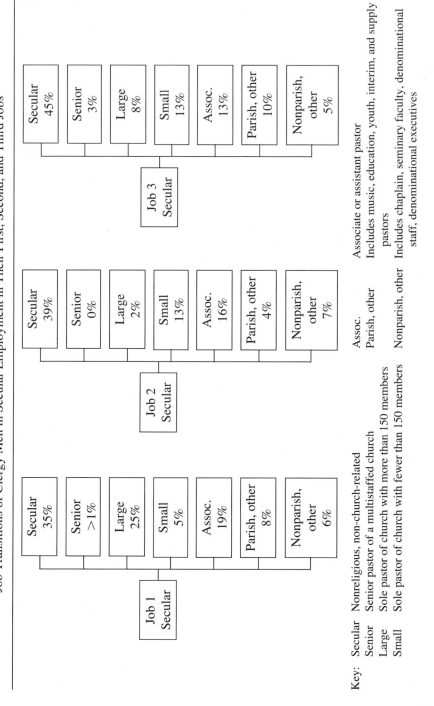

Job 1 Secular

Secular	35%
Senior	>1%
Large	25%
Small	5%
Assoc.	19%
Parish, other	8%
Nonparish, other	6%

Job 2 Secular

Secular	39%
Senior	0%
Large	2%
Small	13%
Assoc.	16%
Parish, other	4%
Nonparish, other	7%

Job 3 Secular

Secular	45%
Senior	3%
Large	8%
Small	13%
Assoc.	13%
Parish, other	10%
Nonparish, other	5%

Key:

Secular — Nonreligious, non-church-related
Senior — Senior pastor of a multistaffed church
Large — Sole pastor of church with more than 150 members
Small — Sole pastor of church with fewer than 150 members
Assoc. — Associate or assistant pastor
Parish, other — Includes music, education, youth, interim, and supply pastors
Nonparish, other — Includes chaplain, seminary faculty, denominational staff, denominational executives

Methodological Appendix

In 1993, the Center for Social and Religious Research at Hartford Seminary received a large grant from the Lilly Endowment, Inc., to study the status of ordained women in Protestantism in the United States. The central goal of the study was to assess the profession of ordained ministry as it is being lived out in the lives of clergy women in the 1990s and to understand how these patterns are the same as or different from those experienced by men. To this end, we designed a twenty-seven-page questionnaire that was sent to 9,894 male and female clergy in sixteen denominations: 5,095 were sent to men, with 2,170 responding, for a response rate of 42 percent; 4,799 were sent to women, with 2,668 responding, for a response rate of 55 percent. The overall response rate was 49 percent. The questionnaire gathered information on many aspects of clergy lives, both personal and professional.

RESEARCH DESIGN QUESTIONS

Denominations Included in the Study

This study originally included the following denominations: the American Baptist Churches,* the Assemblies of God, the Christian Church (Disciples of Christ),* the Church of the Brethren, the Church of the Nazarene, the Church of God (Anderson, Indiana), the Episcopal Church,* the Evangelical Lutheran Church in America,* the Free Methodist Church, the Presbyterian Church (U.S.A.),* the Reformed Church in America, the Southern Baptist Convention, the Unitarian-Universalist Association, the United Church of Christ,* the United Methodist Church,* and the Wesleyan Church. Of these sixteen, the Reformed Church in America handled its own mailing of the questionnaire. We were therefore unable to conduct targeted follow-ups for this denomination and subsequently received only twenty responses from the Reformed Church in America. This low response rate may be due to unobserved factors involved in the distribution of the questionnaire, or it may reflect the efficacy of our targeted follow-up procedures. In any event, we eventually decided to eliminate Reformed Church in America responses from most of our analyses because (1) we were not sure if this population had an equal opportunity to respond and (2) the low response rate introduced the possibility of an unobserved bias in the mailing procedures.

The remaining fifteen denominations include seven (marked by the asterisk) that were part of an earlier Hartford Seminary research study, *Women of the Cloth: A New Opportunity for Churches,* by Jackson W. Carroll, Barbara Hargrove, and Adair T. Lummis (San Francisco: Harper & Row, 1983). In the original *Women of the Cloth* nine denominations were studied, but since the completion of that research, the Presbyterian Church U.S. and The United Presbyterian Church in the U.S.A. merged to form the Presbyterian Church (U.S.A.) and the American Lutheran Church merged with the Lutheran Church in America and the Association of Evangelical Lutheran Churches (a small, breakaway group from the Lutheran Church–Missouri Synod) to form the Evangelical Lutheran Church in America, reducing the number of comparable denominations to seven.

The nine denominations in the *Women of the Cloth* study were chosen at that time because they represented a good cross section of Protestant mainline denominations with the largest representations of women clergy. Today, they are still some of the most active denominations that ordain women. The current project, however, seeks to broaden the study of clergy women to include denominations that are not studied as frequently as these by religious researchers. In this study, we have expanded the distribution of our survey to include denominations of dramatically different theologies, polities, and sizes. We have added smaller denominations, more conservative denominations, and one extremely important liberal denomination.

Unfortunately, our research does not include the historical black denominations (e.g., National Baptists, Progressive Baptists, Church of God in Christ, African Methodist Episcopal Church, African Methodist Episcopal Zion Church, and Christian Methodist Episcopal Church), although approximately one hundred African American clergy appear in our sample in the predominantly white denominations we studied. The decision not to include the black denominations in our study was made in consultation with researchers working on a large survey of African American women clergy concurrent with the fielding of our own questionnaire. We decided not to include historical black denominations to avoid the risk of potentially reducing the response rate of both studies for these groups.

Sample Design

To study the situation of female clergy, we include a comparison group of male clergy in each denomination. In each of these denominations, women represent a minority of the total clergy population (ranging from approximately 1 percent in the Free Methodist denomination to approximately 30 percent in the Unitarian-Universalist Association). This means that a random sampling of less than one thousand clergy from each denomination will not produce enough women for multivariate analysis. Therefore, to obtain a large number of female respondents from each denomination, we oversampled the number of women clergy. Although this solved our size problem, it introduces a proportional bias into the sample that is undesirable when there is an effort to make general comparisons between men and women on some items. To adjust for this skewed representation of women, we have obtained population figures of the proportion of men and women in each denominational group, so that we can weight the sample accordingly. (See Appendix 4.1, "Percentage of Clergy Women in Major Protestant Denominations [1994].")

Generally speaking, we sought a random sample of four hundred women and four hundred men from each denomination. We felt that even with a 50 percent response rate, this number would give us a reasonable number of men and women to perform multivariate analysis both within and across denominational and gender groups. Yet in almost half of our denominations, we found fewer than four hundred ordained women clergy in the entire denomination. In these cases, we asked the denomination for the entire list of women clergy and sent questionnaires to every ordained woman. We then sampled an equal number of men.

Random samples from the larger denominations were obtained with the cooperation of the research and ministry staff in each denomination. First, we asked that they separate their clergy lists into male and female groups and divide the total number in each group by four hundred to obtain some number "n." We then asked that they construct a random sample by selecting every "nth" name from their lists of men and women clergy to come up with a random sample of four hundred names each for male and female clergy. These procedures produced a random sample, stratified by sex and denomination.

Definitions of Clergy

An important concern in research on clergy is the question "Who is clergy?" Each denomination has its own way of defining ordination and ministry. In many denominations there is more than one kind of ordination, and the labels used across denominations vary considerably. For example, an "elder" in the Presbyterian Church (U.S.A.) is a lay person, whereas in the United Methodist Church, an "elder" is a fully ordained clergy man or woman. To make reasonable comparisons across denominations, we have followed the convention established by Constant Jacquet in his cross-denominational surveys of women clergy in 1977 and 1986. We asked denominations to sample only from their lists of "fully ordained" clergy—those who have been ordained "to the highest level of ministry carrying full rights and privileges within their church." (This definition of ordained ministry was developed by Constant H. Jacquet Jr., "Women Ministers in 1986 and 1977: A Ten Year View," *Yearbook of American and Canadian Churches* (1989), pp. 261–66.)

We also found that some denominations included retired and inactive clergy on their lists of ordained members. Since we felt that retired members were more likely to be men than women, we tried to minimize this bias by asking denominations to exclude retired and inactive clergy from their lists before sampling. This is difficult to do, because retirement is an elusive status in a clergy career. When

possible, we also asked for a sample that included only men who had been ordained after 1970. Recognizing that women were not ordained in large numbers
until the 1970s, we felt that such a male clergy sample would make our comparisons with women more accurate. Not all denominations were able to comply fully
with our requests; however, the widespread use of database technologies made it
possible for these requests to be met by the majority of the denominations involved
in our study.

Those who have left active ministry

For some research questions, we became aware that to generalize our findings
accurately so that we could say something about all ordained clergy, it would be
useful to survey ordained men and women who are no longer actively serving in
ministry positions, for reasons other than sickness or retirement. Literature on
clergy, especially women clergy, continually asks why ordained men or women
leave active ministry.

To answer this question, we actively sought a comparison group of persons who
were ordained and subsequently chose to leave the ministry. We discovered, however, that obtaining such a sample was extremely difficult. First, there are varying
ways to define "leaving the ministry." Only a small number of persons no longer
"working as clergy" cut all ties with their denomination by going through the bureaucratic procedures necessary to renounce their ordination. Some denominations ordain for life and do not have procedures for formally leaving ministry.
More often, clergy leave church work yet still feel committed to a ministry that is
independent of affiliations with institutionalized religion. Some clergy no longer
work in congregations but still work within their denomination as administrative
or executive staff in theological schools, hospitals, or other religious institutions.
"Dropping out of ministry" could mean any of these things to the respondents in
our survey.

To locate this comparison sample, we set out to find persons who had "left the
ministry"—defined as someone who no longer "worked directly for the church"
in a local congregation, denominational office, or agency of the church. Locating
such a sample proved to be extremely difficult. Many of these people are no longer
active in their denomination, and there is no record of their whereabouts. They
have lost interest in church and church work. They are no longer on lists of ordained persons. And even when we found some of these people, they had a low
interest level in completing our questionnaire.

We tried a number of strategies to elicit a response from this group. First, we
sought referrals from denominational offices. With the exception of the Evangelical Lutheran Church in America (ELCA), no denomination keeps easily accessible records on this population. Second, we wrote to all two hundred seminaries
affiliated with the Association of Theological Schools (ATS), requesting information on alumni/ae who have "left the ministry." We received a total of twenty
written replies from ATS schools—fourteen of them did not have access to such

information or could not access it readily. Six were able to give a limited response to our request. Unfortunately, most seminaries do not keep track of whether their graduates are ever ordained. Third, we placed advertisements in *Christian Century* and *Daughters of Sarah,* two widely read religious publications. These ads asked persons who had "left the ministry or church work" to contact us in order to participate in a study of ordained clergy. These ads produced about thirty-nine requests for questionnaires. Finally, we included a place on the questionnaire that we sent to clergy for them to list the names, addresses, and phone numbers of clergy who they personally knew had left the ministry. This proved to be the most successful strategy, resulting in 491 names and addresses of once-ordained men and women who, in some way, had "dropped out" of active or visible ministry. Our greatest response was from these personal networks, followed by a small number who responded to our ads. In total, we sent out 530 questionnaires to persons whom we defined as having left the ministry but received only fifty-seven complete responses in our final sample.

Most of these clergy who have left the ministry felt that our questions about ministry were no longer relevant to their lives. Therefore, because the questionnaire was geared toward persons currently active in ministry, we included a cover letter explaining why we needed help and why it was important for us to collect background information from those who are no longer in ministry. The commitment to filling out a lengthy survey about decisions that were often painful was limited, and our response rate for this subgroup was low. This experience shows us that future research efforts need to design instruments that specifically address the situations of these men and women in ways that are sensitive to the often conflicted emotions these persons have about the church and their experiences.

Finally, in analyzing our data, we were able to determine that 485 clergy in our sample (about 10 percent of the total) were persons under age sixty-eight with no paid church-related employment. This was 316 clergy women (12 percent of the women) and 169 (8 percent of the men). Some of these clergy were simply between jobs or taking time off from the workplace for family and the like. The data from this group, however, along with that from fifty-seven clergy who responded to our "dropout" mailing, gave us a sample of clergy who had sensitivity to issues of vocational stability in ministry.

Population parameters

To obtain the population parameters for weighting purposes, we asked each denomination to provide numbers of nonretired, fully ordained men and women. These numbers are the latest collection of figures on the number of women clergy in these denominations. In 1977 and 1986, Constant Jacquet also collected data on the numbers of ordained women from those Protestant denominations that were members of the National Council of Churches of Christ (NCCC) and ordained women. In collecting our numbers, we used the same criteria Jacquet used, namely, nonretired, highest-status, fully ordained clergy, so that we could compare our 1994 information with the number of ordained women in specific denominations at three points in time—1977, 1986, and 1994.

Researchers working with denominational statistics know the problems of collecting comparable statistical information across multiple denominations. For this study, a complicating factor was not only that many denominations have more than one definition of clergy but that they do not break down their counts of clergy in a corresponding fashion. We sometimes found that two offices within the same denomination reported widely different total numbers of fully ordained clergy. In the Episcopal Church, for example, the Office of Ministry initially reported approximately thirteen thousand clergy, while the Pension Board reported between six and seven thousand. We later found that the Pension Board bases its figures on participants in the denominational Pension Plan. Pension plan statistics, however, regularly underestimate the numbers of clergy because not all active clergy are members of a denominational pension program. Furthermore, samples based on such statistics have a systematic bias toward those who contribute to denominationally run retirement plans.

We also found that methods for counting clergy changed considerably between the time periods in which Jacquet collected his data (1977 and 1986) and that in which we asked for our samples (1993). The Assemblies of God reported a surprisingly high number of female clergy in 1986. When we compared these figures with the female clergy reported to us in 1993, we found the numbers had decreased significantly. Noting this anomaly, we contacted the statistician at the Assemblies of God and found that the 1986 number included all ordained females (despite Jacquet's request that they count only fully ordained women). Unfortunately, the majority of the female Assemblies of God clergy reported in 1986 were only locally ordained and did not possess the full rights and privileges of ministry. Similarly, in the United Methodist Church there were approximately thirty thousand United Methodist clergy in 1993, and this number is reported in their 1993 *Annual Minutes*. However, the United Methodist Church had reported only eighteen thousand fully ordained, nonretired clergy in 1986. Since it was unlikely that the number of clergy had almost doubled in seven years, we were able to explain the numbers by noting that the United Methodists changed their method for counting fully ordained clergy ("elders in full connection") in the intervening period.

Although we framed our request for numbers in exactly the same language used by Jacquet in 1977 and 1986, some of the figures we received were still suspect, showing unreasonable changes in the percentages of clergy over time. In each case, we went back to try to confirm the 1977, 1986, and 1994 numbers, sometimes concluding that the numbers came from different sources in different years. Given our interest in looking at trends in the growth or decline of women clergy over time, we asked denominational officials, where possible, to provide us with numbers of female clergy reported in 1977, 1986, and 1994 from the same source. In this way, we were able to maximize consistency over time at the expense of consistency across denominations. This means that in some cases we report numbers that differ from Jacquet's figures in 1977 and 1986.

Jacquet's groundbreaking study on women clergy and his statistics from 1977 and 1986 were published in the *Yearbook of American and Canadian Churches* (1989), and they have long been considered authoritative. They have been reprinted in numerous books, magazines, and articles and have never, to our collective knowledge, been seriously questioned. We respect Jacquet's report as an authoritative source within the field of religious scholarship and suggest that our statistical adjustments should be used as an alternative and supplemental source of data. The careful methods used in collecting our statistics lead us to believe that they are extremely reliable; however, we cannot vouch for the infallibility of the method. Sometimes, despite the most careful planning and wording of requests, sources have uncritically reported numbers they find in their publications or in other sources. Of the data reported in this study, the population figures should be treated with the most caution. Our rigorous methodical survey and the fact that we have rechecked figures with current denominational offices give us confidence that the majority of the figures in this volume are the best figures available for reporting trends on ordained women and men over time in specific denominations. (See Appendix 1.2, "Changing Numbers of Clergy in Major Protestant Denominations.")

DATA COLLECTION

Questionnaire

The questionnaire used in this study was lengthy and detailed (twenty-seven pages). We seriously weighed the relative merits of a more manageable, shorter questionnaire in relation to our response rate. After much consultation and multiple pretests with small focus groups, we opted for the longer questionnaire and made a commitment to devote extra resources to follow-up management. Our decision was influenced by the scale of our effort and our recognition that it was unlikely other studies of this scope or depth would be supported in the near future. We felt that it was important to gather data that would be useful to current and future populations of ordained clergy. We also felt that the opportunity to obtain longitudinal data by replicating key questions from the *Women of the Cloth* (1983) study should be not be missed, even though it lengthened the questionnaire. Finally, we hoped that by designing the questionnaire in an attractive fashion, with strategic uses of white space and frequent opportunities to add individual comments, clergy would be engaged with our project and motivated to take the time and effort to be a part of our study.

Mailing Procedures

The questionnaires, each with a stamped, self-addressed return envelope, were first mailed in the fall of 1993. The mailing of the questionnaires was timed so that they would arrive after the summer holidays and prior to the Thanksgiving and Christmas holiday rush. A month later, we sent a follow-up letter and a second questionnaire. In addition, we sought to increase the commitment of clergy to our study by asking denominational executives to write a letter, on denominational stationery, validating the importance of our work and adding their request that clergy take the time to respond. The letter was sent to us, and we reproduced it and sent it out to all clergy at approximately the same time as the second follow-up mailing. We believe that this official support greatly enhanced our response rate.

Interviews

In addition to the questionnaires, we supplemented our survey with a number of short and long semistructured telephone interviews. Interviewees were chosen from a self-selected sample of survey respondents who indicated a willingness to be further interviewed by telephone.

Short interviews were conducted by research assistants and averaged between ten and thirty minutes. These involved 124 clergy women and the same number of clergy men, distributed over all of the denominations in the study. Those who were called were asked to respond to five open-ended questions on the meaning of ordination, strategies of the job search, the differences between male and female clergy, the greatest challenges faced in ministerial life, and the message they most wanted denominational executives to hear from their stories.

To explore some issues in depth, the principal investigators also interviewed thirty clergy (twenty-six women and four men) in longer depth interviews, lasting anywhere from forty-five minutes to an hour and a half and covering many topics also covered in the questionnaire.

Lay Survey

Recognizing that lay opinions about clergy are important, we developed a separate, shorter questionnaire to send to a limited number of lay persons. We wanted the perspectives of lay leaders who had contact with clergy and were in a good position to evaluate and understand the work of clergy.

The difficulties of identifying a lay population able to comment knowledgeably on the issues in our study were great. Following methodologies first used by Edward C. Lehman in his studies of the American Baptists in "Project S.W.I.M.: A Study of Women in Ministry" (Valley Forge, Pa.: Task Force on Women in Ministry of the American Baptist Churches, 1979); by the United Presbyterians in "The Minister at Large Program: An Evaluation" (report issued by the Vocation Agency, The United Presbyterian Church in the U.S.A., May 1981); and by Jackson W. Carroll, Barbara Hargrove, and Adair T. Lummis in *Women of the Cloth: A New Opportunity for Churches* (San Francisco: Harper & Row, 1983), their study of clergy women, we asked the clergy women in our short telephone interviews if they would be willing to distribute a small number of surveys to lay members within their congregation. The 248 clergy who agreed to do this were sent five lay questionnaires each to be distributed to key lay leaders, as defined by functional position. For example, lay questionnaires were given to moderators, church school superintendents, and heads of various committees in each local congregation. As a consequence, 1,240 lay leaders were asked to complete a lay leaders' survey and return it to us directly in a self-addressed, stamped envelope provided with the questionnaire. In the end, six hundred were returned (351 from women, 243 from men, with 6 failing to indicate gender), for a response rate of slightly under 50 percent.

This method of distribution was both the most economical and the most practical. However, there is an obvious self-selection in the clergy who agreed to distribute questionnaires. We sought to reduce the selection bias by specifying (by office or official role) the lay leaders who were to be asked to complete the questionnaire.

Notes

CHAPTER 1: A NEW SITUATION

1. In the original sample, sixteen denominations were surveyed. We later decided to exclude responses from the Reformed Church in America because they could not conform with our follow-up protocol, creating a bias in the data. (See Appendix 1.1.)
2. Constant H. Jacquet Jr. "Women Ministers in 1986 and 1977: A Ten Year View," in *Yearbook of American and Canadian Churches* (1989), pp. 261–66.
3. The Reformed Church in America self-mailed the survey instruments and did not participate in the follow-up reminders. The Assemblies of God agreed only to send us the names of one hundred male and one hundred female clergy. Both decisions resulted in a low response from these denominations.
4. These figures are distinct from those of female "religious worker," which is also a designated category within the U.S. Census.
5. Reliable trend data for even this small subset of denominations are extremely difficult to collect. Our main sources for the data from 1977 and 1986 are Constant Jacquet's reports in the *Yearbook of American and Canadian Churches* (1977, 1986). In 1994 we called denominational offices directly to collect current data, using Jacquet's defining criteria. Realizing that some of the resulting trends seemed implausible, we rechecked numbers for the Assemblies of God, the Presbyterian Church (U.S.A.), the United Methodist Church, the Episcopal Church, and the United Church of Christ and consequently readjusted some of Jacquet's reported figures for 1977 and 1986. Because our interest is in showing trends over time, we sought to collect data from the same sources for all three time points. Thus, if we found that reporting conventions changed between 1977, 1986, and 1994, we returned to the denominational sources and constructed a consistent reporting scheme for all three time points. This strategy maximizes consistency in the changes reported over time rather than across denominations.
6. See Appendix 1.2 for reported numbers of male and female clergy by denomination.
7. Our numbers include only those clergy with full status, rights, and privileges of ordained clergy. Many denominations have two or more lower levels of ordination that are not included among these numbers. Probably, a higher percentage of women are ordained at these levels.
8. These figures reflect the number of students enrolled in graduate theological education, not the number of those specifically preparing for ordained ministry. It is likely that a higher percentage of the women enrolled may be on nonprofessional career

tracks. *Fact Book on Theological Education* (Pittsburgh: Association of Theological Schools in the United States and Canada), for various years.

9. Barbara Brown Zikmund, "The Struggle for the Right to Preach," in Rosemary Radford Ruether and Rosemary Skinner Keller, eds., *Women and Religion in America: The Nineteenth Century,* vol. 1 (San Francisco: Harper & Row, 1981), pp. 191–241.

10. From a telephone interview with a Church of the Brethren clergy woman.

11. Pamela Brubaker, *She Hath Done What She Could* (Elgin, Ill: Brethren Press, 1985).

12. From a telephone interview with a Southern Baptist clergy woman. See also Nancy Tatom Ammerman, *Baptist Battles: Social Change and Religious Conflict in the Southern Baptist Convention* (New Brunswick, N.J.: Rutgers University Press, 1990), pp. 89–99.

13. From a telephone interview with a Presbyterian clergy man.

14. Barbara Brown Zikmund, "Winning Ordination in Mainstream Protestantism: 1900–1965," in Rosemary Radford Ruether and Rosemary Skinner Keller, eds., *Women and Religion in America: The Twentieth Century,* vol. 3 (San Francisco: Harper & Row, 1985), pp. 339–83.

15. Susie C. Stanley has done extensive work on Wesleyan Holiness women. See her chapter "The Promise Fulfilled: Women's Ministries in the Wesleyan/Holiness Movement," in Catherine Wessinger, ed., *Religious Institutions and Women's Leadership: New Roles inside the Mainstream* (Columbia: University of South Carolina Press, 1996), pp. 137–57. See also Juanita Evans Leonard, ed., *Called to Minister: Empowered to Serve* (Anderson, Ind: Warner Press, 1989); and Rebecca Laird, *Ordained Women in the Church of the Nazarene: The First Generation* (Kansas City, Mo.: Nazarene Publishing House, 1993).

16. R. Eugene Sterner, "Women in the Church of God," in *The Role of Women in Today's World: Six Study Papers* (Anderson, Ind.: Commission on Social Concerns, Church of God, 1978), p. 15, quoted in Stanley, "The Promise Fulfilled," p. 150.

17. Paul Bassett, "The Fundamentalist Leavening of the Holiness Movement, 1914–1940: The Church of the Nazarene—A Case Study," *Wesleyan Theological Journal* 13, no. 1 (1978): 65–91. Two historical resources are useful in understanding the relationship of Calvinist, Reformed-based fundamentalism to women in the church: Margaret Lamberts Bendroth, *Fundamentalism and Gender: 1875 to the Present* (New Haven, Conn.: Yale University Press, 1993); and Betty A. DeBerg, *UnGodly Women: Gender and the First Wave of American Fundamentalism* (Minneapolis: Fortress Press, 1990). See also Janette Hassey, *No Time for Silence: Evangelical Women in Public Ministry around the Turn of the Century* (Grand Rapids: Zondervan Publishing House, 1986).

18. See Stanley M. Burgess and Gary B. McGee, eds., *Dictionary of Pentecostal and Charismatic Movements* (Grand Rapids: Zondervan Publishing House, 1988).

19. See articles in Ruth Wallace, ed., *Feminism and Sociological Theory* (Newbury Park, Calif.: Sage Publications, 1989), esp. Ruth Wallace, "Introduction," pp. 23–33; Jessie Bernard, "The Dissemination of Feminist Thought," pp. 23–33; and Janet S. Chafetez, "Gender Equality: Toward a Theory of Change," pp. 135–60. The quotation is from Bernard, p. 25.

20. "Feminists" come in many varieties, and the types and the names given to the types overlap. Feminists can differ in whether they see women and men as basically equal in abilities or whether they believe women have superior innate qualities of personality compared to men. (Sometimes this dichotomy is called "minimalist" versus "max-

imalist" feminism, or "structural" versus "cultural" feminism.) Those who are called "liberal feminists" simply want the same opportunities and requirements that men have, whereas those who are called "cultural feminists" believe that women's innate higher nature should prevail in society, and that special treatment should be accorded women to help them assert leadership and protect them from those who would exploit or debase them because of their gender. Those who are called "radical feminists" are similar to "cultural feminists" but are more militantly opposed to all or most social systems designed by men. Some feminists believe that the social institutions and systems in place are basically good and have simply been subverted by men for their own advantage—a problem that can be corrected by seeing that women have equal access to leadership positions and other rewards within these institutions and systems. These feminists are sometimes termed "democratic" or "equal rights" feminists. Other feminists believe that the inequity between women and men has been created by these very institutions and systems; therefore, the systems must change before real equality can exist between women and men. "Socialist feminists" make some alterations in the systems and institutions, whereas "Marxist feminists" want to overthrow systems and institutions and start again. These distinctions are further specified, redefined, and blurred when racial, ethnic, and national cultural (e.g., African American, Asian, Hispanic, etc.) versions of feminism are taken into account and become even more varied and elusive when religious values and identities are added.

These definitions and delineations of various kinds of feminists have been developed by Sheila Briggs, "Women and Religion," in Beth M. Hess and Myra Marx Feree, eds., *Analyzing Gender: A Handbook of Social Science Research* (Newbury Park, Calif.: Sage Publications, 1987), pp. 408–41; and in Maria Riley, *Transforming Feminism* (Kansas City, Mo: Sheed & Ward, 1989). Comparisons of the cultural differences inherent in various "feminist theologies" formed through the experiences of women of different races and on different continents are described in Letty M. Russell and J. Shannon Clarkson, eds., *Dictionary of Feminist Theologies* (Louisville, Ky.: Westminster John Knox Press, 1996), pp. 99–120.

21. Feminist spirituality, in Sandra Schneiders's construct, asks women not only to question the underrepresentation of women in social and sacred leadership positions but to challenge male-dominated theology and the conception of God as exclusively male in physical image. Feminist spirituality also has a strong focus on women taking a major role in transforming all social structures, not only to be more inclusive of women but to work for social justice for women and men of all races, nationalities, and socioeconomic locations. See Sandra Schneiders, *Beyond Patching: Faith and Feminism in the Catholic Church* (Mahwah, N.J.: Paulist Press, 1991), pp. 80–110.

22. The seven denominations in which clergy women and clergy men were surveyed in both 1980–81 and 1993–94 are American Baptists, Christian Church (Disciples of Christ), Episcopal Church, Evangelical Lutheran Church in America (previously three Lutheran denominations), the Presbyterian Church (U.S.A.) (previously two Presbyterian denominations), the United Church of Christ, and the United Methodist Church.

23. Jackson W. Carroll, Barbara Hargrove, and Adair T. Lummis, *Women of the Cloth: A New Opportunity for Churches* (New York: Harper & Row, 1983), pp. 93–103 and p. 209.

24. Joy Charlton, "What It Means to Go First: Clergywomen of the Pioneer Generation" (paper presented at the annual meetings of the Society for the Scientific Study of Religion and the Religious Research Association, St. Louis, October 1995).

25. Miriam Therese Winter, Adair T. Lummis, and Allison Stokes, *Defecting in Place: Women Claiming Responsibility for Their Own Spiritual Lives* (New York: Crossroad, 1994).
26. Catherine Wessinger, "Women's Religious Leadership in the United States," in Wessinger, ed., *Religious Institutions and Women's Leadership,* pp. 3–36.
27. Winter, Lummis, and Stokes, *Defecting in Place,* pp. 177–93 passim.
28. See Edward Lehman, *Gender and Work: The Case of the Clergy* (Albany: State University of New York Press, 1993), pp. 52–53.
29. Suzanne Radley Hiatt, "Women's Ordination in the Anglican Communion: Can This Church Be Saved?" in Wessinger, ed., *Religious Institutions and Women's Leadership,* pp. 211–27, esp. pp. 222–23.
30. Susan Kwilecki, "Contemporary Pentecostal Clergywomen: Female Christian Leadership, Old Style," *Journal of Feminist Studies in Religion* 3 (fall 1987): 57–75.
31. For example, see the review discussion concerning negative sanctions faced by uppity, feminist Presbyterian clergy women in Rebecca Prichard, "Grandes Dames, Femmes Fortes, and Matrones: Reformed Women Ministering," in Wessinger, ed., *Religious Institutions and Women's Leadership,* pp. 39–57.
32. Margaret Poloma, *The Assemblies of God at the Crossroads: Charisma and Institutional Dilemmas* (Knoxville: University of Tennessee Press, 1989), pp. 101–21.
33. Not only did women in the Spirit-centered denominations lose influence and autonomy to men in the transition from prophetic to priestly leadership, but without equal access to graduate-level seminary education, they were unlikely to challenge the culture of this denominational cluster, which traditionally affirms women only in a supportive role to men. See Stanley, "Promise Fulfilled," pp. 139–57.
34. Ammerman, *Baptist Battles,* pp. 134–43; and Carolyn Dearmond Blevins, "Women and the Baptist Experience," in Wessinger, ed., *Religious Institutions and Women's Leadership,* pp.158–79.

CHAPTER 2: A COMPLEX LIFE

1. For example, see David R. Covell Jr., *Who Do Men Say That I Am?* (New York: Strategic Research Services Group, Executive Council of the Episcopal Church, 1970); Yoshio Fukuyma, *The Ministry in Transition* (University Park: Pennsylvania State University Press, 1972); Gerald J. Jud, Edgar W. Mills Jr., and Genevieve Walters Burch, *Ex-Pastors: Why Men Leave the Parish Ministry* (Philadelphia: Pilgrim Press, 1970); and Donald P. Smith, *Clergy in the Crossfire* (Philadelphia: Westminster Press, 1972).
2. Jackson Carroll, *As One with Authority: Reflective Leadership in Ministry* (Louisville, Ky.: Westminster/John Knox Press, 1991), pp. 21–23.
3. Teresa Marciano, "Corporate Church, Ministry and Ministerial Family: Embedded Employment and Measures of Success," *Marriage and Family Review* 15 (1990): 171–93.
4. Psychologist Edwin Friedman speaks of the necessity for clergy to engage in "self-differentiation" from the clergy role and set clear boundaries between work for the church and their lives as family members and individuals. See Edwin H. Friedman, *Generation to Generation: Family Process in Church and Synagogue* (New York: Guilford Press, 1985), pp. 246–47.

5. The correlation between being married and the ability to manage boundaries well is not significant for men; for women, the correlation is only .08, significant at .001 level.

6. Edward Lehman, *Gender and Work: The Case of the Clergy* (Albany: State University of New York Press, 1993), p. 192.

7. See Tom Owen-Towle, "Reflections on Marriage," and Carole Owen-Towle, "Ministry and Marriage," in Denise D. Tracy, ed., *Wellsprings: Sources in Unitarian Universalist Feminism* (Oak Park, Ill.: Delphi Resources, 1992), pp. 121–27.

8. The correlation between working and having a spouse who works full-time, part-time, or not at all outside the home, on the one hand, and one's own boundary maintenance ability, on the other, is not significant for clergy men and only .09 for clergy women, significant at the .001 level.

9. The correlations between having any children under age nineteen at home and scores on the ability to handle role and time conflicts between church and family, as measured by our Boundary Maintenance Index, are: for clergy women -.16, for clergy men -.14, both significant at the .001 level.

10. See Catherine Wessinger, ed., *Religious Institutions and Women's Leadership: New Roles inside the Mainstream* (Columbia: University of South Carolina Press, 1996), p. 13, and Rebecca Prichard, "Grandes Dames, Femmes Fortes, and Matrones: Reformed Women Ministering," in Wessinger, ed., *Religious Institutions and Women's Leadership,* p. 49, describe the tendency of younger male clergy to want time from the congregation to be a parent to their children.

11. For example, among the single clergy surveyed, 53 percent of the women and 45 percent of the men have total annual incomes under $25,000, while only 18 percent and 26 percent of the single women and men, respectively, have total incomes of $40,000 and over a year. But among married clergy, the discrepancy between women and men is greater, especially in the higher income brackets—favoring clergy women. Among the married clergy surveyed, only 16 percent of the women and 19 percent of the men have family incomes under $25,000, and fully 59 percent of the women and 45 percent of the men have family incomes of $40,000 a year or more.

12. Edward C. Lehman, *Women Clergy: Breaking through Gender Barriers* (New Brunswick, N.J.: Transaction Books, 1985), pp. 238–41.

13. Julie A. Kanaar, "Survey of Clergy Women Serving in Rural Areas" (report produced for the Division for Outreach and the Commission for Women, Evangelical Lutheran Church in America, Chicago, October 1994).

14. Allison Stokes, "Editor's Preface" and "Conclusion: The Clergywomen and the Laypeople in Relationship," in the Berkshire Clergywomen and Allison Stokes, *Women Pastors* (New York: Crossroad, 1995), pp. ix–xi, 153–64, esp. pp. ix and 159.

15. This quotation comes from a lay leader who responded to another survey sent to a sample of readers of feminist journals or members of feminist organizations; see the survey by Miriam Therese Winter, Adair T. Lummis, and Allison Stokes, *Defecting in Place: Women Taking Responsibility for Their Own Spiritual Lives* (New York: Crossroad, 1994). The quotation was not used in the book. Lesbian clergy surveyed for that study also reported painful experiences in their congregations; see p. 47.

16. Quoted from 1985 ever-divorced statistics obtained by the Associated Press in 1995.

17. Strat Douthat, the Associated Press, "Clergy 'divorce rate same as laity', study finds," *The Orange County Register,* Santa Ana, Calif., Saturday, July 8, 1995, p. Metro 9.

18. J. Michael Parker, "When Pastors Face Divorce," *San Antonio ExpressNews,* January 20, 1996, pp. B 9–10.

19. Blizzard, who died in 1979, looked at these pastoral roles in seven Protestant denominations. A compilation of his major findings, edited by his wife, was published in 1985. See Samuel W. Blizzard, *The Protestant Parish Minister: A Behavioral Science Interpretation*, Society for the Scientific Study of Religion Monograph series 5 (Storrs, Conn.: Society for the Scientific Study of Religion, 1985), pp. 83–109.

20. Clergy over age fifty-five scores: high scores on ability to set clear boundaries = women .20, men .14, significant at .001; and high scores on overall health = women .28, men .l9, significant at .001.

21. See Paula Nesbitt, "First and Second-Career Clergy: Influences of Age and Gender on the Career-Stage Paradigm," *Journal for the Scientific Study of Religion* 34 (June l995): 152–71; and idem, "Marriage, Parenthood and the Ministry: Differential Effects of Marriage and Family on Male and Female Clergy Careers," *Sociology of Religion* 56 (winter l995): 397–416.

22. Among the authors who make this point are Friedman, *Generation to Generation,* p. 27; Lloyd Retiger, *Coping with Clergy Burnout* (Valley Forge, Pa.: Judson Press, l981), pp. 100–105; Elizabeth J. Norell, "Clergy Family Satisfaction: A Review," *Family Science Review* 4 (l989): 69–93; and, most recently, James C. Fenhagen, with Celia Alison Hahn, *Ministry for a New Time* (Washington, D.C: Alban Institute, 1995). These findings are also part of research done by Roberta Walmsley and Adair Lummis for the Episcopal Clergy Family Project, supported by funds from the Trinity Grants Board, the Church Pension Group, the National Episcopal Church, and participating dioceses.

23. Fenhagen, *Ministry for a New Time,* p. 114.

24. The correlations of our four indexes with overall health for clergy women and clergy men are as follows:

	Women	Men
Structural Feminism	−.15	not significant
Spiritual Feminism	−.17	not significant
Boundary Maintenance	.42	.40
Professional Self-Concept	.51	.56

25. The correlation between overall health and structural feminism is -.20 for clergy women in the Spirit-centered denominations but only -.08 for clergy women in the other denominational clusters.

CHAPTER 3: A RELIGIOUS LEADER

1. Martha Ellen Stortz, *PastorPower* (Nashville: Abingdon Press, 1993), pp. 41–42.

2. Jackson W. Carroll, *As One with Authority: Reflective Leadership in Ministry* (Louisville, Ky.: Westminster/John Knox Press, 1991), pp. 30–32.

3. Mission Discernment Project, *To Seek and to Serve: Congregations in Mission* (Cincinnati: Forward Movement Publication, l991), p. 65.

4. Judy Roesner, "Ways Women Lead," *Harvard Business Review* (November–December 1990): 119–25.

5. Stortz, *PastorPower,* pp.109–22, esp. p. 122.

6. Ibid., pp. 108–9.

7. Judy Roesner concludes, drawing from surveys and interviews with women and men executives, that the "second wave of female executives" does not feel constrained to copy the male, transactional command-and-control style of leadership. Rather, as women achieve top executive positions and exercise leadership in these positions, they use a transformational, "interactive" leadership style. Roesner notes that women who use this style "encourage participation, share power and information, enhance other people's self-worth, and get others excited about their work." See Roesner, "Ways Women Lead," p. 120.

   Interpreting her interviews with elite clergy women, Martha Long Ice agrees, "Whereas leadership may be imaged by men as a high position in a hierarchy of command and dominance, women often image leadership more naturally as a central facilitating position in a network of peer-negotiated operations" (*Clergy Women and Their World Views: Calling for a New Age* [New York: Praeger Publishers, 1987], p. 4). This interpretation of women's leadership style is supported by Edward Lehman's 1993 survey results on female and male pastors in four mainline liberal Protestant denominations. Lehman found that although a number of stereotypical differences between clergy women and clergy men did not hold in his study, one did: "More women than men sought to empower their congregation to define their own objectives and find their own ways to pursue them" (*Gender and Work: The Case of the Clergy* [Albany: State University of New York Press, 1993], p. 79).

   According to Ruth Wallace, women "pastors" seem to be accepted by parishioners, even in a denomination strongly opposed to their ordained leadership, because of their leadership style. In her study of priestless Catholic parishes, laity welcome the feeling of inclusion that woman pastors provide through their "collaborative" leadership style. See Ruth Wallace, *They Call Her Pastor* (Albany: State University of New York Press, 1992), pp. 77–85, 153–62.

8. Lehman, *Gender and Work,* pp. 57–66.

9. Mary Clair Klein, "The Influence of Gender on Pastoral Leadership Style," *On the Way* 11 (winter 1994–95): 25–37. See note 7, above, for references to the studies by Lehman and Wallace.

10. Leslie J. Francis and Mandy Robbins, "Differences in the Personality Profile of Stipendiary and Non-Stipendiary Female Anglican Parochial Clergy in Britain and Ireland," *Contact: The Interdisciplinary Journal of Pastoral Studies* 119 (1996): 26–32.

11. Carroll, *As One with Authority*, pp. 22–25, 77–78.

12. Lehman, *Gender and Work,* pp. 134–38.

13. We examined responses to our survey, assessing leadership style by the age at which clergy began seminary as well as current age, on the one hand, and leadership style by current age, controlling for whether these clergy graduated from seminary before or after 1981, on the other hand. Although age at the time of entering seminary has no effect on a pastor's present leadership style, current age does.

14. Lehman, *Gender and Work,* p. 101.

15. Ibid., p. 103.

16. Ibid., pp. 171–77.

17. See Edward C. Lehman, *Women Clergy: Breaking through Gender Barriers* (New Brunswick, N. J.: Transaction Books, 1985); idem, *Women Clergy in England: Sexism, Modern Consciousness and Church Viability* (Lewiston, N.Y.: Edward Mellen Press, 1987); idem, *Gender and Work;* and idem, *Women in Ministry: Receptivity and Resistance* (Melbourne: Joint Board of Christian Education, 1994).

18. It is generally agreed that a strong professional self-concept or self-image helps practitioners deal with the inevitable conflicts and strains in their work settings and retain commitment to their chosen occupation in times of duress. See a review of studies that support this judgment in Jackson Carroll, Barbara Hargrove, and Adair Lummis, *Women of the Cloth: A New Opportunity for Churches* (New York: Harper & Row, 1983), pp. 141–42.

19. John L. Verburg, "Job Satisfaction among Ministers" (paper presented at the annual meetings of the Society for the Scientific Study of Religion and the Religious Research Association, St. Louis, October 1995).

20. Joyce Piper, "Work Stress among Lutheran Clergy Women in the USA and Norway" (paper delivered at the annual meetings of the Society for the Scientific Study of Religion and the Religious Research Association, St. Louis, October 1995).

21. Roberta Walmsley and Adair Lummis, *Healthy Clergy, Wounded Healers: Their Families and Their Ministries* (New York: Church Publishing Corporation, 1997).

22. Even in the 1990s, women seminarians may not feel as affirmed in pursuing a Master of Divinity degree as men do. See Jennifer Butler, "Gender Perspectives on Princeton Theological Seminary: An Attitude Inventory and Analysis of Gender Inclusion" (unpublished student paper, April 14, 1995).

CHAPTER 4: A JOB

1. Data for 1910–40 are from working paper 5; 1950 and 1960 data are from technical paper 18; 1970 data are from *1970 Census of the Population;* 1980 data are from *1980 Census of Population;* and 1990 data are from Equal Employment Opportunity special Tabulations File. Specific citations are as follows: U.S. Bureau of the Census, *The Relationship between the 1970 and 1980 Industry and Occupation Classification Systems,* technical paper 59 (Washington, D.C.: U.S. Government Printing Office, 1989); John Priebe, Joan Heinkel, and Stanley Greene, *1970 Occupation and Industry Classification Systems in Terms of Their 1960 Occupation and Industry Elements,* technical paper 26 (Washington, D.C.: U.S. Government Printing Office, 1972); David Kaplan and M. Claire Casey, *Occupational Trends in the United States 1900–1950,* working paper 5 (Washington, D.C.: U.S. Government Printing Office, 1958); John Priebe, *Changes between the 1950 and 1960 Occupation and Industry Classifications,* technical paper 18 (Washington, D.C.: U.S. Government Printing Office, 1968); U.S. Bureau of the Census, *Census of Population and Housing, 1990* (Washington, D.C.: U.S. Government Printing Office, 1990); Equal Employment Opportunity (EEO) Supplemental Tabulations File (machine-readable data files prepared by the U.S. Bureau of the Census, Washington, D.C., 1993); U.S. Bureau of the Census, *Census of the Population, 1970: Detailed Characteristics, United States Summary* (Washington, D.C.: U.S. Government Printing Office, 1973); U.S. Bureau of the Census, *Census of the Population, 1980: Detailed Characteristics, United States Summary* (Washington, D.C.: U.S. Government Printing Office, 1984).

2. Mark Chaves, "Ordaining Women: The Diffusion of an Organizational Innovation," *American Journal of Sociology* 101 (January 4, 1996): 840–73.

3. When examining the annual earnings of clergy, we consider total compensation. Our survey asked respondents to report their actual cash salary plus the estimated value of their benefits—e.g., housing, car, and educational allowance. Since such benefits are traditionally part of clergy compensation, it is realistic to combine these figures in estimates

of earnings. Furthermore, because of the tax laws regulating clergy compensation, most ordained persons have a fairly reliable estimate of the dollar amount of such benefits.

4. These estimates incorporate population weights to adjust for the oversampling of women in our survey. We also use Huber regression to adjust for cluster sampling within each denomination.

5. Measured by the average weekly attendance at Sunday worship.

6. Trond Petersen and Laurie A. Morgan. 1995. "Separate and Unequal: Occupational-Establishment Sex Segregation and the Gender Wage Gap," *American Journal of Sociology* 101 (2, September): 329–65.

7. Edward C. Lehman, "Organizational Resistance to Women in Ministry," *Sociological Analysis* 42 (2) (1981): 101–18, and "Research of Lay Members Attitudes Towards Women in Ministry: An Assessment," *Review of Religious Research* 28 (4) (1987): 319–29.

8. Arthur L. Stinchcombe, *Information and Organizations* (Berkeley: University of California Press, 1990).

9. Elin Kvande and Bente Rasmussen, "Women's Careers in Static and Dynamic Organizations," *Acta Sociologica* 38 (1995): 115–30.

10. See James W. Fraser, *Schooling the Preachers: The Development of Protestant Theological Education in the United States, 1740–1875* (Lanham, Md.: University Press of America, 1988); and Glenn T. Miller, *Piety and Intellect: The Aims and Purposes of Ante-Bellum Theological Education* (Atlanta: Scholars Press, 1990).

11. Note that the 9 percent overall gap is an average of all denominations and does not distinguish between denominations with specific kinds of placement or employment systems.

12. In the Episcopal Church and the Evangelical Lutheran Church in America, the first job is generally handled by appointment procedures and subsequent jobs are likely to be obtained through an open search process.

13. We are indebted to Jackson Carroll, Director of Ormond Research Center at Duke Divinity School, ordained Methodist pastor; William Lawrence, also of the Ormond Center; Barbara Troxell, former superintendent of the United Methodist Church, currently a professor at Garrett-Evangelical Theological Seminary, for information regarding placement policies in the United Methodist Church.

14. Paula D. Nesbitt, "Marriage, Parenthood and the Ministry: Differential Effects of Marriage on Male and Female Clergy Careers," *Sociology of Religion* 56 (winter 1995): 397–419.

15. Ibid.

CHAPTER 5: A CALLING

1. Jackson W. Carroll, Barbara Hargrove, and Adair T. Lummis, *Women of the Cloth: A New Opportunity for Churches* (New York: Harper & Row, 1983), 93–103.

2. The seven denominations in which clergy women and clergy men were surveyed both in 1980–81 and in 1993–94 are the American Baptist Churches, the Christian Church (Disciples of Christ), the Episcopal Church, the Evangelical Lutheran Church in America (previously three Lutheran denominations), the Presbyterian Church (U.S.A.) (previously two Presbyterian denominations), the United Church of Christ, and the United Methodist Church.

3. Christopher Jencks and David Reisman discuss the reasons behind the establishment

of university seminaries, requiring a four-year college degree to enter, and the expansion of this requirement to even independent and denominational seminaries in *The Academic Revolution* (Garden City, N.Y.: Doubleday & Co., 1968), pp. 209–11, 254.

4. Paula D. Nesbitt, *The Feminization of Clergy in America: Organizational and Occupational Perspectives* (New York: Oxford University Press, 1997).

5. Correlations between the responses to three statements:

A. "Women are changing the meaning of ordination" and "More women should be ordained to full ministerial status in my denomination."

		Congregation-Centered			Institution-Centered	Spirit-Centered
TOTALS		Am. Bap. Christian/ DoC, & UCC	Unitar.- Univer.	Breth. & So. Bap.		
Women		+.12**	+.09*	+.13ns	+.16ns	+.21**	+.09
Men		−.09*	+.00ns	−.04ns	−.33*	−.10*	−.15*

B. "In the ideal church, there will no longer be a need for ordained ministry" and "Women are changing the meaning of ordination."

		Congregation-Centered			Institution-Centered	Spirit-Centered
TOTALS		Am. Bap. Christian/ DOC, & UCC	Unitar.- Univer.	Breth. & So. Bap.		
Women	+.25**	+.28**	+.34**	+.10ns	+.21**	+.12ns
Men	+.07**	+.06ns	+.17ns	−.00ns	+.07ns	−.03ns

C. "In the ideal church, there will no longer be a need for ordained ministry" and "More women should be ordained to full ministerial status in my denomination."

		Congregation-Centered			Institution-Centered	Spirit-Centered
TOTALS		Am. Bap. Christian/ DoC, & UCC	Unitar.- Univer.	Breth. & So. Bap.		
Women	+.11**	+.11*	+.11ns	+.06ns	+.05ns	+.15*
Men	+.07**	+.06ns	+.08ns	+.28**	+.02ns	+.10ns

*Correlation significant at the .01 level.
**Correlation significant at the .001 level.

6. Joy Charlton, "What It Means to Go First: Clergywomen of the Pioneer Generation" (paper presented at the annual meetings of the Society for the Scientific Study of Religion and the Religious Research Association, St. Louis, October 1995). In an even later report on these women, she indicates that roughly half of her sample have left parish ministry and almost all have considered doing so. These "pioneers" may be committed to their calling, but they are defining their ministry in broader categories. See Joy Charlton, "Dropping Out/Staying In: Revisiting Clergywomen in Mid-Careers" (paper presented at the annual meetings of the Society for the Scientific Study of Religion and the Religious Research Association, Albuquerque, November 1995).

CHAPTER 6: AN EXPANDING MINISTRY

1. Of the clergy we surveyed who work in a nonparish ministry position, only one-third of the women (34 percent) and one-fourth of the men (25 percent) say that it is at least somewhat correct (somewhat accurate, accurate) that they work where they do because they dislike parish ministry.
2. Gerald Jud, Edgar W. Mills Jr., and Genevieve W. Burch, *Ex-Pastors: Why Men Drop out of the Parish Ministry* (Philadelphia: Westminster Press, 1970).
3. For example, see David G. Bromley, "Religious Disaffiliation: A Neglected Social Process," in David G. Bromley, ed., *Falling from the Faith and Consequences of Religious Apostasy* (Newbury Park, Calif.: Sage Publications, 1988), pp. 9–28; and Stuart A. Wright, "Leaving New Religious Movements: Issues, Theory and Research," in Bromley, ed., *Falling from the Faith,* pp. 143–65. See also Helen Rose Fuchs Ebaugh, *Becoming an Ex: The Process of Role Exit* (Chicago: University of Chicago Press, 1988).
4. See Richard Schoenherr and Larry Young, *Full Pews and Empty Altars* (Madison: University of Wisconsin Press, 1993).
5. The following researchers have found one or more of these factors to predict clergy *interest* in dropping out, if not actual dropping out: Joy Charlton, "Dropping Out/Staying In: Revisiting Clergywomen in Mid-Careers" (paper presented at the annual meetings of the Society for the Scientific Study of Religion and the Religious Research Association, Albuquerque, November 1995; Gordon Fletcher, *The Lost Shepherd: Why Individuals Are Leaving Full-Time Ministry in the Pentecostal Assemblies of Canada, Alberta District* (D.Min. diss., St Stephens College, 1989); Jud, Mills, and Burch, *Ex-Pastors;* Cameron Lee and Jack Balswick, *Life in a Glass House: The Minister's Family in Its Unique Social Context* (Grand Rapids: Zondervan Publishing House, 1989); Paul Mickey and Ginny W. Ashmore, *Clergy Families: Is Normal Life Possible?* (Grand Rapids: Zondervan Publishing House, 1991); Edgar W. Mills, "Review of Recent Social Science Research on Stress," in Loren B. Mead, Barry Evans, Edgar W. Mills Jr., and Clement W. Welsh, eds., *Personal and Professional Needs of the Clergy of the Episcopal Church* (New York: Episcopal Church Foundation, 1988), pp. 38–67; Elizabeth Norell, "Clergy Family Satisfaction: A Review," *Family Science Review* 4 (1989): 69–93; Lloyd Retiger, *Coping with Clergy Burnout* (Valley Forge, Pa.: Judson Press, 1981).
6. No difference in dropout by age of clergy women was found by Nesbitt either, for Episcopal and Unitarian clergy women. See Paula D. Nesbitt, "First and Second Career Clergy: Influences of Age and Gender on the Career-Stage Paradigm," *Journal for the Scientific Study of Religion* 34 (1995): 152–71.

7. See Paula Nesbitt, *The Feminization of the Clergy in America* (New York: Oxford University Press, 1997); Susan Hill Lindley, *"You Have Stept out of Your Place": A History of Women and Religion in America* (Louisville, Ky.: Westminster John Knox Press, 1996); Mark Chaves, *Ordaining Women: Culture and Conflict in Religious Organizations* (Cambridge, Mass.: Harvard University Press, 1997). Carl Schneider and Dorothy Schneider, *In Their Own Right: The History of American Clergywomen* (New York: Crossroad, 1997).

8. Nesbitt, *Feminization of Clergy in America,* p. 164.

Index